Advance praise for *We Were Th[ere: The Third World]
Women's Alliance and t[he Second Wave]*

"Fifty years ago, the Third World Women's Alliance passionately insisted on interconnections among racism, sexism, and capitalism, inspiring radical analytical frameworks and organizing strategies associated with contemporary conceptions of feminism. We are deeply indebted to Patricia Romney for helping to generate a record of the Alliance's pioneering contributions and thus for ensuring that its revolutionary legacies live on."

> —**ANGELA Y. DAVIS**, author of *Freedom Is a Constant Struggle: Ferguson, Palestine, and the Foundations of a Movement*

"In the 1970s, with the mimeograph as weapon, and in solidarity with international liberation struggles, US women of color turned to one another, across ethnic and racial divides, to recognize their common cause. *We Were There* is the 'origin story' we've been waiting for. Those radical sister foremothers shaped for themselves an utterly prescient (if not always perfect) politic—one to which the tenets of *This Bridge Called My Back*, 'intersectionality,' and transnational feminism remain beholden. Yes, they *were* there, as Patricia Romney, living witness and researcher, fervently attests. And we are so grateful that they were."

> —**CHERRÍE MORAGA**, coeditor of *This Bridge Called My Back: Writings by Radical Women of Color*

"With a narrative that is both engaging and inspiring, Romney's *We Were There* gives us an important insider's view of the Third World Women's Alliance and the powerful sisterhood that transformed the lives of so many women. Now more than ever, we need the voices of women of color activists who were fighting against racism, sexism, and classism in the 1970s to speak across generations and share their lessons learned. The struggle continues!"

> —**BEVERLY DANIEL TATUM**, author of *Why Are All the Black Kids Sitting Together in the Cafeteria?: And Other Conversations about Race*

"In *We Were There*, Sistah Pat has created a riveting collective memory and critique of the TWWA's radical contributions to our enduring movement for justice and liberation."

> —**MELANIE TERVALON**, physician, educator, and activist

"For those who 'were there,' Romney's book rings true with passion, remembrance, and wisdom. For those who were 'not there,' it is a history lesson rooted in honesty, commitment, and the vision of a more just future. From historical artifacts to interviews and portraits of former members, this book includes broad-based examples of solidarity and inspiring personal and collective stories. *We Were There* is a call to action about frequently hidden or denied lessons of the past that we would do well to remember today."

—**SONIA NIETO**, professor emerita, University of Massachusetts Amherst

"*We Were There* brilliantly makes visible and salient the complex and intersectional stories of the 1970s women's movement that have so often been whitewashed and omitted in many educational contexts. This book is a heartfelt and compassionate scholarly exploration of coalition building, education, and activism, centering the work and stories of women of color. Dr. Romney is a gifted storyteller and talented scholar who offers insight and wisdom that helps us, as readers, to better understand contemporary social justice work."

—**MARCELLA RUNELL HALL**, coeditor of *UnCommon Bonds: Women Reflect on Race and Friendship*

WE WERE THERE

The Third World Women's Alliance & the Second Wave

PATRICIA ROMNEY

FOREWORD BY FARAH AMEEN

THE FEMINIST PRESS
AT THE CITY UNIVERSITY OF NEW YORK
NEW YORK CITY

S OFF
A DAVIS
'S ALLIANCE
k City
WE REPRE
& THIRD WO
THE MOST
OPPRESSED
MAN RACE.
THIRD WORLD
WOMEN'S ALLIAN
RICT 65

Published in 2021 by the Feminist Press
at the City University of New York
The Graduate Center
365 Fifth Avenue, Suite 5406
New York, NY 10016

feministpress.org

First Feminist Press edition 2021

 This book was made possible thanks to a grant from New York State Council on the Arts with the support of Governor Andrew M. Cuomo and the New York State Legislature.

First printing October 2021

Cover photograph, *Hands Off Angela Davis*, by Luis C. Garza
Cover design by Sukruti Anah Staneley
Text design by Frances Ross

Library of Congress Cataloging-in-Publication Data
Names: Romney, Patricia, 1944- author. | Feminist Press.
Title: We were there : the third world women's alliance and the second wave
    / Patricia Romney ; foreword by Farah Ameen.
Description: New York, NY : Feminist Press, 2021. | Includes
    bibliographical references.
Identifiers: LCCN 2021031109 (print) | LCCN 2021031110 (ebook) | ISBN
    9781952177828 (paperback) | ISBN 9781952177835 (ebook)
Subjects: LCSH: Women—History—20th century. | Feminism—History—20th
    century. | African American women—History—20th century. | African
    American women—Social conditions—20th century.
Classification: LCC HQ1154 .R73 2021 (print) | LCC HQ1154 (ebook) | DDC
    305.4209/04—dc23
LC record available at https://lccn.loc.gov/2021031109
LC ebook record available at https://lccn.loc.gov/2021031110

PRINTED IN THE UNITED STATES OF AMERICA

For Frances Beal, whose politics, vision, and intellect made the Third World Women's Alliance a reality and without whom there would be no story to tell.

For all the sisters of the Third World Women's Alliance who dedicated themselves to making the world a more just place for women of color, our families, and our communities. And for our brothers who supported us in that work.

For AmFam, my crew of sisters and brothers from the Pioneer Valley—progressive faculty members, teachers, administrators, and social justice consultants—in gratitude for your friendship and your ongoing work for justice.

Contents

Foreword

WHEN PATRICIA ROMNEY first approached me about working on her book *We Were There: The Third World Women's Alliance and the Second Wave*, I expected it to be about a women's movement in third world countries. I'm Bangladeshi American—I grew up in India, and then lived in Bangladesh for a couple years before I came to the United States as a graduate student in 1991. While I'd never heard the term "third world" used in reference to American women, I soon learned that for Pat's organization, the Third World Women's Alliance (TWWA), this internationalist language provided radical insight into the struggles of women of color in the US, and how they could build solidarity.

Rooted in the civil rights movement, the TWWA was a bicoastal group active from 1970 to 1980. They advocated for women of color specifically, because they faced what the TWWA termed a "triple jeopardy" of race, gender, and class oppression. They wanted the women's movement to address issues such as the forced sterilization of women of color, unsafe abortions, infant mortality rates, inequality in wages, and the need for welfare rights. They also questioned sexism in activist organizations.

Thirty years ago when I came to the US, I was shocked to learn that racism and sexism existed in this "first world" country. Classism and sexism are widespread in Bangladesh and India, where there is extreme poverty alongside excessive wealth. Yet both countries have had strong women's movements and broad-based programs to lift women out of poverty. Bangladesh has reduced its maternal mortality rate, achieved gender parity in school enrollment, introduced gender quotas in government, and passed laws addressing violence against women. In a strange juxtaposition to the US, women in South

Asia even hold powerful positions in politics: female prime ministers are not an anomaly.

My family is middle class, which in India meant we could afford to live in a modest house and that my parents could send my two brothers and me to good schools. It was a "traditional" household: my father was the breadwinner, and my mother stayed home and looked after the three of us. Though she had the help of live-in domestic workers (which is common among middle-class families in that part of the world), parenting consumed my mother's time and identity. Part of the reason I left home was to escape societal expectations: to dress "modestly," to get married young to someone from the "right background," to not be "fast" (i.e., have boyfriends). I wanted freedom from all that. But I had a lot to learn about my perception of a perfect life in the West.

As Pat's book unfolds, we see that the TWWA, which launched in New York and eventually started a West Coast chapter, was a product of its time. Its young, prescient members felt alienated by an existing women's liberation movement that didn't address the needs of poor and working-class women of color. They had their own path to follow in their nonwhite communities. One truly telling moment happened on August 26, 1970, when these sisters in arms set out to join the fifty-thousand-strong women's march down Fifth Avenue. The march was in response to Betty Friedan's call for a national strike protesting the fact that women had not yet achieved full equality in the United States despite fifty years of voting rights. When the TWWA women showed up with their "HANDS OFF ANGELA DAVIS" banner, they were first told they couldn't join the march. But they persisted and marched anyway—and in the process helped expand horizons. As Pat writes, "We showed up and we brought the women's liberation we were talking about. We were there!"

These Alliance women became teachers, doctors, physician assistants, social workers, professors, mothers, and wives. Though they were all progressives, the group included socialists, Democrats, and independents. *We Were There* tells their stories as an integral part of the liberation struggles of the era. Pat shows us who these women were, how they embraced their activism, and how their work changed the lives of women, families, and communities. These foremothers powerfully paved the way for future generations of women of color.

Pat emphasizes that theirs was not a movement against men; it was one for justice that was pro-woman, pro–people of color, pro-children, and pro-family. They did not codify and distinguish between the Black power movement, the Chicano movement, etc. "We were in the movement for social change, the movement toward equity and social justice for all," she notes.

As a woman from a third world country, I found this book oddly comforting. I have experienced various forms of racist and sexist discrimination in the US and have been tokenized for my "exoticism." I didn't give it much thought initially, even as I struggled through my first year in a journalism program in Indiana. Although I'd considered myself cosmopolitan, I was judged for my appearance and accent. After grad school, I moved to New York. I enjoyed my years working for national magazines in the city; it was exciting, challenging, and ego-boosting. But after 9/11, for the first time I felt real fear. I was suddenly very conscious of being a Brown Muslim woman. I worried about getting on the subway, the bus, a plane. I watched helplessly when my elderly mother in a wheelchair was frisked at JFK airport because the hooks on her sari blouse set off the scanners.

It was both sad and fascinating to read what Pat and her sisters had faced decades before. Immigrants like me still come to the US (which my father jokingly called "the land of milk and honey") with hopes for a better life. The lucky ones find some of what they came seeking, as I have. But our hopes are dashed when we witness police killings and xenophobia—or when we experience the anti-immigrant hatred promoted by people like Donald Trump, enabling bold public displays of the ever-present, emergent white supremacist movement in this country.

In 2020, we voted in President Joe Biden, who set out to undo the previous regime's regression. He filled his administration with diverse people, including a woman of color vice president, Kamala Harris, who is of both Black and South Asian descent. But Pat's story of the TWWA and their struggle for equality serves as a reminder that race, class, and gender oppression have been with us over the course of many presidencies. The persistent need for women's marches, and the COVID-19 pandemic—which has highlighted the indispensable role women play at home, especially regarding childcare—have shown us we have a long road ahead. So it is with sober realism that we struggle onward in solidarity as women from the third world diaspora.

We have so much work before us. The proliferation of social media and cell phone videos have highlighted the reality of hate crimes. It's also shown us that age is no barrier when it comes to bias. What I've learned over the past eleven years of parenting a Brown child is that discrimination starts very young. I have experienced it on the playground, in mom groups, and in social circles. It's made me realize I may never be fully accepted because I am different, but it's okay. I can find my tribe and comfort zone.

We women of color wouldn't be where we are without trailblazers like Pat and her TWWA peers, who are featured in the "A Luta Continua" sections throughout this book. They are a captivating window into the lives of women who were widely known in movement circles as the standard-bearers for the fight against sexism among activists of color.

Interweaving oral history, research, and first-person memoir, Patricia Romney details how the TWWA shaped and redefined second wave feminism. She highlights the essential contributions of women of color to the justice movements of the 1970s. This book is a reminder to new generations of feminists that solidarity is the only way forward.

We Were There has made me think hard about my dreams for my daughter. What I wish for her is a world where she is not judged on skin tone, gender, or race—a world where she and others like her can work together, strengthen alliances, and build community to empower each other through their deeds and words. As Malala Yousafzai puts it: "I raise my voice not so I can shout, but so that those without a voice can be heard."

—Farah Ameen
June 2021

Author's Note

WE WERE THERE is the story of the Third World Women's Alliance (TWWA), an organization of young women of color who came together in the 1970s "to create a sisterhood of women devoted to the task of developing solidarity among the peoples of the Third World."[1]

Now, fifty years later, the idea of women in the United States identifying themselves as part of the third world seems odd, perhaps even off-putting, but activists of color in our era used that language. An editorial in *Triple Jeopardy* gave a full explanation of our use of the term in the United States: "Within the confines of the United States, the third world consists of the descendants of Asia, Africa, and Latin America. This community is made up of Afro-Americans, Puertoriqueños [*sic*], Chicanos, Latinos, Asian Americans, Native Americans, and Eskimos. We have all suffered from the same kind of exploitation and colonial oppression as our brothers and sisters in our homelands."[2]

My time in the TWWA as a young woman in my mid- to late twenties was formative. I spent three years in the Alliance, some of that time as editor of our newspaper, *Triple Jeopardy*. The radical ethos of the Alliance and the movement made an indelible imprint on my thinking and my character. Just as my sixteen years of Catholic education, eight of them in all-girls or all-women institutions, did.

The Alliance and my sister activists crystallized my political orientation through profound teaching and learning, often through lasting friendship, and sometimes through confrontation and struggle. I learned that the only way to prevail and to lift others in my family and community was to stand up against oppression. This book is my testimony to the Alliance's impact on my life, as well as to its contribution to the struggle for the rights of women, people of color, and all economically and politically oppressed people.

This book is written from my perspective and is not a strictly political analysis. Not all former members of the TWWA will agree with my thoughts or analysis about what our politics were or about how I see the current situation in the United States and what needs to be done. Former Alliance sisters are across the spectrum on the left, but we are all advocates for justice.

The platform of the TWWA called for the support of the family, for full employment, erasure of sex roles, equal education, equitable services, and the right to choose whether to have children. The platform also called for revolution, asserting women's right to defend themselves, advocating for women to learn martial arts, and stating that women had the right and responsibility to bear arms.

The call for revolution was not uncommon during this period in US history. Racial apartheid defined the southern states. Violence was pervasive in America, carried out by disparate forces—by the government during the war in Vietnam; by the rabid racists who killed Martin Luther King, Medgar Evers, James Chaney, Andrew Goodman, and Michael Schwerner, as well as countless Black men and women; and by the police who murdered activists like Fred Hampton. As Max Elbaum wrote, "revolution [was] in the air," and "all society was a battleground."[3]

To be clear, advocating for martial arts and asserting the right to bear arms was about self-defense; TWWA did not promote violence. As an organization, it did not purchase, carry, or use weapons. The Alliance never broke the law; we simply used our First Amendment rights to speak, to march, and to write. Our work was education and advocacy, demonstration and resistance.

I believe the Alliance's platform was, in many ways, visionary. I still support our platform, save for the final assertion

that third world women have "the right and the responsibility to bear arms." Writing this, I must, at the same time that
I reject the call to bear arms, recognize the current situation
in 2020 and 2021.

Police who have sworn to protect lives are still gunning down
Black men and women. Defenses stating imminent danger to
the police ring hollow when we consider why Tasers are not
used in place of guns and why a shot in the hand or leg does not
replace a bullet to the heart. So-called terrorists and bombers
are captured alive, while a young Black teenager with Skittles
and a disabled man selling cigarettes are killed mercilessly.

The murders of George Floyd, Breonna Taylor, Ahmaud
Arbery, and so many more call this ongoing life-threatening
brutality to our attention. Still, the taking of innocent Black
lives continues. And the arming of white militias throughout
the United States, both in and outside of the police, has led to a
response in the Black community.[4] Over the first six months of
2020, gun sellers reported a record 10.3 million in transactions.
Compared with the prior year, that represents a 95 percent
increase in firearm sales and a 139 percent increase in ammu-
nition sales. The highest overall firearm sales increase comes
from Black men and women, who show a 58.2 percent increase
in purchases during the first six months of 2020 versus the
same period last year.[5] In the aftermath of the insurrectionist
siege on the US Capitol on January 6, 2021, I am able to understand (yet still rue) the rise in gun ownership in this country.
God help us all!

The United States already has the highest rate of murder or
manslaughter by firearm in the developed world. I recognize
this country's reliance on guns as a sequela of its creation—
colonization, capturing of Indigenous lands, enslavement of
African peoples, and westward expansion. Some have called
us the United States of Firearms. At the waystation of old age,
I recognize life is precious, and I eschew the use of violence,
which, if at all useful, most often brings only short-term
solutions.

Writing this note in 2021, I am compelled to recognize and
give thanks for today's emergent movements. I celebrate the

Black Lives Matter movement. #BlackLivesMatter was founded in 2013 in response to the acquittal of Trayvon Martin's murderer[6] and has drawn thousands of US citizens together on the streets and in colleges, and in for-profit and not-for-profit groups to protest police violence.

I celebrate the #MeToo movement for naming and challenging the sexual transgressions and violations of powerful men against less-powerful girls, women, and some young men. I commend the #NeverAgain movement against school violence, which arose after the killings at Marjory Stoneman Douglas High School and reminds us that young people are very often our leaders in the quest for social change.

The approach of the TWWA was radical but democratic. Totalitarianism was never part of the Alliance vision. I am disturbed now by the things I did not know about the harsh practices and mass murders that took place during the Cultural Revolution in China. And I marvel that I, a person who views travel, as my parents did, as one of the most important means of education, did not recognize and speak up about some of the practices of nations like my beloved Cuba, where freedom of movement and travel is restricted even today. And it seems clear to me that nations that prohibit worship are doomed to fail. One does not have to believe in God, but the right of citizens to worship God as they define God is a right that must be defended.

We have seen the fall of the Soviet Union and the struggles of socialist Cuba. We are witnessing the human-rights abuses of the People's Republic of China and the evil of North Korea. Yet we also see, if we choose to look, the strengths and benefits of some of those nations. I note China's success in combating COVID-19 and the success of countries with democratic socialist practices—like Norway, Sweden, Denmark, Finland, New Zealand, even Canada and Britain—where social safety nets exist and healthcare and education are provided more fully and equitably to all citizens, as their Gini Index coefficients illustrate.

As I reflect on the 1970 demands and goals of the TWWA, I see them as calls for basic human rights: education, healthcare, jobs. Despite the straightforward simplicity of these ideas, racism continues to plague our society; women are still harassed, raped, and underpaid; the poor and working poor of all races and ethnicities continue to be exploited. In 2015, *Fortune* magazine dubbed the United States the richest and most unequal nation in the world.[7] America—sometimes called "the world's greatest democracy"—has yet to find enduring solutions to many of the concerns raised by the Alliance in the 1970s.

The women of the Alliance took a stand against economic exploitation, knowing in our hearts what Zora Neale Hurston had put into words: "There is something about poverty that smells like death. Dead dreams dropping off the heart like leaves in a dry season and rotting around the feet."[8] We took a stand against sexism, knowing from our own experience what Audre Lorde later put into writing: "There are so many silences to be broken."[9] We took a stand against racism, knowing, as Jean-Paul Sartre wrote, that "racism is built into the system."[10]

While there may be legitimate critique of our philosophy and approach, I ask all readers to evaluate us through the munificent lens of history. What I celebrate and honor in this writing is our struggle for human rights for women and people of color, and an end to oppression and exploitation. What I intend to lift up is our struggle for equity and justice. And here there is no question: all Alliance sisters still living continue that struggle today.

Introduction: The Need for This Story

Each generation must out of its relative obscurity discover its mission, fulfill or betray it.

—*FRANTZ FANON*, THE WRETCHED OF THE EARTH

The Call

"Women of color were not involved in the women's liberation movement!" This was the pronouncement my Hampshire College students made with great certainty and sighs of resignation in the late 1980s when I asked why their independent research papers on the women's movement of the 1970s described only the contributions of white women. When I inquired further, they responded that they *had* searched and were disappointed to discover that women of color had not been involved in the women's movement. To confirm this conclusion, they cited a statement by bell hooks that had put an end to any further inquiry on their part.

In her 1981 book *Ain't I a Woman*, hooks wrote that Black women in the women's movement "were by and large silent." She continued,

> Our silence was not merely a reaction against white women liberationists or a gesture of solidarity with black male patriarchs. It was the silence of the oppressed—that profound silence engendered by resignation and acceptance of one's lot. Contemporary

1

black women could not join together to fight for women's rights because we did not see "Womanhood" as an important aspect of our identity. . . . Consequently, when the women's movement raised the issue of sexist oppression, we argued that sexism was insignificant in light of the harsher, more brutal, reality of racism. We were afraid to acknowledge that sexism could be just as oppressive as racism. We were a new generation of black women who had been taught to submit, to accept sexual inferiority and to be silent.[1]

My students loved the work of bell hooks. Eloquent and scholarly, writing both personally and politically, she spoke both to their hearts and their progressive politics. She was widely read and a much sought-after speaker on the college circuit at the time, and because of that, my students felt no need to question her assertion.

Progressive, feminist, and mostly white, my students were busy exploring the sixties and the seventies, decades that had profoundly changed the face of America. Theirs was not simply an intellectual curiosity. They had personal and political reasons for their interest. Born in the early 1970s, these young college women were the first immediate beneficiaries of the women's movement. Many of them had been raised by liberal, progressive, or radical parents who in their youth were active in the justice movements of the sixties and seventies. They grew up hearing about Students for a Democratic Society (SDS), Student Nonviolent Coordinating Committee (SNCC), the Young Lords Party, the Black Panther Party, and the National Organization for Women. They heard their parents' stories about the freedom rides of the 1960s and the women's demonstrations on the fiftieth anniversary of suffrage.

My white students were also engaged in exploring and defining their own identities as women and sometimes as gay people or as Jews. My students of color, though few in number, knew racism from their own experience, and many of them were beginning to explore their identity as women. They all wanted to understand the era of activism into which they had been

born and were eager to make their own mark as student scholars and activists.

Sister hooks's statement and my discussions with my
students about their research was the starting point for this
book. I was eager not to have the work of women of color
rendered invisible in the literature on second wave feminism.[2]
From my students' perspective, hooks was an unquestioned
authority, but I knew that what she wrote was not true for all
Black women. As a Black woman myself, I had been a part
of the women's movement from which women of color were
supposedly absent. The Black women, *and* Latinas, *and* Asian
women, *and* Middle Eastern women[3] with whom I worked in
the Alliance were in no way silent about their oppression as
women. We were deeply involved, and we asserted our rights
in vocal and active ways.

From 1970 to 1974, I was a member of the New York Chapter of the Alliance. I, along with many other Black women and
other women of color throughout US history, *had identified
sexism* as part of our experience and had joined together to fight
for women's rights.[4] We had overcome our fear of our brothers' condemnation (and some did condemn us), and we had
taken the necessary risks to expose our oppression as women.
We did not resign ourselves; on the contrary, we announced
our commitment to wage a struggle for women's liberation in
conjunction with a struggle against racism and imperialism.
We fought vigorously and visibly to assert the role and importance of women in the movement, and I was concerned that
the vital contributions of women of color to the second wave of
feminism were missing from the history books. I felt compelled
to set the record straight.

The conversations with my students in the late eighties and
early nineties led to my research focusing on the activism of
my own cohort, the sisters of the Third World Women's Alliance (TWWA). I discovered that my students were correct about
the lack of documentation of our movement. I found no information about the Alliance and very little about the activism of
women of color during this period.

The Research

My research on the Alliance has continued over the last twenty-five years, alongside the business of everyday life: earning a living, raising three children, caring for elderly parents, being a guardian for my disabled brother, and now grandparenting. Over time, the story of the Alliance has found its way into the literature, being recounted in theses and dissertations, as well as in articles, books, and film. The organization is now a frequent topic of conversation in both Black history and Black politics classes, as well as women and gender studies programs. Yet from my perspective, the record remains incomplete and in some important aspects inaccurate.

Kristin Anderson-Bricker's article "'Triple Jeopardy': Black Women and the Growth of Feminist Consciousness in SNCC, 1964–1975" in Kimberly Springer's excellent book *Still Lifting, Still Climbing: African American Women's Contemporary Activism* locates the history of the Alliance in the emergence of feminism among Black women in SNCC and deftly distinguishes this emergence from the feminism among white women that occurred three to four years earlier. She follows with a detailed discussion of the early years of the TWWA but incorrectly dates the end of the TWWA, stating, "Despite the ideological consistency of the Third World Women's Alliance, the organization disappeared shortly after the summer of 1975."[5] The Alliance actually lived on until 1980, deepening its analysis and activism.

In their book published in 2000, *Dear Sisters*, Rosalyn Baxandall and Linda Gordon published an Alliance statement dated 1968 and cited it as being retrieved from an undated issue of *Triple Jeopardy*. It read, "And to the white women's liberation groups we say . . . until you can deal with your own racism and until you can deal with your OWN poor white sisters, you will never be a liberation movement and you cannot expect to unite with Third World peoples in a common struggle."[6] But *Triple Jeopardy* was not published until the September/October 1971 inaugural issue, and the name Third World Women's Alliance was not adopted until 1970; 1968 was the period of organizing within SNCC as the Black Women's Caucus and later the Black Women's Liberation Committee. The statement does bear a resemblance to the TWWA platform that was published in *Triple Jeopardy* but is not as complete. The distinctive difference is that the statement Baxandall and Gordon cite contains several paragraphs about the Alliance's perspective on white women that did not appear in the official platform in *Triple Jeopardy*.

We are certain from incorporation papers filed January 3, 1969, that that was the year Fran Beal and the Black Women's Liberation Committee, a forerunner of the Black Women's Alliance and the TWWA that evolved later, was incorporated in New York City. As we discovered, the dates are at odds and the origin and date of this "statement" are unclear. With the source unclear, I can only hypothesize that this statement was an earlier iteration of the platform. I have not been able to verify its authenticity, but the statement as quoted does reflect the sentiment of Alliance sisters and does align with conversations we had about our relationship to white women during my time in the Alliance.

In 2001, Linda Burnham (see portrait on p.165), a member of the Bay Area Chapter of the Alliance and cofounder of the Women of Color Resource Center in Oakland, California, published the article "The Wellspring of Feminist Theory." In it, she places the Alliance at the center of the early thinking about "the concepts of the both/and of Black women's reality, the simultaneity of their oppression, and the intersection of race, class and gender."[7] Burnham's interview by Loretta Ross in 2005 for the Voices of Feminism Oral History Project was rich in detail about the Alliance, but as Burnham said there, the Alliance "is something some articles have been written about, but it deserves a more comprehensive treatment."[8]

Max Elbaum's 2002 book, *Revolution in the Air*, describes the Alliance in the context of SNCC's demise and details how Black women evolved from SNCC to become the Black Women's Alliance and then in 1970 expanded to include other women of color. He also notes that "TWWA pioneered in developing and promoting the concept of 'triple jeopardy' (and published a newspaper of that name) that women of color faced the combined and intersecting burdens of capitalism, racism and sexism."[9]

Steven Michael Ward's 2002 dissertation, "Ours Too Was a Struggle for a Better World: Activist Intellectuals and the Radical Promise of the Black Power Movement, 1962–1972,"[10] gives a detailed history of the development of the TWWA, but he relies solely on a review of the literature, which was not very extensive at that time, and on conversations with Beal. In addition, he situates the Alliance in the Black Power movement, with a brief acknowledgment that the organization came to include other women of color and had other leaders of color but continues to describe it as a Black feminist organization. And though Ward does cover the period up to 1972, he omits the growth of the Bay Area Chapter, which was developing in 1971 and 1972.

Benita Roth's *Separate Roads to Feminism*, published in 2003, covered the Alliance and mainly gets it right, notably crediting the TWWA with establishing early "the concept of Black feminist organizing as intersectional,"[11] but her work suffers some of the shortcomings of other research, most notably that she defines the Alliance as a Black feminist organization. She makes note of Puerto Ricans joining the group, but most unfortunately for a book titled *Separate Roads to Feminism*, she does not focus on the ways in which Black, Middle Eastern, Puerto Rican, Chicana, Japanese American, Chinese American, Korean American, and other women of color came together in the Alliance.

Joon Pyo Lee did the best job of capturing the multiracial, multicultural nature of the Alliance in her 2007 master's thesis, "The Third World Women's Alliance, 1970–1980: Women of Color Organizing in a Revolutionary Era."[12] She reviewed the Alliance's archives and interviewed several former members, including myself.

Iris Morales's *Through the Eyes of Rebel Women: The Young Lords, 1969–1976* is a welcome and unique contribution to the literature—in addition to the extensive details about the activism of women in the Young Lords, the book documents both the presence and activity of Young Lords women in the development of the Alliance and the support of Alliance women in the work of the Young Lords and the movement in New York City.[13]

Ashley Farmer's 2017 article "The Third World Women's Alliance, Cuba, and the Exchange of Ideas," published on *Black Perspectives*, does a beautiful job of describing Cuba's impact on the Alliance. We also impacted our fellow brigadistas in the national program that was the Venceremos Brigade. And we were influenced as well by China, Vietnam, and revolutionary struggles for independence all over the Caribbean and Latin America.

At the time of this writing, it is apparent that the literature on the TWWA is expanding at a very rapid pace. Of note is Ariane Vani Kannan's excellent and detailed 2018 dissertation, "The Third World Women's Alliance: History, Geopolitics and Form," which explores the Alliance's contribution and participation in defining the US third world and "building lifelong activists." Through an examination of the archives and the "behind the scenes organizational labor" of the Alliance, Kannan endeavors to make a contribution to the field of rhetoric and composition.

Despite my appreciation of the growing literature on the Alliance, I still feel the need for the more comprehensive treatment that Burnham called for. Readers can learn about the work of the Alliance in New York or in California but usually not both. Histories of the Alliance often reflect extensive interviews with Frances M. Beal, its founder and an undisputed authority on the Alliance, but other voices are lacking. Some of the publications are important political treatises, but they omit the texture of the lived experience of members. Some focus on the Alliance's voice for the rights of women of color but neglect the work against imperialism and classism. Most do not mention the international perspective of the Alliance, sometimes placing the Alliance within the context of nationalist movements.

Writings about the Alliance, then, most often depict the organization as a Black women's organization and include its politics solely under Black feminism. This is of particular concern to me because one of the unique strengths of the Alliance was that it was an organization open to all *women of color*, not of a single racial or ethnic group. In fact, the cover of *Triple Jeopardy*'s first issue illustrates this clearly: it is a drawing of three women—one Black, one Asian, and one Latina. From my perspective, this accomplishment needs to be asserted and understood. As you will discover here, many former members agree.

Becky Thompson, an anti-racist feminist and writer, saw a problem with the reporting on the women's liberation movement and did her part to right the historical record in 2002 in her article "Multiracial Feminism: Recasting the Chronology of Second Wave Feminism." And Chela Sandoval, feminist scholar and third world theorist, wrote of a "hegemonic feminism" that, according to Thompson, "marginalizes the activism and world views of women of color, focuses mainly on the United States, and treats sexism as the ultimate oppression."[14] This feminism, she wrote, "deemphasizes or ignores a class and race analysis, generally sees equality with men as the goal of feminism, and has an individual rights-based, rather than justice-based, vision for social change."[15] Thompson placed her frame on "multiracial feminism," which she defined as "the liberation movement spearheaded by women of color in the United States in the 1970s that was characterized by its international perspective, its attention to interlocking oppressions, and its support of coalition politics."[16] This is exactly where the story of the TWWA fits. We were a group of women of color focused on multiple and intersecting oppressions, centered deeply in a systemic class, gender, and race analysis, and committed to transnational politics.

My Perspective and Goals

I believe the important role of the Alliance in the multiple liberation struggles of the seventies has been miniaturized by the extant literature. As if to affirm this, on October 30, 2005, the Women of Color Resource Center in Oakland presented its annual Women of Fire Award to the TWWA, saying,

> TWWA is widely recognized, both among scholars and among today's activists, as a critical player in the activism of the 1970s

and as a primary source of new thinking on issues of gender, race, and class. In the past few years, several articles have been written about the role of TWWA in the development of "women-of-color feminism" and about the relationship between TWWA and the anti-racist and anti-imperialist movements of that time.

The Women of Color Resource Center award signaled that the Alliance had had a profound impact on the lives of young women and was recognized as a part of their legacy. It confirmed my resolve to tell a fuller story about the Alliance, one that I hope will illustrate the uniqueness and the prescience of its politics by documenting its history in greater detail than I have found in the literature. I hope to illustrate that the Alliance was indeed "a wellspring," not only of Black feminist theory as Burnham proclaimed, but also of activism and theory building that united women of color and educated the progressive movement.

Where I can, I will correct inaccuracies and demonstrate that although there certainly were Black women like the ones hooks describes, there were others of a different sort as well. Burnham states it most clearly:

> Significant players in the emergence of Second Wave feminism were women who, as activists in the Civil Rights, Black Power, Puerto Rican Independence, Chicano Liberation, Asian self-determination, and Native American sovereignty movements, began to identify and object to manifestations of sexism within their organizations, communities, and broader society. As an oppositional movement, women of color feminism challenged the suppression of women's full initiative in the struggle for social justice.[17]

The Alliance helped to shape and define both the women's movement and influence the other liberation movements of the period. I intend to illustrate that the activism of women of color was not only unquestionable but also essential to understanding that era. While the media has turned the leaders of the movements of the sixties and seventies into what I might call "celebrity activists," the millions of people who fought for social change and social justice in the United States at that time were ordinary citizens, largely unknown. The members of the Alliance were among those activists. Not one of the former Alliance women has become a household name. That was never their goal. Like the acorns described in James Hillman's book *The Soul's Code: In Search of Character and Calling*, these women pushed beyond their edges. Their principal passion was to change themselves and the world around them. To accomplish this task, they strove to become freedom fighters, calling for justice for themselves and their sisters and brothers.

Although I locate the Alliance in the second wave of feminism, I will also demonstrate that it was an active organization in the anti-imperialist, anti-racist movements of the 1970s and was one of the earliest organizations to foreground the shared importance of race, class, and gender. It is noteworthy also that hooks changed her perspective about Black women and activism in the period, writing in 1984:

> While Betty Friedan was writing about "the problem that has no name," addressing the way sexist discrimination affected highly educated white women with class privilege, Septima Clark, Ella Baker, Fannie Lou Hamer, and Ann Moody, along with individual black women across the nation, were challenging the sexism within the black civil rights movement.[18]

I hope to demonstrate that the Alliance continued that work into the Black Power movement, Latino and Asian American movement, anti-war movement, and women's movement.

Did the activists of the 1960s and 1970s give up social change goals and settle into traditional middle-class lives of self-interest and self-aggrandizement? Did they rework their ideologies as a new era emerged? Were any core values preserved? I hope to answer these questions by documenting Alliance members' current lives and sharing their perspectives from the vantage point of their senior years.

Finally, I propose to challenge some of the erroneous assumptions and assertions about the activism of 1970s women of color and to demonstrate that there were:

1. women of color who were feminists, predating the literature on "womanists," "feminisms," and "third world feminisms";
2. women of color who were internationalists, predating the literature on what is now known as transnational feminism;
3. women of color who came together across ethnicities and race and "operated together as a political category"; and
4. men of color who fought with us for the rights of women of color and who, therefore, can rightly be called "third world feminists."

I interviewed thirty-three individuals who were involved with Alliance work: twenty-seven women and six men. It was a revelation and inspiration to see who these activists became and to witness the degree of progressive orientation they retained. As Alliance sisters reflected on their times, on their organization, and on the women's, civil rights, and power movements of their youth, they spoke about what activism meant to them then and what it means to them now.

In the wake of the 2016 election in which white working-class voters played a pivotal role and writing in the waning days of the Trump presidency, I want to raise for reflection and conversation the attention that the Alliance gave to issues of social class and share our perspective on the role of white people in educating and supporting the white working class.

We Were There is written for women of color—for women of color activists, first and foremost—but also for others who may wonder why we took the stand we did and how we dared. It is also for men of color who just don't get this feminist stuff and for our brothers who truly do. It is for our white sisters with whom we have raised the "race question" and fought for our rights. It is written for young people who are not easily drawn to the study of history. It is written for my young colleagues who now live the concept of intersectionality, bringing together in their lives and their work the struggle against racism, sexism, homophobia, gender norms, and more. They carry the torch by virtue of who they are and what they do, and I am proud and happy to have the opportunity to know and work with them.

And this book is written for workers of all races, genders, and cultures—the people who built this country with their hands, muscle, and sweat. People like my carpenter grandfather who worked closely with Secretary of Labor Frances Perkins to advance union rights for people of color; like my brother, also a carpenter, who worked with Fight Back to bring down racial barriers in New York City's building trades; and my uncles and my cousin who also fought those fights. I have not forgotten them. This story, this telling, is for all of them, so they will know that a group of activists many decades ago believed in the interrelatedness of oppression and struggled to sustain attention to the importance of the working class.

What You Will Find Here

What follows is the story of one organization among the innumerable others in which women of color were active. In the 1960s and 1970s, a group of ordinary, yet uncommon, activist women of color—young, committed, passionate, visionary— truly did help to change this country. These women became teachers, doctors, physician assistants, social workers, professors, mothers, grandmothers, wives, socialists, Democrats, independents, and always progressive.

Here I endeavor to put into words what women like Burnham and other Alliance sisters put into action. *We Were There* tells the story of the women of the Alliance from their beginnings in New York City to their emergence as an integral part of the liberation struggles of their era. By sharing who these women were, how they came to their activism, and how their work changed the lives of women, families, and communities, both then and now, I aim to shed light on the contributions of these women who were widely known in movement circles as the standard-bearers for the fight against sexism among activists of color. I have not shied away from discussing some of our shortcomings and errors. Ultimately, I hope this story will offer current and future generations of women knowledge of their foremothers and a guide to the behaviors, strategies, and practices that successfully created a powerful, progressive movement of women of color—a movement not *against* men but a movement for *justice* that was pro-woman, pro–people of color, pro-children, and pro-family.

All quotes on Alliance materials are either from the archives housed in the Sophia Smith Collection at Smith College in Northampton, Massachusetts, or from editions of *Triple Jeopardy* found online at Independent Voices on JSTOR. All quotes from Alliance members are either from the archives or from personal interviews with members.

You will find the phrase "the movement" throughout the book. I use it because it was the phrase used by my cohort in the Alliance. We worked intersectionally. We did not codify and distinguish the Black Power movement, the Chicano movement, etc. This we left to others. We were in the movement for social change, the movement toward equity and social justice for all. We called it simply "the movement."

As I write this story, I struggle with voice. Sometimes I speak in the first person, sharing my thoughts and experiences. Other times, I write about what "we" did. When I use "I," it is because I was there, a part of the organization and the work it did in New York. I also sometimes write about the Alliance in the third person when discussing the branch in California, where I was not a member, or when I write about the New York Alliance before I joined it or after I departed. No matter the voice, I embrace the TWWA as my own, and I identify as one of the millions of women across the globe who stood and mobilized and became part of the second wave of feminism, as well as part of the anti-racism, anti-colonialism, internationalist, and workers' movement.

I also struggle with memory. In my interviews with Alliance members, it became clear that we all do. None of us could remember in any great detail what would have been interesting aspects of particular meetings or specific things said—it was all simply too long ago. What the reader will find is substantial information about what we read and studied, what we wrote, and the actions we undertook. Hopefully, this will provide sufficient information to understand who we were and what we fought for.

It has been said that we go into the past to know how to act in the present. In the 1970s, the Alliance took up its mission. It is my deepest hope that reflecting on this organization and the lives of the women who were a part of it will inform and inspire present and future action for equity and social justice—for women, for people of color, for workers, and for all of us.

A Luta Continua: Alliance Women Today

*Women's equality has made positive gains but the world is
still unequal.*
          —International Women's Day, 2014

THE PROGRESSIVE THEORIES we studied and the consciousness we nurtured in the TWWA continue to shape former members'
activism today. Our activism continued in 1991 after Anita Hill testified
during Senate Judiciary Committee hearings for Clarence Thomas's
nomination to the Supreme Court that while she worked for Thomas, he
had sexually harassed her. Powerful men publicly questioned her truth-
fulness and character. In response, on October 11, 1991, African American
women declared in a statement in seven newspapers, including the
New York Times, "The seating of Clarence Thomas is an affront not only
to African American women and men, but to all people concerned
with social justice. We are particularly outraged by the racist and sexist
treatment of Professor Anita Hill, an African American woman who was
maligned and castigated for daring to speak publicly of her own experience of sexual abuse." Black women who were past members of the
Alliance, including myself, were among those signatories.

Though not all former TWWA members consider themselves to be
socialists, and the term "revolutionary" as applied to movement activists perhaps has seen its day, Alliance women are still active in the
struggle against racism, classism, and sexism.

For this book, I interviewed former Alliance members to illustrate what they have done to move the world toward greater equity

and liberation and how their lives exemplify key TWWA values. I have presented these women as I first encountered them twenty to thirty years after their time in the Alliance. Many of them have moved on to retirement; most are continuing their activism. I hope the individual portraits interspersed throughout this book reveal the uniqueness of each person and the uniqueness of their work toward progressive values. Their activism differs. Their sectors of engagement differ. Still, in all, you will see attention to race, gender, and, very often, social class.

Thinking of the Alliance mantra, I invite you to pose this question as you read about each Alliance sister: "Are you inspired to live like her?"

TWWA Sisters: "Hasta la victoria siempre"

Vicki Alexander: Works tirelessly to serve children and families (p. 164).

Frances M. Beal: Channeled the fire of revolutionary spirit to nascent radical women of color, and her activism never waned (p. 34).

Brenda Boho Beato: "Even though I left the Alliance, it never left me" (p. 36).

Linda Burnham: "The Third World Women's Alliance is the foundation for my outlook" (p. 165).

Rebecca Carrillo: "I do see myself responsible to future generations. That doesn't go away" (p. 167).

Christine Choy (Chai Ming Huei): Retained her character, her languages, and her conviction that there should be economic equality and justice (p. 38).

Concha Delgado Gaitán: Ever the educator and organizer, she is always focused on empowerment and justice (p. 170).

Lenore French: Works with artists who have banded together around public art initiatives and protecting affordable housing, finding commonalities as multiracial artists (p. 41).

Stella Holmes Hughes: "I can see now the linear step between the Alliance's commitment to self-determination and my work with women experiencing domestic violence" (p. 67).

Milagros Pérez Huth: A former teacher, she still lives on the Lower East Side and is active in community struggles (p. 69).

Georgette Ioup: "My passion for most of my life has been the Palestinian cause. I'm angry about the injustice!" (p. 118).

Cheryl Johnson Perry League: "I have the confidence that the Alliance instilled in me over many years. I am always advocating around minorities and women, making sure minorities and women are represented" (p. 71).

Miriam Ching Yoon Louie: Has dedicated her life to advancing social movements—"women of color, immigrant women workers, grassroots Asian communities, and other kindred troublemakers" (p. 172).

Barbara Morita: With her perspective on the world and her service to communities around the globe, she truly lives the Alliance's goal of serving the people (p. 174).

Michelle Mouton: An activist who is of the community and who still lives in its heart (p. 188).

Shirley Nakao: "I still believe I'm a leftist. I still believe in core socialist thoughts. There are aspects of socialism that would better this country" (p. 190).

Ann-Ellice Parker: The word "empowerment" finds its way into her current practice of working with families on end-of-life issues (p. 190).

Yemaya Rice Jones: "This was a pivotal time, and we were hyper aware of how important it was for us to define our role in the struggle for equality" (p. 120).

Patricia Romney: "From each according to his ability, to each according to his need" (p. 121).

Melanie Tervalon: Lives the vision of the TWWA, bringing together community and family and engaging in an ongoing quest for justice for women and children (p. 192).

Renata Tervalon: "All the knowledge I gained in the Alliance, I poured into my son because as I learned in the Alliance, culture is passed down via women" (p. 195).

Zelma Toro: "Through working with Alliance sisters you got to know the line, what work style was expected out of you, how to put together a program that reflects your goals" (p. 196).

Barbara Webb: Brings her commitment and her activism to the field of education, honoring the Alliance's call for education to increase knowledge about "the history of third world women and their contributions to the liberation struggle" (p. 124).

Nancy Hing Wong: The Alliance "helped uplift me from this feeling that my family or I was personally responsible for the status we had. In the Alliance, I had an epiphany" (p. 197).

Ana Celia Zentella: Has a lifelong dedication to disenfranchised, under-represented, underresourced people of color, together with a lifelong focus on women and children (p. 125).

PART I

East Coast Organizing

CHAPTER 1

August 26, 1970

Women's consciousness is changing, and it's irrelevant to me whether 500 or 5,000 women turn out. This is already a huge success.

—*BETTY FRIEDAN*[1]

AUGUST 26, 1970, was, in many ways, a very ordinary summer day in New York City—warm but thankfully not too steamy. WMCA radio in New York rated Stevie Wonder's hit song "Signed, Sealed, Delivered (I'm Yours)" number one among its top forty. The Mets lost (nine to seven) to the Atlanta Braves. On television, *All in the Family*, starring Jean Stapleton as Archie Bunker's "dingbat" wife, Edith, reigned supreme.

It was also the day that women came together in never-before-seen numbers to demonstrate their passionate commitment to equal rights.

Much of the affluent population of the city had retreated from the August heat to summer sojourns in the Catskills, the Poconos, the Hamptons, Fire Island, Sag Harbor, the Vineyard, and other exurban and rural destinations. Poor and working-class folk contented themselves with Orchard Beach and the open fire hydrants of the five boroughs.

Frances Beal awoke that morning with her mind fixed on the many things she had to do before going to the demonstration. It was a Wednesday and she had taken the day off from work. She got up, showered, and picked out her light brown curly Afro, hair that was both soft and nappy, as if paying joint homage to her Black father and her white Jewish mother. A thirty-year-old divorced Black woman with two children, a full-time job, and more than full-time activism, she threw on a dress that was perhaps a bit too short then woke her daughters, Ann, eight, and Lisa, seven, and got them dressed.

Fran dropped the girls off at her mother's and then headed over to the Third World Women's Alliance (TWWA) office on the second floor of the rectory at St. Peter's Church in the Chelsea section of Manhattan to meet with other Alliance sisters and pick up their banner. They traveled together uptown to the demonstration, banner in hand.

Hands Off Angela Davis

What the women saw when they arrived at the demonstration astounded them. They were used to demonstrations of scores, hundreds, and maybe even a couple of thousand people. On this day, fifty thousand women filled the streets on and off Fifth Avenue, blocking the thoroughfares and filling the expanse of the avenue from curb to curb, completely overrunning the one lane the police had allocated for their march down Fifth Avenue.

Women were everywhere—individuals, small groups, whole organizations had come out in unbelievable numbers in response to Betty Friedan's call for a national strike to bring attention to the reality that despite fifty years of voting rights, women had not yet achieved full equality in the United States of America. In New York, the idea of a strike had evolved into a "march." Thousands of women started parading down Fifth Avenue to Bryant Park, a 9.6-acre park adjacent to the main branch of the New York Public Library on Forty-Second Street and Fifth Avenue.

Contingents of women joined the march, holding up posters and banners that had not been fully visible while they convened on the side streets. Huge posters made of oak tag were stapled down the middle to two-by-fours. The ends of bedsheets were wrapped around wooden two-by-fours and stapled, forming enormous banners. All were emblazoned with words and pictures: the names of the women's organizations, revolution-ary slogans, caricatures, and women's liberation symbols. As women joined the parade route, they raised their signs high or walked behind their handmade banners, proudly holding them steady and widespread as they marched. Thousands simply walked arm in arm, the words on their silk-screened T-shirts proclaiming their political views.

Radical feminists like the Redstockings and mainstream feminists like the National Organization for Women (NOW) were there, as were hundreds of groups representing all kinds of political viewpoints along the feminist continuum, their perspectives succinctly encapsulated on signs or on clothing. The political diversity was astounding. Friedan, the founder and president of NOW and the march's organizer, carried a poster that read "Women Need Constitutional Equality N.O.W." A sign on top of a car urged "Women Artists Unite." The Working Women's Contingent's sign read "Child Care Centers for Work-ing Mothers/Open All Jobs to Women/Equal Work, Equal Pay." Another poster read "End Human Sacrifice, Don't Get Married . . . Washing Diapers Is Not Fulfilling." Acerbically, another read, "Oppressed Women. Don't Cook Dinner. Starve a Rat Today." Women protesting the war in Vietnam were there too, with signs that read, "Sisterhood Is Powerful—End the War," "The Women of Vietnam Are Our Sisters," "I'm No Breeder for Man's War!"

In the midst of this bustle of activity, Fran and the hand-ful of her Alliance sisters approached the march's gathering point carrying their banner, with four simple words painted in the center in bold, black block letters: "HANDS OFF ANGELA DAVIS." In the upper-left corner, they had painted the Alliance logo, the well-known symbol for "woman" distinguished by the addition of a power fist rising up from the base of the circle. The fist clutched a raised rifle that intersected the circle from left to right, with the barrel lifted up. Across the bottom of the banner in smaller letters were the name and address of the organization: Third World Women's Alliance, 346 W. Twentieth Street, New York City.

As the women of the Alliance approached, Lucy Komisar, the parade coordinator and vice president of NOW, moved toward them. It was her job to check in all organizations and give them their places in the line of march. She looked at the Alliance women and at their banner and said, "The Angela Davis banner you are carrying has nothing to do with women's liberation." The Alliance women would not be allowed to march.

KOMISAR'S STATEMENT WAS a way of saying, "You don't belong here." This was ironic because the group almost didn't go to the march that day. Alliance members had been reluctant to participate because they did not see themselves as "women's libbers." In fact, they were critical of the racism and middle-class orientation of the "white women's movement." Friedan, who'd called for the Women's Strike for Equality that day, was a prime example of that white middle-class orientation. Her 1963 book, *The Feminine Mystique*, is said to have ignited the second wave of feminism, but Alliance women were critics of her work. Very little of what she wrote in *The Feminine Mystique* related to the experience of poor and working women of color. Among us, we characterized Friedan's "problem that has no name" as the problem of unhappy and unfulfilled suburban housewives who, despite their college education, were confined to driving carpools and making decisions about which new household appliance to purchase. These were not the issues that galvanized poor and working women of color who had problems they could easily name: heroin in their communities, limited access to good jobs, a need for welfare rights, racism, and lack of adequate healthcare. An article in *Triple Jeopardy* tackled this distinction directly, contrasting the affluent summer visitors to Atlantic City's beaches with Atlantic City's West Side "slum area where mostly black and poor people live. . . . The children pass their time playing in the streets because they can't afford to go to the other side of Atlantic City where the rich folks play where the rides are located."[2]

The history of women of color in the United States, college educated or not, was different from those of white women. Native women had been forced off their land, had walked the Trail of Tears, and had often been murdered along with their men and children as the British and Spanish colonizers "settled the land." Much the same had happened to Mexican women in the Southwest. Asian women were working in laundries, restaurants, and factories across the United States. Black women, forced to work during enslavement and needing to work in the postbellum years to help support their families because of the low wages and limited employment of Black men, did not know the "luxury" of some of the problems that Friedan described.

The women of the Alliance were working women, single parents, students who knew they had to find jobs and develop careers because they would have to rely on their own earnings to support themselves and help their families in the future. Few of the sisters had the luxury of not working and being able to stay home and raise their children.

Friedan represented a privileged experience that neither the Alliance sisters nor their communities in "El Barrio," the Bronx, or Fort Green, Brooklyn, shared. Because of all these issues, Alliance members had thought long and hard about marching, and it hadn't been an easy decision to show up that day.

August 25, 1970, was the fiftieth anniversary of the passage of the Nineteenth Amendment to the United States Constitution, which gave women the right to vote—after great struggle and effort by early suffragettes. Many Black women participated in the early struggle for voting rights for women, including prominent figures like Sojourner Truth and Ida B. Wells, as well as ordinary Black women like the southern Black suffragettes.[3] Hispanic women like Adelina Otero-Warren took part in the United States and in England. Sophia Duleep Singh and Bhikaiji Cama were among the South Asian women who played vital roles in the suffragette movement. In 1890, however, white women wanted the support of white men, from the North and South, racist and anti-racist, and they began to exclude women of color from their ranks. And the right to vote for Black women was not fully ensured until the 1965 Voting Rights Act. Thus, the fiftieth anniversary of women's suffrage was really the fiftieth anniversary of white women's suffrage.

The women of the Alliance were children of the 1940s and 1950s, and they understood that, despite the Nineteenth

Amendment, there was still a great deal of containment and control of women in the "Father Knows Best" era in which they were raised. Condoms or diaphragms were the only forms of birth control available during the fifties, and women were dependent on their doctors (mostly male at the time) to prescribe diaphragms or on men to buy condoms because convention and etiquette prevented women from purchasing them at a store.

Some changes began to take place in the sixties because of women's activism. In 1965, the Supreme Court ruled in *Griswold v. Connecticut* that the law against birth control violated marital privacy. Birth control pills, which had been approved in 1960, became more widely available. An amendment including the word "sex" was added to the Civil Rights Act of 1964, prohibiting discrimination by sex in the workplace. In 1968, women protested the Miss America Pageant, calling it sexist, and the Roman Catholic Church decided to permit nuns or schoolgirls to read the epistle of the Mass but only in severely limited settings. These changes fueled women's desire and empowered them to seek more change and greater liberation.

Abortion was still illegal in most states until 1973, and women were dying or rendered sterile in attempts to terminate pregnancies. Horrifying methods included inserting coat hangers or tubes filled with turpentine into vaginas and up to the uterus to try to end pregnancies. Women drank poisonous substances in an effort to expel their fetuses. They tried to avoid bearing children not simply because they did not want them but also because they could not afford them, and without resources and husbands, they would be ostracized, and their children would be dubbed "illegitimate." Pregnant girls were often turned out of their parents' homes and forced to drop out of school. These closed doors became barriers for their future lives and well-being.

Some women could find skilled medical personnel to perform a safe abortion despite the illegality, but this was not easy. These women who could afford abortions were often left to suffer in the most harrowing of circumstances. Out-of-wedlock pregnancy was such a disgrace that when showing up at the clinic to have an abortion, women would have to wear a wedding ring, and then there was the question of cost. Illegal abortions were expensive.

Fran had an illegal abortion when she was seventeen. When she returned home after her first year at college, she learned that a close high school friend had died after an attempted illegal abortion. At the same time that some women were trying to end unwanted pregnancies, women in Puerto Rico and Black women in the South were undergoing rampant, state-sponsored forced sterilization,[4] as four articles in the 1973, 1974, and 1975 issues of *Triple Jeopardy* later reported.[5]

Even giving birth was a traumatic experience in the 1960s—women in the United States were not allowed to have anyone but medical personnel with them in the labor and delivery rooms. Fathers were not allowed in, and doulas did not yet exist. Women spent five, ten, fifteen hours—sometimes days—in labor with no one to support them. Women suffered then (as they still do now) from high rates of cesarean sections, and when they tried to nurse their babies, they were shamed and isolated to discourage them.

Ordinary day-to-day living was not without its constraints either. Although there were half-day nursery schools for the children of rich families, day care was not widely available for working mothers. Another problem existed in employment: classified ads for men and women were segregated and thus limited job possibilities for women. Even women with a college degree found their options often limited to secretarial work, teaching, or nursing, all honorable professions but with inadequate pay and limited opportunity for advancement. Men's higher pay was justified by the claim that they were "the breadwinners" and "the heads of household."

Nurses did not yet have the increased responsibility and status that began to occur in the 1990s. There were only a few women lawyers, professors, and doctors. Voicing the zeitgeist of 1956, five male psychiatrists stated that they believed "female ambition was the root of mental illness in wives, emotional upsets in husbands, and homosexuality in boys."[6] Women with careers were forced to justify themselves. In response to an article titled "The Woman in the Gray Suit" by Sloan Wilson,

Reka Hoff, a lawyer, asserted, "If unmarried, their career is designated a 'substitute' for marriage; if married, their career is designated a 'substitute' for motherhood; if a mother, their career brands them as selfish and neglectful."[7]

Women's participation in athletics was also limited. Basketball was one of the few sports in which women could and did participate, but they were only allowed to play half-court and could only dribble the ball three times because they were deemed too fragile to exert themselves.

Rape and spousal abuse were not commonly reported, because if women called the police or pressed charges and took the complaint to court, they were likely not to be believed. They were often humiliated in the process and were then further threatened by their male abusers. Clothing was an issue too! Women who wore pants in public were open to derision and in certain places, like the college I attended, we were forced to wear dresses, stockings, and heels to dinner. Women's birth names were cast aside when they were married. For example, a woman born Mary Jones would be addressed by her husband's name after marriage, becoming Mrs. John Smith.

Women could not be ministers in most Protestant denominations. In some states, women could not serve on juries. It was difficult and often impossible for women to get credit, bank loans, or purchase cars. Although the proportion of women among college students in 1958 was 35.2 percent, fewer than 10 percent of doctorates were awarded to women. In *A Century of Higher Education for American Women*, Mabel Newcomer reported that three out of five women attending coeducational colleges were taking secretarial, nursing, home economics, or education courses, and the percentage of women receiving professional degrees in the 1950s had not been as low since before World War I.[8]

It was even harder for women of color. Impacted by the same sexism as white women and damaged by the same racism that affected men of color, vast numbers of African American women were confined to domestic work in the 1950s. In a 1970 *New York Times* article, Dorothy Height is quoted saying, "With all the advances that black women have made—and we are in every field occupied by women—it is still true that we are in predominantly household and related services with a median income of $1,523."[9] Large numbers of Mexican, Mexican American, and Filipina women spent their lives as migrant workers. Untold numbers of Chinese women on the West Coast were exploited in factories, and women from Indigenous populations on the nation's reservations were invisible and stricken with poverty and discrimination. Recent Puerto Rican migrant women were often limited to working as machine operators in the garment and textile factories of New York and Massachusetts. The bodies of women of color, controlled by rape, oppression, and extinction during enslavement and colonization, were still not their own in the middle of the twentieth century.

Alliance women experienced oppression as women, along with their oppression as people of color, and they wanted to express solidarity with the demand for women's rights, but there was ambivalence as well. The TWWA supported equality for women. They certainly acknowledged the progress women had made in achieving the right to vote, but most Alliance members were not believers in the electoral process. They saw little substantive difference between the Democrats and the Republicans, and they believed little could be achieved by voting. These were the realities that led the women of the Alliance to think they should march that day.

"IT HAS EVERYTHING to do with the women's liberation *we're* talking about," Fran responded to the NOW parade coordinator's assertion that the Alliance's sign had nothing to do with women's liberation. She did not relent. She insisted and persisted. Like the tree planted by the water in the old civil rights song, Fran would not be moved. The sisters of the Alliance did indeed march that day. Fran was stationed at the right corner of the banner, lifting it high with Affreekka Jefferson, Barbara Goff, Karen D. Taylor, Stella Holmes Hughes (see portrait on p. 67), and others.

I was twenty-six years old on that August day and I, too, marched down Fifth Avenue with the Alliance contingent. My compañero at that time, Joaquín Rosa, had told me there was to be a demonstration about women's issues, and he'd encouraged me to go down to the march that afternoon. Joaquín and I were both activists in a community organizing group called Latin Action. I was nervous because I didn't know anyone in the Alliance and really didn't have a sense of what I was going to. Joaquín had stressed that the Alliance was an important organization, and for weeks, he had urged me to go. One problem was that I didn't know any of the women, but there was something else too. Somehow, it felt like Joaquín was pressuring me to go, and that bred my resistance. I learned later in an interview with Lucas Daumont, former chairperson of Latin Action, that there had been an organizational directive for me and Zorina Costello, another Latin Action sister, to attend the demonstration.

This wasn't unusual. Most movement organizations encouraged their members to participate in other organizations whose missions aligned with theirs. Latin Action's agenda was the liberation of Latinos in the United States, the Caribbean, and Central and South America. The Alliance supported the liberation struggle of Latinos and other people of color around the world. Thus the politics and values of these two organizations were in alignment.

Overcoming my resistance, I met up with Zorina, and we went together. I was familiar with Fifth Avenue, having paraded down that street with my Mother Cabrini High School classmates in four consecutive St. Patrick's Day parades from 1958 through 1961, and again in 1963 when I was a student at the College of Our Lady of Good Counsel in White Plains, New York. This time the "uniforms" were different, and there were no "best school" marching trophies to be won. As I joined the sisters on the march down Fifth Avenue, I felt an immediate sense of solidarity and connection. I had experienced racism all my life as the only Black student in my classes from fourth grade through college. I'd had my own illegal abortion at age twenty-two, performed by a nurse who put "a clamp" on my uterus and sent me home to endure thirty-six hours of labor until the embryo was expelled. My parents had been working people in a household where two incomes were necessary. My brother was serving in Vietnam. I had been involved for several years in Latin Action, working to organize communities in the South Bronx, but, as a non-Latina, I was always a bit on the fringe. I fit easily into the definition of "third world" and for the first time did not have to explain myself any further. Energized by the other women and inspired by the speeches at Bryant Park, I realized by the end of that day that I would become a part of the Alliance. I had found my place in the movement.

The Alliance had a purpose in the march that day. They wanted to stand up for women's rights, and they also wanted to emphasize a difference between the TWWA and the many white women's organizations that marched. The Alliance banner expressed solidarity with the most well-known Black woman activist of the time, Angela Davis, an avowed communist freedom fighter. The words on the banner were meant to focus onlookers on the Alliance's solidarity with her. The crucial, though perhaps less obvious, subtext was the message that the Alliance's mission was the same as Angela's: to wage an ongoing struggle against racism, sexism, and class oppression.

Among the signs enjoining women to stand up against their male oppressors, the simple statement on the Alliance banner spoke volumes. It called for the liberation of a woman—a Black woman—who in her quest for freedom spoke and acted against racial oppression, systems of class advantage, and capitalist and imperialist hegemony. The banner expressed cogently the politics of the TWWA and eloquently captured its particular vantage point and position in the women's movement, while simultaneously placing us in relation to the militant Black liberation movement.

With fifty thousand other women, the Alliance marched all the way down to the rally at Bryant Park. There among the speakers, including Friedan, Gloria Steinem, and Congresswoman Bella Abzug, three Black women also spoke: Eleanor Holmes Norton, chairperson of New York City's Commission on Human Rights; Florynce Kennedy, a feminist lawyer and frequent speaker at women's liberation rallies; and Alliance member Barbara Goff.

Fran had been asked to speak, but she had delegated the task to Barbara. Understanding that building a revolution meant developing a cadre of leaders, Fran always worked to empower other sisters. This inclusive leadership style was in fact a distinctive element of TWWA organizing.

Fran had read the speech Barbara prepared. She approved of the message, especially the part where Barbara asserted that "revolution, not reform, is the answer." With Barbara's speech, the Alliance publicly announced its place in the 1970s women's movement, which later became known as the second wave of feminism. Standing up for women and people of color and taking an anti-imperialist stance, the Alliance was present on a day that changed the conversation about women's lives in the United States.

We brought our version of women's liberation, our form of feminism, to the march on Fifth Avenue. It was a feminism that declared race an integral, inseparable issue in the struggle for the liberation of women. Barbara spoke to an audience of fifty thousand people at Bryant Park and named us as revolutionaries, not reformists. Our presence and our perspective were documented in the *New York Times*, the most widely respected mainstream paper in the state. We were beginning to influence the women's movement.

In New York City that day, women took over the Statue of Liberty, a lawsuit was filed against the Board of Education to press for more women in administration, and women demonstrated at the New York Stock Exchange with placards that read, "We won't bear any more bull."

Actions took place around the country as well. As the National Women's History Museum wrote in a blog post, "This was the largest protest for gender equality in U.S. history. There were demonstrations and rallies in more than ninety major cities and small towns across the country,"[10] alerting the world that women still did not have equal rights in America. Feminist scholar Jo Freeman wrote that this day was "the first time the potential power of the feminist movement became publicly apparent . . . and with this the movement came of age."[11]

It turned out that Friedan seriously underestimated the number of women who would be present at the largest women's demonstration on American soil, up until that time. Fifty thousand women were on Fifth Avenue in New York City on August 26, 1970—and the women of the TWWA were among them.

Our participation that day—the encounter with Komisar, our presence and our banner, Barbara's speech at Bryant Park, and the coverage that followed in the *New York Times*—helped to expand the vision of what women's liberation and feminism meant. We showed up, and we brought the women's liberation we were talking about. We were there!

A Luta Continua: Alliance Women Today

Frances M. Beal
TWWA Founder, Activist, Writer, Mother, Grandmother

Lenin said when asked about the appropriate type of education for women: "Women should be taught to run the state." It's part of what made me a revolutionary.

Frances M. Beal is a self-defined "Black radical" and a founding member of the Student Nonviolent Coordinating Committee (SNCC) and Black Women's Liberation Committee (BWLC, which evolved into the TWWA). She has committed her life to political activism, asserting that "what I struggle for is a social and economic transformation that better serves working families and the poor in the US."

Fran was six or seven years older than most of the New York women who joined the Alliance. She was the foremother who illuminated the way for younger activists who had not been part of the civil rights era struggles in the South. Fran channeled the fire of revolutionary spirit to nascent radical women of color who were ready kindling, needing only the right spark to ignite their activism and help them make sense of their outrage about injustice.

Fran is the most renowned and frequently interviewed member of the Alliance. I interviewed her four times for this project. She is author of the widely celebrated article "Double Jeopardy: To Be Black and Female," first printed in pamphlet form by the Alliance and later published in 1970 in both Robin Morgan's *Sisterhood Is Powerful* and

Toni Cade Bambara's *The Black Woman: An Anthology*. Fran helped to disseminate awareness of race, gender, and class issues that became the early triumvirate of progressive feminists of color, and she maintains that what "Alliance women justly assert is the original praxis and articulation for the academic concept of intersectionality." She bolsters this by quoting SNCC's language about the "intersection of class and race."

The daughter of a Marxist Jewish mother and a Black Christian father, Fran fully identifies as African American. This is how she was seen and treated in the majority white community where she was raised. This is how she was experienced and how she identified when studying at the Sorbonne, and this is what she knew from struggling in the South with SNCC in the late 1960s.

Talking with Fran is like sharing a conversation with a movement history book, an opportunity for a one-on-one tutorial with one of the great activist-thinkers of the sixties and seventies. She is always excited about ideas, always defining what she sees before her—in you, the person with whom she is talking, and in the world. She is always a step ahead, sorting, categorizing, remembering, codifying, and correcting. She is eloquent, her language full of evocative metaphor. When she recalled what it was like to finally be free of the "horrible girdle" that constricted her and other young women of our era, she said, "You couldn't walk; couldn't run; couldn't be free. . . . It was like shaking off the chains of a Victorian era that lasted well into the twentieth century."

After TWWA came to an end in New York, Fran moved to California and worked with the Alliance there as well as the Marxist group Line of March, covering Black politics for its newspaper, *Frontline*. She spent seventeen years at the American Civil Liberties Union of Northern California. When the Alliance folded in California, Fran's activism didn't wane, although she has returned to the family tradition of quilting as she ages. She worked for the National Council of Negro Women during the time she was in SNCC and the Alliance. In 1982, she became an associate editor for *Black Scholar* magazine, and in 1992, she became a writer and journalist for *Crossroads Magazine*. As a columnist for the *San Francisco Bay View*, in 2000, she wrote weekly columns on national Black politics. From 1987 to 2005, she was a legal assistant and then a research associate for the ACLU's Racial Justice Project, where she worked with Michelle Alexander on racial profiling issues. After retiring, she continued her work as a lifelong peace advocate, supporting the struggle for Cuba's sovereignty, African liberation, and an equitable peaceful settlement between Israel and Palestine.

Having reached the age of eighty at the time of this writing, Fran stays involved with politics and is engaged with social media. She threw her energy into the 2020 elections, working with Black Folks for Bernie Bay Area. Her Facebook page shows that she supports Food and Water Watch, the Schomburg Center for Black Culture, Mobilization for Health Care for All, Oakland Rising, Peace Action West, and the Rosenberg Fund for Children. She attributes her sense of social consciousness to watching her mother take up struggles for justice and to stories her father told her about racial injustices. They gave her the belief "that when something was wrong in society, you should get together with others and do something to change it."

Brenda Boho Beato

Teacher, Mother, Grandmother, School Leader

The Third World Women's Alliance was my first twinkle of women being empowered, women being able to do anything.

Brenda Boho Beato was on her hands and knees on her front walkway, laying pavers, when I arrived for our interview. Her beautiful octagonal home in upstate New York had been lovingly and painstakingly constructed, renovated, and maintained by both Brenda and her husband, Tom. Working on the house is one of the major ways she spends her time.

Running road races is another of her passions, along with maintaining a vegetable garden and tending to abundant flowering plants. These were not things she learned growing up in the projects on First Avenue in Harlem. Her current vigorous physical activities must certainly have been born in the Alliance, I recall thinking. "That period," she told me about the organization's influence on her life, "was my first twinkle of women being empowered, women being able to do anything."

Sitting on her comfortable deck, surrounded by abundant flowerpots and the flower-filled gourds she designs and makes, we talked about her years since the Alliance. She directed her political energy toward education, and this became her way of "working to change the world." She and her husband were teachers at different schools. "Every day, with every one of those children, I tried to make the world a better place," she says. Whether with a hug or an innovative lesson plan, she strove to keep them connected and engaged. She retired in 2010 after thirty years of teaching.

She also worked hard to mentor younger teachers as a union representative for the Middletown Teachers' Alliance. She was chair of its political action committee and recalled when "we had no contract and the action committee had to come out . . . to get a contract and what we did was we sent out leaflets. . . . We pretended there were a lot of people on the action committee, and we scared the bee-jeebies out of them and finally the contract was done." Speaking about her fellow teachers she says, "If people had a question and they were afraid of bringing it up, I was not afraid of bringing it up. I never had a problem bringing anything up."

Brenda spoke with deep conviction about her belief that individuals don't "own" one another, referring to her husband, her children, even her mother. She talked about supporting her children in developing their own family traditions.

Reflecting on Tom (who later passed away in 2017) she said, "You don't own Tom; you let Tom be." Brenda describes Tom as "the love of my life" and "my partner," feeling the term captures their relationship. "He'll always be my partner," she says. "The kids say that's a term for gay people, but we got it from the movement."

Brenda was speechless when I handed her the Alliance's platform, the statement of purpose and values she hadn't seen in almost thirty years. She exclaimed as she read. "Oh, wait a minute; I remember this. . . . To create a sisterhood of women. That was one of the reasons I was there. It promoted a sisterhood." Her excitement reached a high point when she got to "we do not believe that any person is the property of any other" and "all people must share equally in the decisions which affect them." "Here it is," she said. "I keep saying, 'I don't own anyone.'" There was so much in the platform that Brenda still believed in. "It laid a big foundation in my life," she said. "Even though I left the Alliance, it never left me. It became an integral part of me."

When we spoke about Brenda's years as a teacher, she was critical of the increased testing in public schools. "Years ago, I found that my eleven- and twelve-year-olds had more of an understanding of their history than they do now because New York State has 'testized.' All it does is test, and all teachers do is teach to the tests," she says. "They're no longer learning anything else other than what's on a test. So, what doesn't get taught is history—what you're about. What is your culture? They have no clue. The more tests are given, the less and less of that is being taught to students. So, if they don't know it in the sixth grade, you won't know it in the seventh . . . eighth grade. . . . So by the time they leave high school, they learn less and less about themselves."

Brenda worries about the young women she taught in middle school. "They are stronger than the boys in middle school," she said. "They will kick your ass and not think about it twice. The girls are much more aggressive than boys now. Girl-on-girl fights. Forget about it; it's blood. Being in the classroom in an inner-city school, you see an aggressiveness among females that you've never seen before." Her statement reminded me of Grace Boggs's comments about youth in Detroit: "Deferred dreams now wreak the same negative outcomes in girls as in boys."

When I ask Brenda to sum up the impact of the Alliance on her life, she speaks with confidence, "I'm not a shaker or a mover on big terms, but I'm there. Making sure that things are flowing for people."

Christine Choy (Chai Ming Huei)
Filmmaker, Professor, Mother

They isolate you. Racism is how they do it.

In an apartment huddled between the Garment District and Koreatown on the West Side of New York City, I interviewed the renowned filmmaker and former TWWA member Christine Choy. Her apartment is as idiosyncratic and artistic as Christine herself. Its huge, almost floor-to-ceiling windows overlook the Hudson River, directing my eyes up to the sky and buildings that top the New Jersey skyline to the west. Inside, my gaze is drawn to the East, to China and Korea. An opium bed rests reminiscently in the living room. The parquet floors illuminate the placement of her mother's vintage Asian furniture, and a tiny curving flight of white steps leads up to a loft where her son sleeps when he visits. "Minimalist," she murmurs as she follows my gaze.

But Christine's life has been anything but minimalist. She came to the United States in 1969 with a huge leather suitcase that she could barely lift and headed to Sacred Heart School where she had been enrolled.

"Oh God, Patricia. I had hell with my name. I had a hell. When I arrive, my name was Chai Ming Huei, which no one could pronounce. So the nuns said, 'Well, you look so innocent we are to give you a Catholic name, Theresa.' So I became Theresa," but they still had trouble with the rest of her name, so she finally changed it herself, settling on Christine Choy.

She had traveled a long way from the People's Republic of China, first to Hong Kong, then to South Korea, followed by a brief stay in Japan, then back to South Korea, to Hawaii, and, finally, to New York. But because her X-rays showed some calcification in her lungs due to the touch of tuberculosis she'd had in Shanghai, she was quarantined at the sanatorium at Grasslands Hospital in Westchester County.

When she returned to Sacred Heart School, she was given a private room so as not to contaminate a roommate. She hated American food and didn't quite know how to eat it. She was embarrassed to eat in the dining hall, so she'd sneak bits of food back to her room where she ate alone.

"They had a dorm that had a box, for those who were willing to give their old clothes to Theresa, to me, because I didn't have warm clothes. So I walk around the school with other people's clothes." Unfamiliar with American clothing, she was often laughed at for mistakes she made in her attire (she once wore a bed jacket to a party).

Before she was a teenager, Christine had lived in four countries and experienced life under four political systems.

"I had already lived in a Communist state, which was the People's Republic of China, Shanghai. Lived in Hong Kong—at the time it was a colony of Britain. We moved from there to South Korea, which is a neo-colony of the United States." She remembered her time in South Korea: "Which I hated because at the time 99.9 percent of the population was starvation and 1 percent were filthy rich—the ones associated with the US army." This experience was especially difficult, she said, because, "I was already politicized. . . . When we were kids (in China) the first textbook was dialectical materialism. And everybody was supposed to be equal? It was like a nightmare."

While living in Korea, Christine became interested in film while watching American movies. In the seventies, Chris became a member of Newsreel, a radical film company with chapters around the country. In the mid-seventies, she was a key leader in the transformation of the New York Chapter of Newsreel into a separate organization, Third World Newsreel (TWN), which still produces films today—most recently, *Making the Impossible Possible: The Story of Puerto Rican Studies in Brooklyn College.*

During her years in the Alliance, Chris made a film about Marilyn Jean Buck, feminist poet and revolutionary; traveled to Cuba to visit liberation activist Assata Shakur; and drew and sketched scores of illustrations for *Triple Jeopardy* decrying capitalism and racism and asserting the power of women. She was the New York Chapter's main graphic artist, and during our interview, she gifted me with copies of many of her sketches, which frequently appeared in *Triple Jeopardy* and on Alliance posters.

Christine has traveled a long way since that time and has retained her character, her languages, and her conviction that there should be economic equality and justice. She has made more than fifty films. Her best-known film *Who Killed Vincent Chin?* was released in 1983 and nominated for an Academy Award. *Teach Our Children*, *From Spikes to Spindles*, *Inside Women Inside*, *To Love, Honor, and Obey*, *A Dream Is What You Wake Up From*, and *Fresh Seeds in a Big Apple* preceded it; many more followed.

"The only time I went back to South Korea was making a film, *Homes Apart: Korea*. I filmed in North Korea first then filmed in the South which enraged the government." She went back to China often. First, "to establish the NYU campus there." Then afterward to make a film about her childhood friends and later a film about the June 4, 1989, Tiananmen Square protest, "which is in the process of completion."

Today, she is on the faculty at New York University's Tisch School of the Arts. She is making a film about Tupac Shakur and his influence on the new generation. She continues her work as teacher, mentor, and filmmaker, and, speaking in an accent that demonstrates her long-term loyalty to her heritage, she makes clear that her films will continue to serve as political and humanist statements exposing injustice. "Racism, sexism," she says, "are rampant today. Disgusting!" Regarding social- ist politics? "Marxist? I'm not into isms. Has a lot to do with my eclectic background. Even though China has its problems, if China had not been communist, it would be completely invaded by Western ideas, and it would be falling apart."

With her characteristic humor, she ends our last conversation by stating, "Lord, we are getting old. I knew [Patrice] Lumumba who got killed by the FBI as well as Mutulu [Shakur] who is still in jail. So I will be one of the first people in line for the COVID vaccine."

Lenore French
Activist, Artist, Community Builder

I've used the lessons of the Third World Women's Alliance all my life.

Lenore French calls herself a "third-generation rabble-rouser." Describing those three generations, she recalls, "My grandfather's work as a postal clerk connected him with the National Alliance of Postal and Federal Employees, the first African American union in the US. My father, Joseph French, broke barriers as the first African American trained in neurology at Johns Hopkins, and he also marched with Dr. King in Selma in 1965." Her mother, too, was an activ- ist. "She worked with the Women's League for Peace and Freedom, and that inspired her to take me to the national March on Washington against the Vietnam War in 1969."

While a student at Harvard, Lenore began to read *Triple Jeopardy* and connected immediately with the articles. She took a semester's leave in the spring of 1973 to join the TWWA in New York.

At Harvard, Lenore was active in the divestment movement and part of the group that planted five hundred black crosses in the snow in Harvard Yard to protest the university's holding of stock in Gulf Oil, the largest American investor in Portuguese-held Africa. Each cross signified the death of a thousand Africans at the hands of Portuguese colonizers. According to French, "That image—the dramatic presenta- tion of black crosses against white snow—made a lasting impression and created a visceral understanding of the role art can play in systemic change." Later that year, she and fellow students occupied the offices of then-president Derek C. Bok. Their actions, aided by public outcry, led to Harvard divesting itself of its Gulf Oil holdings.

Diversity drew Lenore to the Alliance. An African American woman of multiracial background, she said, "Looking around, I recognized the common denominator among disenfranchised groups. Though it had been explored in my family, that was my own, personal pathway to Marxism." She cherished her time working with Christine Choy, Ana Celia Zentella, and Fran Beal. She recognized that Alliance women fully represented the triple jeopardy of women and related this to her own experience: "In those days, even in political circles, men were very dismissive of women's voice . . . of the role sexism played in the narrative of our history." While working with the Alliance, Lenore focused on the arts and culture for *Triple Jeopardy*.

Now living in Los Angeles, Lenore continues to use art as a tool for social justice, and retaining her "class consciousness," she works with multiracial artists "on cultural equity and inclusion in public art initiatives and protecting affordable housing." She also finds the separate racial demographics in Los Angeles unsettling and reports that Latinos commit 50 percent of the hate crimes against Black folks in LA. When she thinks about the Alliance, she recalls the importance and impact of gaining strength through unity: "I've used this all my life."

Informed by Joan C. Williams's book *White Working Class: Overcoming Class Cluelessness in America*, which she describes as "a scathing review of elite ignorance that led to the Trump presidency," Lenore is part of a local coalition between the Latino (mostly Oaxacan) community and artists in LA.

In addition, Lenore founded Green Communications Initiative, a nonprofit that inspires responsible consumption and environmental justice, and cofounded the Venice-Mar Vista Arts Coalition, a coalition of nearly thirty arts institutions, nonprofits, and individual artists.

CHAPTER 2

From Double Jeopardy to Triple Jeopardy
The Genesis of the TWWA

*They could talk all night about liberation and freedom as it
related to race, but when it came to the question of women,
they were going back to fifteenth-century Africa in order to
see a feudal relationship.*

—*FRANCES BEAL*

SNCC

The TWWA had not been around very long when Alliance sisters
decided to participate in the 1970 Women's March in New York
City. The organization had just evolved a few months earlier
like a subterranean rhizome planted at least a decade before.

In 1960, a sit-in was staged at a Woolworth's lunch counter
in Greensboro, North Carolina, where, as in most restaurants
throughout the segregated South, Black people were refused
service. Carryout service, or takeout, was the only option for
Black folks in most restaurants and not all restaurants offered
that option. Although the staff would not serve them, Black
students sat at the lunch counter and refused to get up, a
tactic first used in the 1940s by Howard University Law School
students. The Woolworth's lunch counter sit-in in Greensboro
lasted several days, drawing news coverage, shocking citizens
living in the North and the West, and inspiring other sit-ins at
restaurants throughout the South.

Spurred by these actions, Ella Baker, executive secretary of the Southern Christian Leadership Conference (SCLC), convened a conference at Shaw University in Raleigh, North Carolina, on Easter weekend, April 16, 1960. The goal of the conference was "to coordinate these sit-ins, support their leaders, and publicize their activities."[1] Its result was the emergence of a new organization, the Student Nonviolent Coordinating Committee (SNCC), an organization based on the students' nonviolent approach to social change.

SNCC grew quickly, expanding beyond its southern Black student roots, drawing white civil rights activists from around the country, and sponsoring the now famous freedom rides. Initially facilitated by Baker's nonhierarchical leadership style, SNCC grew to become one of the most powerful organizations advancing desegregation in the 1960s. SNCC then expanded its activism to tackle other aspects of segregation. Despite having the legal right to vote, Black people in the South were being stopped at the polls and asked for identification that they didn't have and shouldn't have needed. Poll taxes were created and levied to prevent poor Black folks from exercising their constitutional rights. In response, SNCC developed freedom rides for activists from the North who went to the South and with activists there engaged in massive voter registration drives.

TWWA's founders Fran Beal, Mae Jackson, who ran SNCC's fundraising arm in New York City, and Gwen Patton, a member and lifelong activist, were SNCC staffers. Fran experienced racism firsthand during her childhood in Binghamton, New York, where she and her brothers were often called the "N" word, and her brothers were sometimes beaten up because of their race. She deeply felt the "race prejudice, religious prejudice, and reactionary political temper"[2] of the town and was shaken by the murder of Emmett Till in 1955. Her parents were active leftists. Fran recalls her mother picketing the showing of *Birth of a Nation* in Binghamton during Fran's childhood. Inspired by a college speaker who spoke about segregation in the South, Fran became an activist in college, joining the NAACP in 1958 and picketing Woolworth's stores in the North because of their racist hiring practices in their southern stores.

Gwen had a long history in the South. She spent time with her grandparents there every summer and as early as age nine began to resist the ignominies of segregation. At sixteen, she moved to Montgomery, Alabama, to live with her grandparents after her mother died, and she immediately joined the Montgomery Improvement Association and later became involved with both the SCLC and SNCC.

During Fran and Gwen's time in SNCC in the early to late sixties, the organization became a powerful change agent in the struggle for civil rights in the South. It developed a wider role as well, becoming one of the first Black organizations to come out against the war in Vietnam and, according to Fran, playing an instrumental role in "hammering the last nails in the coffin of the McCarthy era."

Although McCarthyism, the campaign that Senator Joseph McCarthy waged against alleged communists in the US government, lasted from 1950 to 1954, with traces remaining in the sixties, Fran recalled,

> McCarthyism was everywhere. People lost their jobs. People were accused of being Communists and people were asked to tell on each other. There was a complete undermining of Constitutional rights—of due process, free speech, and free assembly. They used loyalty oaths to keep progressive movements in line. SNCC played an important role in terms of refusing to sign the loyalty oath and still demanding racial justice and racial freedom. It was in a sense spitting in the face of the remnants of McCarthyism. In many ways, the civil rights movement, the active challenge of white supremacy, and Jim Crow in the South, essentially broke the back of McCarthyism.

Women who worked with SNCC were integral to its success, and Fran's perspective was that "SNCC was less sexist in some ways than some of the other organizations. . . . SNCC women were playing some leading roles—not roles where they were there for the TV cameras but roles at the concrete place of organizing. . . . A number of Black women came to the fore in terms of the struggle."

"Still," she continued, "women in SNCC, like women in most

other organizations of the time, were often limited to less prominent roles in the organization and because of this and because of the not infrequent expression of 'backward ideas' [about women] . . . it was very easy to begin to see that being a woman is no different, in terms of the oppression and exploitation she feels."

Responding to some of these concerns, a group of Black and white women staffers went to an SNCC staff meeting in the spring of 1964 carrying placards protesting their role as always being the ones to take minutes. Later that year, several SNCC staffers wrote about gender inequities in a paper titled "The Position of Women in SNCC."[3] Distress about women's roles in SNCC grew when word spread that Stokely Carmichael, then a field secretary with SNCC, responded to the report by saying, "The only position for women in SNCC is prone." Although this comment was never confirmed, Carmichael's widely reported statement intensified frustration among SNCC women and other women activists.

Female SNCC staffers would sometimes complain in private about these things and, over time, they continued to vocalize their concerns. Fran and Gwen pointed out that the important committees were staffed by men, that clerical work was assigned to women, and that in rare cases when women were in leadership positions, they often had to defer to men when major decisions were being made.

Fran remembers clearly that it was the women in SNCC who were expected to clean and do the laundry and that a division of labor based on whether one was male or female was taken for granted. Women were expected to type and answer the phones; men were the project organizers and leaders. In one troubling case that Fran recalled, a woman voluntarily surrendered leadership of a project to a man, even though she was clearly more suited to the role, because she felt it was the time for Black men to step forward in leadership. "She ended up, of course, leading from the sidelines because she was the stronger person . . . more creative, and it created a very bad dynamic because, in fact, she was the one that should have been the leader because she was the one who was capable," Fran says.

Although Gwen did have some leadership responsibilities, she, too, spoke up about the inequities. In the South, she said, "women were doing some of the most dangerous work, carrying a package at two o'clock in the morning. And it had to be so surreptitious." She and James Forman, who was SNCC's executive secretary between 1961 and 1966, were very close, "like two peas in a pod," she recalled. "I loved him, but I had to ask him, 'Why do you have these young girls running around doing the brothers' bidding? If a brother needs a package let him carry it.'"[4]

Gwen also remembered the gender difference in clothing during that time period. In those early days of the movement, "the men were wearing fatigues and combat boots, and we were in African dress wearing gelees and long, wrapped dresses, and it was basically 'go bring me, go get me, go fetch me.' I refused. All of that, and we were never a part of strategy, never a part of the planning."

Gwen also noticed the division of labor that relegated women to think about and take care of the children. "We had a conference at the Commodore Hotel around the war in Vietnam and the overall human rights/civil rights movement, and as people were registering for the conference, a sister asked, 'Why are women always shunted into workshops dealing with children?'"

When working to assist in the building of the League of Revolutionary Black Workers in Detroit in 1968 and 1969, Gwen spoke to SNCC leadership about her own concerns. She posed the question "of brothers relegating us to second-class status," stating it was "symbolic of 'you walk behind us.'"

Frustration grew deeper with the publication of Eldridge Cleaver's *Soul on Ice* in 1968. According to Fran, SNCC leaders were very impressed with the book, and Cleaver was immediately catapulted to the forefront of the Black Power movement. SNCC members, she recalled, began taking the book to events, selling it, and heralding it as "really revolutionary."

"So I got a copy of the book, and I read it. And I was absolutely horrified by Eldridge's attitude toward women. And Gwen Patton read the book and had the same reaction."

Other SNCC women had similar responses. So much so that,

according to Fran, SNCC women "actually wrote something up, which we called 'Soul on Fire' . . . a woman's response, a Black woman's response. . . . The basic thing about it was that we ended up saying, Cleaver's book 'is great because he practiced raping Black women, so that he could get up to the point of raping white women?!'"

The paper "Soul on Fire" has never been found, but Fran identifies the reading of *Soul on Ice* as one of the major motivations for the coming together of SNCC's Black Woman's Liberation Committee. "We needed some kind of Black women's committee within SNCC, because we just felt that the level of consciousness [about sexism] was not there."

Several SNCC women continued to talk about these issues and decided they needed to have an "organized forum" to take up some of these questions. They were not coming from an adversarial anti-male position; rather, they wanted to look at the status of the Black woman in society. In December 1968, Fran presented a paper on sterilization abuse and reproductive rights at a national SNCC staff meeting, at which SNCC's BWLC met for the first time. On December 27, 1968, Gwen wrote a letter from New York, outlining the proposed ongoing BWLC. SNCC voted to have an SNCC BWLC (also sometimes called the Black Women's Caucus) "to investigate some of the conditions under which black women function." Both Forman, then head of the International Affairs Commission, and H. Rap Brown, SNCC chairman, supported the decision.

"On the one hand, it was a period in which we were talking about freedom and liberation and changing things," Fran recalled. "So, you can't sort of be talking about liberation and freedom as a Black person and be a Black woman and not feel oppressed and exploited by exploitative behavior." But not everyone agreed about moving in the direction of examining conditions, the specific conditions of Black women. There were SNCC people who were very opposed to the idea. They could see being anti-racist, but they couldn't quite shift their lenses to see the oppression of women. Some of the opposition to the founding of the Black woman's caucus came from women as well as men. Fran recalled the perspective of some women:

"Being Black is hard enough. If we have to take up this women thing, too, it's just too much. You know, we've got to support our men."

SNCC women who were concerned with the woman's perspective recognized that these male chauvinist attitudes (as we called them then) were not just confined to SNCC. They were also troubled by the regressive manner in which women were being treated and portrayed in many of the cultural nationalist organizations of the day. Maulana Karenga's US Organization and Amiri Baraka's Congress of African Peoples were casting women in what Fran and other sisters considered a false and very backward fifteenth-century view of the role of women in which they were expected to be subservient and leave leadership to the men.

Women were expected to maintain the household and have babies for the revolution. As Baraka reportedly said to his male followers, "Keep them barefoot and pregnant." This statement also resounded throughout the movement's progressive ranks. The sentiment about having "babies for the revolution" was another phrase that was promoted by a number of cultural nationalist men, and abortion often was viewed as a genocidal plot against Black people. This kind of thinking was also mirrored in the Nation of Islam, which was drawing many young Black men. In that organization, there was a strict dress code for women—they had to cover themselves from head to toe, could not wear slacks, and were not allowed in leadership positions. Fran remembered,

> I already had two children and had just come out of a relatively oppressive relationship. And had, in the beginning of that relationship, gone along with a lot of things. Women are supposed to be at home and taking care of the family and keeping the house clean, and men are supposed . . . you know, these very prescribed roles for men. So, I think there was a certain personal aspect to it for myself, too. I was already almost thirty, where some of these guys were like in their early twenties, and I was the one that had two children I was trying to support by myself. So, this "babies for the revolution" didn't exactly go down all that well.

SNCC women were not the only ones who witnessed and protested the male chauvinism of Black movement organizations. In her book *Labor of Love, Labor of Sorrow*, Jacqueline Jones notes that "Ruby Doris Smith-Robinson, Kathleen Cleaver, and Angela Davis also spoke out against the tendency of men in SNCC to cry 'matriarchal coup d'état' whenever we women were involved in something important."[5]

Although she served as the chair of the Black Panthers from 1974 to 1979, Elaine Brown decried the fact that in the early days of the Black Panthers, "women in the organization were largely considered, at best, irrelevant. A woman asserting herself was a pariah. A woman attempting the role of leadership was making an alliance with the counter-revolutionary, man-hating, lesbian, feminist white bitches."[6]

Another major concern of SNCC Black women was *The Moynihan Report: The Negro Family, the Case for National Action* (1965). Daniel Patrick Moynihan, a sociologist who had become assistant secretary of the Labor Department in the Kennedy Administration, conducted a research project to determine the causes of Black unemployment and the increasing number of single Black women and their children on the welfare rolls. His aforementioned report introduced the idea of "the black matriarchy." The concept suggested that the Black family was weak because of the absence of fathers in the home. Although Moynihan did identify slavery and racism as the source of Black matriarchy and pressed for welfare departments to remove the requirement that aid could only be given if there was no man in the household, this information and his goals seemed to get lost in the message. Many in the Black community felt that by identifying Black matriarchy as a problem in the development of Black children and the well-being of the Black family, Moynihan had placed the blame on the *victims* of racism—on Black women and mothers.

The concerns about male chauvinism and sexism did not, however, encourage SNCC women to move toward any of the white women's liberation groups. Sexism experienced in the civil rights movement was not unique. White women also experienced sexism, but the racism of white women led Black women to question both white women and the white women's movement. Even during the struggle for women's suffrage, bias and discrimination against Black women had been a problem. In 1913, Black women were asked to march at the back of the Woman's Suffrage Demonstration in Washington, DC.[7] And while working with SNCC, some of the sisters had negative experiences with white women. Gwen had clear memories of her experiences with white women activists in the South. She had escorted a group that included Joan Baez and Judy Collins on a trip through Lowndes County, Alabama, so the women could get "the lay of the land." There was a plan to develop a freedom school in Alabama, one similar to the Mississippi Freedom School. Gwen recalled the women commenting on the "beauty" of the cotton fields and how much this bothered her. From her vantage point, cotton represented oppression and hardship, not beauty.

Gwen returned from showing the white visitors around Lowndes County with the strong sense that the women understood little or nothing about the experience of Blacks in the South. She reported it to Forman, saying, "We're not going to have an Alabama freedom summer. These women have no understanding of the human condition. Our children will be out of school until October to pick the cotton. In January, they'll leave school again to pick the cotton."

Gwen and other SNCC women wanted to involve more Black women in the struggle, but she also noted that white women were not interested in that effort. "They had the wherewithal to organize southern Black women to bring them to a more prominent place, but they wouldn't buy it." From Gwen's point of view, they were more focused on anti-war activity, leaving the question of the elevation of Black women in the background.

On another occasion, Gwen recalled that during a rally to protest the war in Vietnam in Washington, DC, she and other Black activists chose to hold a rally at Banneker Field at Howard University instead:

I was speaking at Banneker Field at Howard. I opposed the nonsense of going into Washington, although I was very big in the anti-war movement. Staying at Banneker Field was an alternative I organized. Left [wing] white women had no sensitivity to DC. It was a Black city with no voting rights. How they trashed the city! There was no money to clean it up and DC was under receivership at that time. They made no connection between the human condition of people in DC and the anti-war movement. The people of mostly Black DC were invisible!

Another important figure in the building of SNCC's Black Women's Caucus was Mae Jackson. Mae worked in the SNCC fundraising office in New York City. This office, initially called Friends of SNCC, supported the organization's civil rights organizing in the South. Their job was to give parties and sell posters, books, and calendars, all of which were part of both fundraising and marketing. Mae remembers, "We would get orders and fill orders. The regular shit work. All done by hand. The day-to-day work that people don't think about when you have a civil rights organization."[8]

She recalls that they sold Julius Lester's children's books and that they received a lot of help from Harry Belafonte's sister Shirley and his then-wife, Julie. She became involved in building the Black Women's Caucus at SNCC because, as she said, "confronting all of that sexism in the office forced you to." And Mae become one of the incorporators of the BWLC and stayed with the organization in the early days of the Black Women's Alliance.

Mae saw the sexism, but she was also aware of the strengths of Black women. She described Fran as "a force to be reckoned with," saying Fran was really the engine for the development of the Black Women's Caucus. "I think it was more of Fran's idea to do something. She was not to be played with. She came in there like a whirlwind." Recalling Gwen, she said, "She could play poker with the best of them. When we had no money, we would give a poker party at my house, my mother would cook fried chicken, and sell whiskey. And Gwen would play all night, and she always won at least $500. My job was to top off her beer and keep her ashtray clean."

Despite the strengths of SNCC women, Mae remembers that

male dominance still reared its head from time to time: "One time we bought a mimeograph for the office with the money Gwen won, and a guy came in and started talking shit to us. I suggested he take some fliers and go drive a cab and stop telling us what to do."

These historical events were all crucial to the developing consciousness of some of the SNCC women. Larger issues affecting women stayed on their radar—inequality in SNCC, the regressive movements of cultural nationalists, the failure of white feminists to understand Black women's needs, and the state of women in the country and the world—and contributed to what followed. In the end, sexism and male chauvinism experienced in the collectives of brothers and sisters working together for the liberation of Black people were both irritants and stimuli.

SNCC's BWLC

The BWLC of SNCC formed in December 1968. Quite soon, it expanded to include women who were not SNCC members: students, welfare mothers, and women from other organizations as well.

On January 3, 1969, the BWLC incorporated in New York and met for the first time at SNCC's offices in St. Peter's Church. The signers of the articles of incorporation were Frances Beal, Mae Jackson, and Gwen Patton. From that point on, events began to move at lightning speed. On January 6, 1969, on behalf of the BWLC in Washington, DC, Gwen proposed a March 1 meeting in Atlanta. In March 1969, a BWLC planning and organizing meeting was convened in Atlanta. Gwen, its chairperson, wrote, "The time has come for us to sit down to seek answers to some of our major problems. We need to take time out to regroup and to redefine some basic concepts and ideas."[9]

To help sisters prepare for the meeting, Gwen distributed three pages of provocative questions designed to prompt thought and develop discussion. The questions were organized under six headings: female, male-female, Black-white, family, philosophy, and revolution. There were scores of direct and daring questions to consider, fashioned from assertions, questions, and debates that were ongoing in the movement:

> What is a woman? What is her purpose and function? Is a black woman different from a white woman? Are babies problems? Does capitalism say babies are problems? Can you organize for the Revolution if you have children? Who is a castrator? Is the black woman one? Were Sojourner Truth, Harriet Tubman castrators? Can the black woman take a leadership role in the struggle? What is nation-building? What is genocide? Does the birth control pill play a part in this? What is communalism, socialism, communism? Should the black woman believe in the Third World concept? What is revolution? What will revolution offer to our people? Is it worth fighting, killing, and dying for? Does the black woman feel that she can fight, kill, and die? Will she take up a gun? Will she pay for the ammunition?[10]

Thirty women attended the meeting and a deep level of shared consciousness-raising occurred. The women were empowered by the realization that not only was there a place for them in the struggle but also a need for an organization that would help other Black women understand their power and their unique contribution.

The Black Women's Alliance

In April 1969, just four months after incorporation papers were filed and one month after the March convening, Fran wrote to her friend Julia Hervé in Paris, telling her of her hopes and plans for organizing Black women, saying, "We hope to be able to create a revolutionary ideology for ourselves." Fran told Julia that a "Black Women's Alliance" had developed and that the organization wanted to "engage in those activities which we feel will improve the conditions of black people and particularly the condition of the black female."[11] The organization began to hold open meetings; all Black women were welcome.

Organizing efforts were deepening. Black women from all

walks of life—both liberal and more leftist women—came to talk about what it meant to be Black and female. They didn't agree on everything. There was no universal agreement on politics, but as they talked, several of the women began to think that they should publish something. "In that era, the mimeograph machine was said to be the favorite weapon of the left," Fran recalled. Toni Cade Bambara, who later became a well-known fiction writer, was there. Gayle Lynch was another participant. A supervisor in a clothing factory, she had not been involved in any political movements before; she simply started coming to meetings and ended up staying for a year or more. Eleanor Holmes Norton, who was then a young lawyer, and would later become chairperson of the Equal Employment Opportunity Commission and serve in the House of Representatives as a delegate from DC, attended. Black feminist Maxine Williams also attended.

Using the movement's "favorite weapon," Fran and these five women published the first of many writings coming from the developing group. Fran recalled, "It was the absolute first publication trying to take up all the nonsense going on about Black women."

They titled their collection *Black Woman's Manifesto*. Gayle's introduction announced the articles' purpose and substance: "The black woman is demanding a new set of female definitions and a recognition of herself as a citizen, companion, and confidant, not a matriarchal villain or a step stool baby-maker. Role integration advocates the complementary recognition of man and woman, not the competitive recognition of same."[12] Numerous copies were printed and circulated, raising consciousness among Black women already in the movement and drawing more Black women into the movement. The collection was later republished and distributed by the Alliance.

Of particular importance in the evolution of the Alliance, and perhaps even more broadly for women of color in the movement, was Fran's paper in the *Manifesto*, "Double Jeopardy: To Be Black and Female," which has been extensively anthologized over a period of many years.[13] The article advanced several key concepts. First, it identified capitalism as the source of racism and male chauvinism. Tracing the history of Black male disemployment and Black women's limited employment opportunities, mainly in the service of white people, Fran cited the economic exploitation and psychological damage done to Black people in America. Second, she set the record straight on Black women and oppression by declaring that Black women were raped by white colonizers and exploited by the system by being placed in the most exploitative jobs in the country, serving as maids, wet nurses, domestics, garment workers, hospital workers. She critiqued those Black men who asserted that Black women were less oppressed and especially called out those Black men who maintained that they were being oppressed and castrated by Black women. She clarified that Black women had not only been equally oppressed but also at times were being used "as the scapegoat for the evils that this horrendous system has perpetrated on Black men."

Third, Fran identified the ways that the reproductive rights of nonwhite women—those in India, Puerto Rico, and Black women all over the United States—were being violated with sterilization abuses, testing of birth control pills, and abortion-related deaths caused by putting poor women of color at "the mercy of the local butcher." And she stated her views on Black women's relationship to the white women's liberation movement. Although she was clear that the woman's movement was not monolithic, she declared that "any white group that does not have an anti-imperialist and anti-racist ideology has absolutely nothing in common with the Black women't [sic] struggle." Further adding, "If the white groups do not realize that they are, in fact, fighting capitalism and racism, we do not have common bonds." The reader will of course recall her confrontation with the NOW representative on August 26, 1970.

The anti-capitalism, anti-imperialism, and Marxist orientation of Fran's writing had a history. In addition to having leftist parents, Fran lived in France and studied at the Sorbonne during the anti-colonialist period. The activist writing of the Marxists there, as well as Simone de Beauvoir's book *The Second Sex* (which she "struggled through in French"), informed her perspectives. SNCC, too, had its Marxist elements, and differences between the advocates of nationalism and the advocates of Black Power and Marxism were one of the fissures that led to organizational collapse. The International Affairs Commission of SNCC, to which Fran was connected, had a Marxist orientation, and she was aligned with Forman, who headed the newly formed commission when it was established in June 1967. Forman had said, "Working on international affairs, I felt that I could help inject an anti-imperialist position not only into SNCC but into the black movement as a whole."[14]

As the Black Women's Alliance was growing, SNCC was coming apart. Once Jim Crow had been vanquished, the organization's momentum diminished, and its ongoing purpose became unclear. This was illustrated through leadership struggles over the organization's direction, as well as the overall splintering of the civil rights movement. Through all of this, the fledgling Black Women's Alliance held together.

The Alliance was strengthened by the many new women who joined the founders. Beverly Ojeda, Patricia (Kisha) Green, Yemaya Rice Jones, Stella Holmes, and a sister named Affreekka Jefferson, among others, all became part of the Black Women's Alliance. Beverly's husband, along with my compañero Joaquín, was a member of Latin Action in the Bronx and Kisha's partner was a Black Panther. Affreekka's identity as a lesbian helped to shape and strengthen the Alliance platform.

Yemaya came to New York in January of 1970, bringing an already high level of consciousness about race and gender. She had been living in the South when members of the Ku Klux Klan assassinated four little Black girls at the 16th Street Baptist Church in 1963. She had been president of the student body at Morristown College, a two-year Black college in Morristown, Tennessee, when Martin Luther King Jr. was assassinated in 1968 and the students engaged in a rally to demand more rights. About one hundred students had demonstrated, but interestingly, it was eleven women, "coeds" as they were called then, who were expelled.[15]

Yemaya began meeting with the BWLC when she moved to New York with her partner, Mohammed Hunt, who was an

SNCC member. She recalled that SNCC "was on the wane" and said of her work there, "I couldn't type, so I folded letters. SNCC loved women to type and stuff." Recalling BWLC, she said, "We felt a need for us to have our own organization," to have a voice in defining "the role of women in the movement."[16]

Stella joined the Alliance in the same time period. She was a student in a new college entrance program called Search for Education, Elevation, and Knowledge (SEEK), created to bring Black and Puerto Rican students onto the City College campus. Well-known for its excellent education, and dubbed the "working-class Harvard," until 1976, City College was completely tuition-free for all qualified students. Stella told me her story:

> All of us were in the SEEK program and . . . we did not feel wanted. We did not feel accepted. We were upset that they had this big, sprawling campus in the middle of Harlem. Harlem at that time was surrounded by poor, Black, destitute people, and yet you had this enclave. You had a school that owned the best property, the finest property, property that they wouldn't rent to us. And the school, we felt, was our school, so the students formed the Black and Puerto Rican Student Committee [BPRSC] and aimed to take it over. That was the politics around BPRSC. They wanted the school to address the special needs that Blacks came with, SEEK students came with.[17]

As Stella's involvement in BPRSC deepened, she noticed what SNCC women had observed: leadership was male, and there was little room for consideration of women's needs. In her search for a woman's organization, Stella found the Black Women's Alliance. She recalls that the meetings were at first informal. "They were trying to recruit women. As many people as you could get could come just to explore. It was at the fifth or sixth one of these meetings that we decided we would be the Black Women's Alliance."

This group of sisters came after those who had written *Black Woman's Manifesto*, and they went in a more socialist direction. Stella had learned about the Venceremos Brigade from her partner and future husband, Bernard Hughes, who had been on the Second Venceremos Brigade, and she brought the idea of participating in the Third Brigade to the women in the newly formed Black Women's Alliance. Many of them, including Colette Ali and Yemaya, decided to go. A single parent with two children, Fran stayed behind.

Stella said it was in Cuba that she first met someone who called herself Chicana. "We just learned so much about what it meant to be a member of the third world," she recalls meeting Native Americans and people from different parts of the African continent. These members, who were by now almost all of the Black Women's Alliance, became more internationalist and more explicitly left wing after their time in Cuba, which led to the next evolution in the organization.

Becoming the Third World Women's Alliance

During the late spring and early summer of 1970, another significant transition occurred. Affreekka had a partner who was Latina, and she wanted her to be able to join the Black Women's Alliance. Several Puerto Rican women in the city also expressed an interest in joining, saying they had nothing like the Alliance in their community.

In response to those requests, Kisha, a key leader in the Black Woman's Alliance, proposed the Alliance expand to include Puerto Rican women. Yemaya recalls, "TWWA was all about inclusion. We stood for women of color supporting each other regardless of sexual orientation, religious belief, or cultural differences. This was a revolutionary line of thought in the seventies. It was transcending. We knew as we defined ourselves first as the Black Women's Alliance it was important to broaden our vision if we were to project lasting change."

Members discussed the proposal and concluded that "since our oppression is basically caused by the same factors and our enemy is the same," they would open the doors of the Black Women's Alliance to Puerto Rican women, as well as all women of color who might be interested. "Although Asian, black, Chicana, Native American and Puerto Rican sisters have certain differences, we began to see that we were all affected by the same general oppressions."[18]

Using the common terminology of the era in which "third world" connoted people who had been colonized and oppressed,[19] they chose Third World Women's Alliance as the organization's new name. The thinking was that in the United States, "the third world consists of the descendants of people from Asia, Africa, or Latin America." As stated later in *Triple Jeopardy*, "We have all suffered from the same kind of exploitation and colonial oppression as our brothers and sisters in our homelands."[20]

After this decision was made, the women of the newly formed TWWA went to the Adirondacks on retreat and wrote their platform, as was the norm for all political organizations of the era. The Black Panthers, the Nation of Islam, and the Young Lords all wrote and then published their platforms in their newspapers. The Alliance officially established itself by printing its new platform in the inaugural issue of *Triple Jeopardy* in September 1971.

With the concept of an alliance of sisters now expanded, more women from third world communities joined. Latinas had an interest in the empowerment the Alliance offered. As Fran had written about and presented at the SNCC conference earlier, sterilization was being practiced on Puerto Rican women as a result of US policies,[21] and for a fifteen-year period before birth control pills were marketed in the United States, Puerto Rican women were subjected to birth control pill experiments without the benefit of today's rules about informed consent.[22]

Machismo was a fact of life that many Latinas of that era had to face. There were many positive aspects to the culture of machismo, such as a sense of responsibility for family and many ways to understand the growth of machismo as a response to a racist culture (see Earl Shorris's book *Latinos: A Biography of the People* for a description of the origins of the term). Yet the reality of the oppression and sometimes the brutalization of Latin women justified by concepts of male supremacy were undeniable. As Puerto Rican sisters would soon describe in the second issue of *Triple Jeopardy*, "Machismo has always been a very basic part of Puerto Rican culture. Machismo means male chauvinism, it also means 'mucho Macho.' It means a man who puts himself at the head of everything without considering the woman."[23] Puerto Rican women joined the Alliance whether or not they had been involved in politics before. Latinas who were lesbians and afraid to reveal their sexual orientation could join, and at least one closeted lesbian whom I knew well was a member of the Alliance.

A few Chinese American women who lived in Chinatown and experienced and witnessed the poverty there joined the Alliance or participated in its events. One notable Asian American member was Christine Choy (see portrait on p. 38), a young filmmaker who worked first for Newsreel, an activist filmmaking collective, and later helped found Third World Newsreel. Some young Asian American women knew of the legacy of the feudal systems and cultures of their heritage, which cast women in subservient roles. Others would only learn some of their history later when their Alliance work led them to do research on Asian American women and when *Triple Jeopardy* published articles about India, Japan, China, and Korea.

The history of Japanese American women was more present because the women of this generation were born during or immediately after the relocation and internment camps of the 1940s. Anyone who was Japanese American had parents, aunts, and uncles or other family members who had spent time in the camps.

Asian American women were familiar with the history of the garment factories on both coasts in which their foremothers had worked under harsh conditions for generations. (Latin women also shared this history on the East Coast.) In 1970, when the Alliance was initiating its efforts, Asian American women had the lowest income levels of all women when compared with men. "Filipino American women earned 47.5 percent, Japanese American women 43.7 percent, Chinese American women 39.6 percent, and Korean American women 37.0 percent of white men's income."[24]

The Vietnam War sparked the consciousness of young Asian Americans at that time. Although anti-Asian sentiment may have seemed to have abated or disappeared after World War II, it resurfaced in the United States as the word "gook," used for the Vietcong and by association all Vietnamese, became part of the national vocabulary, and pictures of Vietnam's napalmed children and villages became a prominent and disturbing daily feature on the evening news and the front pages of daily newspapers. In the Alliance, Asian American women would join with other sisters of color who were recognizing that Black and Brown men were being conscripted to Vietnam to kill "another people of color who are, after all, our brothers and sisters."[25]

With the expansion of the Alliance, Black membership also increased. Black women's legacy of oppression during the years of their history in the United States was emerging. In his 1989 book *I Dream a World*, photojournalist Brian Lanker wrote, "Black women whose ancestors were brought to the United States beginning in 1619 have lived through conditions of cruelties so horrible, so bizarre, the women had to reinvent themselves."[26]

Other third world people had similar stories. Although it may appear that some were "voluntary immigrants," they, too, experienced the racism and oppression of the United States. With the renaming of the organization, women from all of these groups could find a welcoming home.

More Women of Color Join the Alliance

After the Women's March, Zorina Costello and I wanted to learn more about the Alliance, so we both joined. She stayed for a short while, but I remained.

The seeds of my consciousness about women, race, and economic injustice predated my participation in the Alliance. I had gone to an all-girls high school and a women's college where my sense of myself *as a girl and a woman* (although not my sense of self as a Black person) was unencumbered by a sense of limitation. My mother was a strong woman. She fought for life from the moment her mother died while giving birth to her, and she succeeded through many life experiences that would have laid others low.

I can still picture the Bronx tenement where my widowed Auntie Mazie and her five living children resided. The cracked marble steps up to their apartment and the broken mailboxes under the stairs on the first floor were the subject of nightmares, as my subconscious mind struggled to overcome the sense of darkness and danger I felt when I went downstairs with my older cousins to pick up the mail.

After college, I was employed as a caseworker for the New York City Department of Welfare. My job was to monitor and "assist" mostly Puerto Rican welfare families in the South Bronx slums, families whose immaculate apartments, carefully and thriftily furnished with plastic-covered furniture and decorated with plastic flowers, stood in colorful, gleaming contrast to the decaying tenement buildings and the dirty city streets where they lived. I had also spent several years teaching in the New York City public schools, where I witnessed the inadequate funding of schools in the South Bronx. This, combined with the racism I experienced and saw directed toward the students (and the few teachers of color teaching in New York City in that era), opened my eyes to the structural inequalities of our society. And the union strikes following the incidents in Ocean Hill Brownsville in Brooklyn and the movement for community control of schools hit me hard, as I and my two colleagues Pete Bronson and Bill Schwarz broke the United Federation of Teachers strike at PS 50 in the Bronx so that we could continue to teach our students, who were sorely in need of schooling.

I grew up in a community that was all white, save for our family, and attended Holy Cross School where my brother and I were the only children of color. In high school, I was the only Black child in my class, and in college, I was the only Black student at the College of Our Lady of Good Counsel in White Plains, New York. I experienced racism in my early life that for many years I did not perceive as such and racism that did so much psychological damage I would spend a lifetime working to overcome it. I had risked my life with an abortion soon after college, and I understood the importance of freedom of choice. And I felt the sisterhood on the march that August day.

Coming from a family with a high degree of ongoing postdivorce conflict and in a first marriage where my husband and I struggled with class and cultural differences, I found a kind of safe haven in the Alliance.

Along the route of the march on August 26, 1970, was a young Puerto Rican woman named Brenda Boho (later Beato; see portrait on p. 36). Just out of high school and working with a group of high school students from the Wagner Projects who were pressing for a youth community center there, Brenda had never heard of the TWWA. When I interviewed her in 2007, she had no memory of seeing the Alliance contingent that day. She did recall, however, that she and her friend Bernadette ("Puerto Ricans never travel alone," she joked) were on the sidelines looking at the marchers. Brenda talked about seeing hundreds and hundreds of white women without bras, and people on the sides yelling at them.

"What a sight!" she reflected. "Here were these women who in some way, *how* I wasn't exactly sure, made me feel empowered deep inside—even though at the time, I didn't know that word. That day some kind of hope was awakened. That was my first twinkle of women being empowered, women being able to do anything."[27] Brenda recalled that one of the phrases the marchers repeated again and again on that day was, "Sisterhood is powerful. Join us now."

Introduced to the Alliance by fellow student Kisha Green, Brenda joined while she was at Queens College in New York. She was a member of a Puerto Rican student organization there that was affiliated with the Puerto Rican Socialist Party. Brenda had a lot of problems with her campus organization when it came to women's issues.

"Anytime women brought up issues that concerned women, you were 'against the revolution' or 'against change' because [they would say that] it wasn't the issue of women that should be the focal point," she recalls. "I mean I went to parochial school for twelve years in order to be a secretary, and I was supposed to be one. That's all we could aspire to. Be a secretary. Even though I didn't know how to type. I was a terrible typist. I didn't know stenography. And when I graduated, I had no hope. There was nothing there for me. I was twenty. I was old already because by eighteen, you're supposed to be married and have a family."

For these reasons, Brenda's identity as a woman was a major issue for her. Brenda joined the Alliance almost without making a conscious decision to do so. "I went to a meeting," she said. "I went to another meeting. And then I just stayed."

On the day of the march, Cheryl Johnson Perry League (see portrait on p. 71) was getting ready to return to school in September to teach her fourth graders at Our Lady, Queen of Angels in Harlem. Cheryl was active in the anti-war movement but wasn't even aware of that day's demonstration. Introduced to the Alliance by a friend some months later, Cheryl brought her organizing skills, as well as her commitment to developing women's leadership.

Milagros Pérez Huth (see portrait on p. 69) had immigrated to New York from Puerto Rico when she was ten. She was not even thinking about the women's march on August 26. To her way of thinking, the only thing that should be on the minds of people in the country at that time was the war in Vietnam. "We could end this war, if all progressive people would focus on it," she remembers thinking. Everything else, in her mind, was "a distraction" from this most pressing issue.[28] Months later, she, too, would join the Alliance.

Georgette Ioup (see portrait on p. 118), a Lebanese American woman and Palestinian activist was not at the march, nor was she in New York on that day, but she remembers watching on television while visiting her mother in Pennsylvania. Most of the Ioup family was there that day—Georgette, her older brother, his wife, and her younger brother—sitting at the table having lunch. They watched news clips from the parade and overheard a discussion about what women wanted. Georgette's mother was appalled: "What do you think of all this nonsense? All these demands! Isn't it crazy?" Georgette clearly recalls the younger generation's response: "All of us in unison said, 'No!'"[29]

Georgette joined the Alliance a few years later. In the early seventies, she was a member of the Third World People's Coalition in New York, a group of people from different organizations that dealt with issues of oppression in the third world. Members were Filipino, Arab, South African, African American, and Latino. She met Fran at a coalition conference at Princeton University and shared her thoughts on how male-centric the Coalition was, saying, "none of you men have stood up to" the oppression of women in your countries.

She recalls that Fran called her after the meeting saying, "You're on the wrong foot. This is not the issue in the third world. It's the system that oppresses women, not the men. Yes, there are issues, but these are not the main thing. We can work out these issues very well. We need them as partners to do the real fighting."

Fran invited Georgette to attend an Alliance meeting. Soon after, during the time of the oil embargo and the Palestinian conflict with Egypt and Syria, Georgette became a member, bringing to the sisterhood a deeper understanding of the Palestinian perspective.

By autumn 1970, under Fran's leadership, Alliance membership had grown to about forty-five and included women who were Asian American, Latina, Middle Eastern, multiracial, and of African descent. The women were largely working class, with some college students and a few college graduates in the group—most, if not all, first-generation college students—and also women who had been or were currently on welfare. With its purpose clearly defined, the Alliance continued to grow and expand over the next ten years, solidifying its place in the liberation movements of that era.

The expansion was based on an understanding of women's oppression through a process that included inquiry, the study of history, and the process of writing and publishing what was learned. This was conjoined by the building of relationships beyond the boundaries of our own ethnic and racial groups. Based on these discussions, as well as *Black Woman's Manifesto* and the concept of double jeopardy, Alliance members were beginning to build theory and practice that would shape the trajectory of our lives.

A Luta Continua: Alliance Women Today

Stella Holmes Hughes

Social Worker, Mother, Grandmother

I can see now the linear step between the Alliance's commitment to self-determination and my work with women experiencing domestic violence.

With this statement, Stella begins our most recent conversation. Just one of scores of conversations we have had since our time together in the TWWA.

After many years of working with homeless mentally ill clients, Stella is now a director in one of the largest domestic violence programs in New York City. Her agency is headed by people of color and shelters women and children, and their pets if they have them. "Sheltering pets is important," she adds, "because a lot of times the abusers abuse the pets too."

It is easy to see "the linear step" between Stella's early life and the work she has been doing for decades in some of the poorest New York City neighborhoods.

"My parents were hard-working people in low-wage jobs. My mother a nurse's aide and my father a factory worker." It was hard going. "My parents would rather we starve than get government assistance and, therefore, many a day and night we did."

Stella's mother was mentally ill, most likely suffering with undiag-nosed schizophrenia, and "that impacted her ability to parent." The lack of mental health services for poor people was a reality of life in the fifties, and being Black made it worse. There was no treatment. Because of that, Stella spent a large part of her teenage years living at Villa Loretto in Peekskill, New York. There her high intelligence was identified, and she was skipped ahead in school.

It would be easy to take an up-from-the-ashes view of Stella's life, but she sees herself as "part of something bigger." She believes that "the context is everything." "I grew up surrounded by a community of Black and Puerto Rican children and families who experienced poverty, drug addiction, mental health problems, and racism," she recalls. Although problems were real, so was the sense of community, leading Stella to assert, "It was my experience as a child with that community, all of whose families were affected by racism, that resulted in my thirst to be part of the freedom of my people."

Her political awakening came when she became a student in the SEEK program at City College in New York City. "There were students, mostly men, who were taking on the garb and the rhetoric of revolution." Stella knew nothing about "revolution," but she was well aware of inequity. The then-beautiful City College campus, with its grand buildings and acres of land, stood in sharp contrast to the shabby hotel on Seventy-Second Street and Broadway where the mostly Black and Brown SEEK students had classes during their first year.

The revolutionary rhetoric of the brothers was appealing. She found a way into their organization when she met Bernard Hughes, whom she eventually married. On their first date to the Liberation Bookstore on 135th Street and 7th Avenue in Harlem, she was shocked when he said, "When you and I get together, when you come to see me or I come to see you, you better have your brains on. Don't leave your brains at the doorstep and be this little sex poodle. I want to surround myself with people who think."

Stella became an active member of BPRSC, but she noticed something. "There was little room for women to question what we were reading. I came from an oppressed background where I had no voice, and with the BPRSC, I was back there again!"

She found a group of women who were getting together monthly, trying to form an organization. She attended a few meetings and became one of the founders of the Black Women's Alliance and, subsequently, a leader of what became the TWWA.

After her movement days, Stella returned to school and got her master of science degree from the Columbia University School of Social Work. She has risen to management positions in New York City's mental health and social service agencies, all the while fighting the structural racism that still pervades those agencies. In her current position, for the first time, she is able to say, "Racism is one thing I no longer have to fight at work."

But then there is something else about Stella—a gift all her own that makes her a connector, an empathizer, a person so filled with compassion that she will hug a client when that is the client's deepest need. COVID-19 be damned! A gift that leads people to call her for solace and direction in their most difficult moments of grief and loss. She is a person who continues in the struggle against race, class, and gender inequities, yet never missing the beating of the human hearts within that struggle and all the while loving the work she does.

Milagros Pérez Huth
Teacher, Writer, Mother, Grandmother, Community Activist

I never gave up the support I had for the community.

Immigrant, dedicated mother, prizewinning author, and community intellectual—perfect descriptors for Milagros Pérez Huth. The photo of her in a peacoat with a Puerto Rican flag threaded through the buttonhole appears to be the most frequently portrayed cover of *Triple Jeopardy.*

Milagros was born in Puerto Rico. "I came to this country when I was ten," she says. "I came to join my mother who had migrated with my older sister. You know the usual story—to get a job, to get settled, and send for the other children. I lived with my grandmother and my aunt." When I ask her if there were any men at home, she replies, "My father died when I was three or four years old. Only women at home— my grandmother and my aunts." And her face transforms as it seems to dawn on her that her early history in a family of women was probably an influence on her later membership in the Alliance.

Milagros's life in New York included finishing school, doing factory work, and eventually joining the SEEK program at Queens College.

She recalled life in her late teens and twenties. "I worked in factories. On Canal Street. On Twenty-Third Street. Doing little jobs like packing toys. One factory was some machine that made coin wrappers—one of those jobs that people say are terribly monotonous and dehumanizing, but I didn't stay in those jobs that long." She experienced racism in that work. "I usually worked with white people, European immigrants who were like racists already. They had not been in this country too long, but they were already looking at you like you were some freak."

Although not a joiner by nature, Milagros joined the Alliance when she was about twenty-seven years old, describing that decision as "an instinctual thing, a gut feeling. It's like they say, 'water seeks its level.' It was a powerful experience. I'm not a feminist. It just always felt like a great sisterhood. I'm interested in women's issues. I read mostly women authors." She was drawn to the Alliance mainly because it comprised women of color yet didn't make women's issues the sole or even the central issue, and she found it "nurturing and not dogmatic. . . . We had a sense of family among us, of taking care of each other." She had thought about joining the Puerto Rican Socialist Party, but "I felt as a woman I was more accepted and more likely to be heard in the Third World Women's Alliance."

In my interview with her, Milagros talked about how the Alliance changed her. "It was part of my development, my growing up, and in that respect, it's one of the things in my life that has significance for me," she said. "It was my step going forward." She also spoke about the importance of Black women in the Alliance as role models for her and how, as a rather shy young women, she could shore herself up by saying, "I know very strong Black women and therefore I am also strong." Some forty-five years later, Alliance women continue to have an impact on her life. "It's like some families have forefathers, forbear-ers who were exceptional and give you strength, moral and spiritual strength. The Third World Women's Alliance helped me in that respect."

Milagros also became a member of the Young Lords Party. She knew Young Lord Felipe Luciano from Queens College and consid-ered him to be brilliant and impressive. For her, there were pros and cons to the party. She liked the focus on Puerto Rico, her homeland, and the connection to struggles in Latin America, but at first she didn't like the way she felt they were imitating the Black Panthers. For her, it was easier to relate to Alliance women, and she was more comfortable there, but she loved the Lords' strong community ties and orientation, and eventually she affiliated with them. In particular, she respected their work with Lincoln Hospital and their confrontation with the New York City Sanitation Department because it didn't provide the same services to the Puerto Rican community as it did to wealthy neighborhoods. "It was very exciting . . . because you were constantly waging struggle. My aim in life was not just nationalism. . . . I felt a worldwide connection with socialism."

As the daughter of a factory worker, Milagros has remained attentive to social class. She became a teacher, still lives on the Lower East Side, and is active in community struggles. Her politics are consistent. "I still consider myself a socialist," she says. "I do question what's going on in China, and some of the communist countries, and in Cuba. I do question and want to have honest conversations about that. You can't be just saying it's wonderful. We're at a point in history where we have to talk about a lot of what we accepted as truth."

Cheryl Johnson Perry League
Public Administrator, Program and Public Policy Advocate, Mother, Grandmother

Every day I advocate to improve the quality of life for African American women and girls.

Founder of the Bay Area Chapter of the Alliance, Cheryl Johnson Perry League is now the first vice president of programs for the National Coalition of 100 Black Women, Oakland Bay Area Chapter.

Cheryl grew up in New York City in a Baptist family where education was such a priority that "my parents enrolled me and my sisters in Catholic schools so that we could receive the best education possible." She attended Catholic schools from elementary through high school, and she was teaching at Our Lady Queen of Angels, in what was then called Spanish Harlem, when she joined the Alliance.

Cheryl became a member of TWWA because of the initiatives directed toward the empowerment of women and people of color and remains deeply committed to those objectives. "I enjoyed being a change agent during my time at the Alliance," she told me. "It is truly all about getting women active in the community. I enjoyed the activities, the work, and building relationships. I was always organizing around something."

She started attending consciousness-raising sessions with the Alliance in New York City, and before she knew it, she was recruited to go to Cuba. After the Brigade, she decided to move to the Bay Area, and when Fran Beal asked her to form an Alliance chapter there, she quickly agreed. "Connect and organize" was her mantra.

Since those days, Cheryl has remained engaged in community service. She was a member of the Niagara Democratic Club and cochair of the Fundraising Committee working for Jesse Jackson's Rainbow Coalition and for Congressman Ronald Dellums. She was a contract compliance officer for the Title 7 Litigation Unit with the Legal Aid Society of Almeda County, advocating on behalf of minorities and women in all careers.

For almost thirty years, she worked at the Port of Oakland, ultimately as director of its Office of Equal Opportunity, where she ensured that minorities and women had a level playing field for employment, promotions, and contract opportunities. She became a member of the National Forum for Black Public Administrators and in 2003 was elected its national president. She now serves as a board member for the National Coalition of 100 Black Women, Inc. and is an active member of the Oakland Bay Area Chapter.

Currently an activist for African American women and girls, she works to change the quality of their lives. "I am fortunate to have had mentors throughout my career and in my years as an activist. Their guidance and belief in my desire to learn provided me with much confidence, especially during my time in the Third World Women's Alliance. I continue my work as an advocate," she says, a big smile lighting up her face.

CHAPTER 3

The New York Chapter (1970–1977)

Platform, Theory, and Praxis

The main objective of the women in other Third World countries is the liberation and self-determination of their peoples. They understand clearly that there is no freedom for them as women unless everyone is free. Our goals here should be the same; self-determination and the liberation of our people; freedom for us all.

—TWWA PLATFORM[1]

FROM THE TIME of the TWWA's origin as the BWLC in SNCC and after the Alliance's participation in the 1970 Women's March, the organization continued to grow, highlighting the need for a clear statement of TWWA's mission and vision. As noted in chapter 2, just before the Women's March, the founding members of the newly formed organization had gone on retreat in upstate New York to write an organizational platform.

The TWWA Platform[2]

The platform, published in the SNCC newspaper and in *Triple Jeopardy* in 1970, included the Alliance's history and goals and formulated its position. It immediately addressed three myths: the myth of the Black matriarchy, the myth that Black women were not as oppressed as Black men were, and the myth that a women's organization would be divisive to liberation struggles.

The Alliance statement on Black matriarchy (predating, by nine years, Michele Wallace's 1979 book *Black Macho and the*

Myth of the Superwoman), declared, "A matriarchy denotes a society where the economic power of a group rests in the hands of the women *and we all know where the economic power of this nation rests*" (italics added). Contradicting the thinking of many people at the time, the Alliance combated the "widespread concept that by some miracle, the oppression of enslavement for the black woman was not as degrading, not as horrifying, not as barbaric as it had been for the black man," declaring, that "in any society where men are not yet free, women are less free because we are further enslaved by our sex," and stating that "a true revolutionary movement must enhance the status of women."

The final myth was contested by directly posing the question, "Is a third world women's group divisive to the liberation struggle?" The Alliance's unequivocal response was, "A third world women's group can potentially be one of the most revolutionary forces confronting the U.S. ruling class." In the platform, Alliance women urged "our brothers" to understand that we were an organization that stood "for the liberation for women and the Third World" and that the Alliance would play an important role in training women of color for leadership roles. The platform ended with the following powerful statement: "It is the position of the Third World Women's Alliance that the struggle against racism and imperialism must be waged simultaneously with the struggle for women's liberation, and only a strong independent socialist women's group can ensure that this will come about."

Based on a manifestly anti-imperialist agenda that was pro-woman, pro-worker, and pro–third world, the Alliance platform explained its expansion to include all third world women as a recognition of our common exploitation as "domestic workers, hospital workers, factory workers and farm laborers . . . and garment workers." We declared solidarity between Asian, African diaspora, Chicana, Native American, and Puerto Rican sisters.

The ideological part of the platform began with a statement about the right of all people to be free. It made a distinction between oppression and exploitation, stating that under imperialism, minorities were oppressed, and the white majority was wounded, too, through its ongoing exploitation as workers or what was sometimes referred to as "wage slaves." The section ended with an assertion that our struggle was against a system that exploited the minority and majority as well. Then the platform took up seven topics that the Alliance saw as fundamental to the liberation of all people: family, employment, sex roles, education, services, women in our own right, and self-defense.

Family

We advocated for communal households, extended families, and the sharing of all housework by men and women. The history of reproductive abuses (forced sterilization and experiments with birth control), conducted largely on Latinas in Puerto Rico, Dominican women in New York City,[3] and African American women in the South, led the Alliance to state, "There shall be no forced sterilization or mandatory birth control programs which are presently used as genocide against third world women and against other poor people." We recognized that some women would choose to have babies, even without the so-called benefit of wedlock, and the platform declared, "There is no such thing as an illegitimate child."

Employment

The Alliance platform demanded that workplaces put an end "to the racism and sexism that forces third world women into the lowest paying service jobs and which ensures that we will be lowest paid of all" and called for "guaranteed full, equal, and non-exploitative employment controlled collectively by the workers." To support this, we called for universal free day care, like that in Cuba and China.

Sex Roles

The Alliance's platform demanded an end to all rigid sex roles and urged role integration wherever and whenever possible. The platform also made a progressive statement on same-sex relationships, stating that women had the right to love others of their own sex without fear or shame and that "the oppression and dehumanizing ostracism that homosexuals face must be rejected and their right to exist as dignified human beings must be defended."

Education

We asserted our rights to education and to the determination of "our own goals and ambitions." We demanded self-determination and full participation "on all levels of the struggle," and that schools teach "the history of third world women and their contributions to the liberation struggle, their relation to society and the knowledge of their bodies." Self-knowledge was central to education, we believed, and when women came to know themselves, they could free themselves of rigid, limiting sex roles, develop skills, and determine their own goals and ambitions.

Services

We identified that, based on our race and our class position as members of the third world, we received services that were "inadequate, unavailable, or too expensive," which guaranteed that those services were "administered in a racist, sexist manner." We believed that our rights included "all services necessary to human survival—health care, housing, food, clothing, transportation and education." Healthcare services, we believed, should be free and should be controlled and administered by those who benefited from them.

Some of us had direct experiences of those inadequate, racist services. When I was pregnant with my first child, Maceo, I was for a brief time on Medicaid. My husband, Joaquín, was still in college, and although I was a college graduate who had always been employed, I needed to stop working during the last days of my pregnancy and for a few months after giving birth, to take care of my newborn. My being on Medicaid meant the doctors and nurses had a stereotypical and classist view of who I was. When I would ask intelligent questions about my pregnancy, they wondered if I was a nurse. They seemed shocked that a Black woman on Medicaid would have any knowledge at all. As if a Medicaid recipient would certainly not read nor remember information about her pregnancy and would certainly not engage in intelligent inquiry with her care providers. After Maceo was born, I was placed in a ward—six mothers to a room—and was shamed for breastfeeding my baby. Joaquín was refused permission to see our son in the nursery. He was darker than Maceo was at that time, and the hospital workers didn't think he was the father.

Women in Our Own Right

The penultimate section of the platform addressed a mission that I highlight throughout this book: specifically, a call on "all organizations & institutions [to] deal with third world women in their own right as human beings and individuals, rather than as property of men and only valued in relationship to their association or connection with some men." We wanted to be seen as full human beings, not simply adjuncts and servants to men. We were determined to be free to make our own decisions and, most importantly, to participate in all levels of the struggle for our own liberation.

Self-Defense

In the final section of our political platform, we declared our right to bear arms in self-defense. We lived in an era of whites bombing Black churches in the South and right-wing citizens and government officials murdering and assassinating our leaders, and we saw armed struggle as a necessity for full self-defense.

Our platform was the foundational document of our vision of the kind of women we wanted to be and the kind of society we wished to live in. We declared ourselves as third world women with a clear political agenda: pro-socialist, pro–women's rights, anti-racist, anti-colonialist, pro-family, and pro–community organization.

Organizing Begins

With its purpose clear—to create "a socialist society where we can live as decent human beings, free from the pressures of racism, economic exploitation, and sexual oppression"—the Alliance developed and attracted new members.

The plight of our people was intense. In New York City, heroin abuse was at an all-time high. Drug addicts hung out on the corners of the streets in poor communities. As Jesús Papoleto Meléndez wrote in his poem "junkies are very skillful people," published in *Triple Jeopardy*, they were our families.

> they are sisters & brothers
> mothers & fathers
> cousins & aunts
> of you & i
> we are extensions of them
> they are that part of you & i
> . . . .
> & junkies we need you
> the revolution needs you
> to wheel & deal
> chug-a-mug
> & jive
> & get funds for our cause.[4]

We wondered: Who was selling the drugs? Where were they coming from? Who was profiting from them?

We were driven by our questions and by our need to understand our own experiences more deeply. We were trying to understand the economic inequities of people of color here and abroad. We were trying to understand why women were limited to the "female professions," why people of color were thought to be inferior, and why there was so much poverty among our people.

We wanted to understand why some people had so much and some so little. We needed to answer the question of why we and our communities were so disadvantaged. Why was racism so entrenched? Who benefited from it? How could we understand the historic, long-term subjugation of women? Why was our story so different from Betty Friedan's?

Why were the front lines of the Vietnam War filled with Black and Brown soldiers? Why, in God's name, were we in Vietnam anyway?! Our brothers were being drafted into the army to fight in Vietnam while simultaneously being discriminated against in the United States. My own brother and his fellow Marines—all in uniform—were refused service at a restaurant in the South. My first husband, Joaquín, a Black Puerto Rican from the South Bronx, got his front teeth kicked out by "fellow" sailors while he was stationed in the South because he danced with a light-skinned Puerto Rican woman friend who was presumed to be white.

Alliance women conceived of our work in two realms. Internally, we educated ourselves about our bodies, our current realities, our history, the situation in other third world countries, and the current situation of women in third world nations. The external dimension of our work involved reaching out to other women of color and connecting with activists of color both to educate them about women's issues and to participate with them in the struggle for liberation.

Consciousness-Raising and Study

Consciousness-raising was an important starting place to educate ourselves and others. The term "consciousness-raising," first used in China in the 1920s and 1930s, was the process of becoming politically aware or conscious. Feminists in the United States in the late sixties and seventies gathered together in consciousness-raising groups to discuss and analyze women's lives and roles. In the Alliance, the term related to learning about ourselves and our bodies.

One memorable Alliance meeting involved a consciousness-raising session based on the Boston Women's Health Collective book *Our Bodies, Ourselves: A Book by and for Women*. There was no other book like it at the time. As the authors stated in the introduction to a later edition of the book, "In 1969, there was practically no women's health information easily available, and every fact we learned was a revelation."[5]

This perfectly described our experience at one meeting of the Alliance. We sat on metal folding chairs in the TWWA office on West Twenty-Sixth Street with a copy of a sketch from *Our Bodies, Ourselves* taped to the wall. It showed a woman lying flat on her back, knees bent, feet on the floor, legs open wide, exposing her sexual organs. The parts of the diagram were labeled: the hood of the clitoris, the clitoris, the urethra, the outer lips, the vagina, and the inner lips—even the anus. This was so unknown to many of us and so vitally important that we reproduced the illustration and published it in *Triple Jeopardy* with an article describing this part of the female anatomy.[6] And we continued to publish many articles about women's reproductive and gynecological issues, including childbirth, abortion, venereal disease, and sterilization.

As I remember it, Fran was the only woman in the room who'd had children at the time of this session. She undoubtedly was aware of at least some of these parts of her own body. I was twenty-six, a college-educated woman, and I had never heard of a clitoris. I did not even have a name for my vagina. My mother's instruction to me about bathing, given with a wry little smile, was "wash up as far as possible, and down as far as possible. And don't forget to wash possible." In her little ditty, the word "possible" represented the unmentionable vagina.

We sat and stared and puzzled at the portrayal of the clitoris, which many of us had not heard of or, to our knowledge, ever touched or felt. Perhaps some of us in surreptitious masturbation felt some clitoral pleasure "down there," but we did not know its anatomical source. Even doctors were still writing about healthy female orgasm only being achieved as a result of vaginal penetration. It was incredible to me to have this kind of conversation, to read this kind of material. For our generation, it was revolutionary. I remember wriggling uncomfortably at the book's suggestion that we take a mirror and look at our vaginas to see what they looked like. Some sisters who were not timid did exactly that. I, still gripped by my Catholic school background and its repressive messages, did not.

Learning about our bodies in that way for the first time definitely assisted many of us as we became pregnant and began to have children. During pregnancies, we continued our study and our activism. Like other members of our generation, we were among the first women who were allowed to have their partners in hospital delivery rooms. We dedicated ourselves to studying Lamaze birthing methods as passionately as we studied Marx. We refused pain-relieving drugs because we wanted our babies born drug-free, and, perhaps more importantly, we wanted our partners to be able to be with us in the delivery room and men had to leave once medication was administered.

Moving more and more to de-medicalize our deliveries, some of us began having our babies outside of the hospital. I had my second child, Imani, in 1976, one of the first babies in the US delivered by midwives at the Maternity Center of New York, the first independent birthing center in the United States. Later, some members began having home deliveries.

As Yemaya said years later, "Our consciousness-raising sessions were transformative. They ingrained in us the necessity to live our lives with true love and understanding for our sisters."

A central part of our study and education was our foundation in the socialist literature of dialectical and historical materialism. In the Alliance, we were exposed to Marxist and socialist literature, in part because that was the prominent political analysis of many leftist activists and intellectuals in the sixties and seventies. More directly, many SNCC members and leaders had moved toward Marxist-Leninist thinking in SNCC's final days. Since its early days, SNCC had also focused on international struggles, particularly on the African continent. In 1967, it established a Foreign Affairs Commission and named former SNCC executive secretary James Forman as head of the Commission. Jim was an expert on Marxist thought, and he came to the Alliance to teach us.

Brilliant, principled, and an encouraging teacher, Jim met with a fifteen-member core group three times a week for six weeks of political education on the principles of dialectical and historical materialism. In these theories, we found a convincing philosophy to ground our work for social change. The Hegelian philosophy of dialectics connected to the principles of Marxist materialism was a theory of change that posited that the world functioned and progressed by means of the struggle between opposites. The core dialectical paradigm for Marxists was the class struggle—rich against poor, working class against owning class. This was a binary view of the world: good/bad, up/down, empty/full. According to the theory, one side of the binary (the dominant side) was described as the thesis and the other side as the antithesis. An intellectual (and political) struggle between the opposites (the thesis and the antithesis) was believed to lead to the emergence of a synthesis.

As soon as a synthesis of the two opposing ideas emerged, this new synthesis would become the new thesis and an antithesis would evolve in response. A new struggle would ensue, and a new synthesis would be developed. This was thought to continue endlessly, with each new thesis in the class struggle helping society to spiral forward to greater levels of equity and development. The intellectual and economic struggle between the owners (dominant/thesis) and the working class (subordinate/antithesis), for example, would lead to a revolution from which a new, more just economic order would emerge.

The relationships between the two binaries of thesis and antithesis were also called "contradictions." There was the class contradiction, the race contradiction, and the contradiction of the sexes, among others. We knew that perfection could never be reached, and we believed that new contradictions would always be developing in the new society. It was our conviction that these struggles would help society to continue to make progress, and in light of this, we called ourselves progressives.

The philosophy of materialism was another part of our reading and study with Jim. Materialism was the idea that the only thing real was the physical world of substance. This philosophy taught that nothing ever died and that everything was in a constant state of transformation. Materialists were anti-idealists, believing neither in organized religion nor in the existence of spirit. Religion and the belief in spirit and after-life, materialists believed, had been used like a drug to mollify the oppressed people of the world, encouraging them to place their faith and hope in an afterlife as a way to blind them to the perpetrators of the hardships of their current lives. Studying with Jim, we evolved into Marxists, eschewing religion as what Marx called "the opiate of the masses."

Looking back, the lack of a spiritual outlook is hard to understand, given that for most of us, faith in God was deeply a part of our various heritages as women of color, regardless of our current state of belief. For me, the new materialism was not difficult to embrace. I was already in a crisis of faith precipitated by my parents' divorce (which I had prayed to God to prevent) and my emergent libidinous yearnings, the satisfaction of which did not mesh with Catholic teaching. Several of us were still practicing Catholics, like Ana Celia Zentella (see portrait on p. 125), but many of those with religious backgrounds had turned away from God or felt God had turned away from them. As adolescents and young adults in rebellion against the oppression and exploitation we saw around us, it all made sense. The philosophy fit with our sense of agency, our position that we, the people ourselves, needed to change the world because there was no God who would make that happen for us, and there was no afterlife on which to place one's hopes.

We all cherished studying with Jim. Cheryl Johnson remembers that Jim gave her her first Red Book[7] and Brenda Boho Beato recalls "James Forman coming in, and my taping his talks and listening to them over and over." Jim was twenty to twenty-five years older than most of us, who were in our late teens or twenties, and we respected the depth of his knowledge and his history of activism. He taught us, too, about change and the difference between quantitative and qualitative change, showing us through illustrations how quantitative change could lead to qualitative change. I will always remember his example of how a qualitative change took place as a person changed from sober to drunk by imbibing more and more alcohol, thereby increasing the quantity of alcohol in his system.

In our work with Jim and in our committee meetings, we also read from the socialist literature, which spoke directly to the issues of class, race, and gender. Ana Celia, despite her years of study and exposure from her travels, first encountered these treatises in the Alliance and joyfully declared herself a Marxist-Leninist.

We read Fran's paper "Double Jeopardy: To Be Black and Female," in which she located the oppression of women within the context of capitalism and the exploitation of workers.[8] Citing Sojourner Truth, the paper reminded us that we have never had the "luxury" of being protected and spared from the hardship of life as white women supposedly were. Fran's paper critiqued the attitude of "some" Black men who blamed us for their oppression and suggested that enslavement was not as brutal for Black women as it was for Black men. She stated that Black women were happy and proud to see Black men rise up and claim their rightful place but asked that they do this as our partners, not at our expense. This paper set the tone and the frame for everything we did throughout the life of the organization. We claimed a partnership with men of color while critiquing any sexist or anti-woman biases they might have. We are with you, we asserted, but remember, we are walking side by side.

Through our work and study, we moved from the two-faceted idea of double jeopardy to the fuller awareness of our triple jeopardy—that we were oppressed by the intersecting realities of our subordinate positions as women, women of color, and poor and working women. Here, we were beginning to develop a theory of our own.

The class issues raised by the socialist literature were compelling to us. We were not familiar with other literature that had a class analysis. Some of us, like Brenda, had emerged from families where economic disadvantage was the main oppression felt. Stella had come from a family damaged by economic privation, largely the result of racism and the lack of mental health services. Many sisters had lived through the social class deprivations about which we read.

Others of us were somewhat better off. Both of my parents, for example, were working people, neither college graduates nor professionals, but we were an economically secure working-class family, so I knew that racism alone did not determine economic advantage or disadvantage. My father's description of life in Trinidad in the era of British colonization, where Indian indentured servants suffered through years of oppression and bondage, and his many stories about the dire poverty of some Trinidadians who lived in corrugated tin housing along the roadside, brought economic issues center stage for me even before I first visited Trinidad at age sixteen. There I found a society strictly segmented by class and color and unlike anything I'd ever seen in the United States. The color bias of my own multiracial Trinidadian family was shocking to me. Witnessing this bias as a teenager, years before I ever saw the poverty of the rural South, led me to keep my eyes fixed on the issues of social class and race in the international arena. Other Alliance sisters were also of West Indian heritage, and, together with the Puerto Rican and Asian American sisters, we brought international perspectives to our work in the Alliance.

Christine, for example, recalls moving with her family from China, where class divisions were not so clear, to Korea in the early 1950s during the Korean War. She recalls, "Over 300,000 American troops were stationed there. People were living in the gutter and in tents, drinking rainwater. There were beggars covered with black mud. If you did not give them money, they put mud on you."[9] She saw segregated American GIs in Korea and observed how the Koreans looked down on the Black GIs.

After immigrating to the United States, Christine was the one who was looked down on. "I sensed this subtle discrimination," she said, "even at Sacred Heart [school]." There was the "charity" of having clothes donated to her. There was also her experience of exclusion after being put in a separate residence hall room because she had lost her X-rays during her travel to the United States and could not prove she did not have tuberculosis.

When, in the Alliance, I read James Boggs's *Racism and the Class Struggle*, my attention to the issues of economics and social class was strengthened. Boggs was an African American Chrysler autoworker in the sixties; his emphasis on the struggle of workers struck a chord with me. Most of the men on my mother's side of the family were carpenters. My grandfather, and later my brother (as a member of New York's Fight Back),[10] fought for the inclusion of Black carpenters in New York City's carpenters' union. Although my own work did not involve labor, as my father often reminded me, I came from a family of construction workers, and I was proud of that history.

All Alliance women read and studied and tried to learn more. There was not a lot of debate about Marxist theory itself. It made so much sense to us. But there was ongoing discussion and struggle around the hierarchy of contradictions. We readily agreed that racism, classism, and sexism were outgrowths of capitalist imperialist structures, but we struggled with the question of which type of oppression—racism, sexism, or classism—had the highest valence. These conversations about race, class, and gender were ongoing. Which oppression was worse? Was one aspect primary? What about the interrelationships between the three types of oppression? At first, we saw racism, sexism, and economic oppression as additive: aspects that were added on top of one another to make life more and more difficult. It was both this (racism) and that (sexism) and then that (capitalism). But as we talked and reflected, our thinking became more complex. And we posed different questions. What was worse: Being a Black lesbian or a Black woman with disabilities? Was it worse to be a Latin man on drugs or a Latin woman working in a sweatshop?

Despite the perhaps trivial-sounding nature of these questions, we were pushing ourselves to think in more complicated ways. Did it even make sense to make these kinds of comparisons? And, perhaps most important, we asked ourselves, what created the context for the emergence of these forms of oppression and exploitation? What were the constituent factors?

We read whatever we could find about the history of our communities and the heroin epidemic that was ravaging them. We followed the Vietnam War. And what we read and learned was dutifully written about in *Triple Jeopardy* to inform our sisters and brothers. Taking heed from the lyrics of the Last Poets's 1970 song "When the Revolution Comes," we were careful not to "party and bullshit."

There was a sociocultural aspect to our study. We became sisters in the struggle, as well as friends. We liked each other. We dated brothers from organizations whose politics we shared; I dated and later married Joaquín Rosa from Latin Action/Latin Union. I introduced Brenda to her future husband, Tommy, who was a Latin Union member. Brenda later recalled, "In the Alliance, you found people who were like you, who were educated, who wanted to learn."

These were the days before ethnic studies and women's studies departments, before there were courses focused on women and people of color, before even the inclusion of topics and readings about women of color in mainstream courses. I had never read in college a book written by a Black person. As a Spanish major, I had read only one piece written by a Puerto Rican—a poem by Luis Palés Matos.

Alice Walker's *The Color Purple* had not yet been published. Toni Morrison's *Beloved*, a book that informed a nation about the psychological impact of enslavement on women, had not been written. Walker had not yet "rediscovered" Zora Neale Hurston and shared her work with the world. Sally Hemmings's story had not yet been told. The headlines about enslavement were about men being sold away from their families, not about mothers being left to raise families alone or even being sold away themselves.

Other stories had been written, like those of Linda Brent, Jarena Lee, Ida B. Wells, and Julia Foote. But without Black studies and women's studies programs, few Americans, even educated ones, especially those like me from predominantly white institutions, were familiar with these women and their stories. We were not alone in this; white women's history was also unknown, as Sheila Rowbotham's 1973 book *Hidden from History: 300 Years of Women's Oppression and the Fight Against It* made abundantly clear.

Because our history (both as women and as women of color) had been buried, we learned more in the Alliance about ourselves and our people than we ever had in school. Ana Celia, who had been in the Peace Corps prior to joining the Alliance, said that it was her first introduction to reading political treatises. "It was," she said, "my training in the international perspective, and this whole triple jeopardy idea."[11]

This, too, was a time when there was no feminist language, when the language of "all men were created equal" was still being used. When we read about enslavement, male voices and male stories, like that of Frederick Douglass, dominated. We did not yet know about *Incidents in the Life of a Slave Girl*, which was published in 1861 but did not resurface until the 1980s. Stokely Carmichael didn't mention women in his 1966 Black Power speech at Berkeley when he said, "Now it is clear that when this country started to move in terms of enslavement, the reason for a man being picked as a slave was one reason— because of the color of his skin." Again, at Garfield High School in Seattle in 1967, he omitted women when he said, "You've watched the red man and the white man on TV? Fighting with each other? If the red man is winning, then the white man calls for the cavalry."[12] And he didn't mention women in other public speeches at the time, as far as I can ascertain.

Getting an understanding of the structures that enforced our oppression and developing a correct analysis of how they operated was paramount to us. We had to understand the system in order to dismantle it. We worked hard at getting our analysis right so we could share it with other women.

We were reading all the time. We read movement newspapers published by other organizations—*Pa'lante*, published by the Young Lords Party; *Mohammed Speaks*, by the Nation of Islam; *Black Panther*; and the *Guardian* (the leftist publication with the largest circulation at that time). The Vietnam War and the politics of repression were daily experiences in our lives, and we could not trust the mainstream press to tell our stories truthfully. Because of that, we read movement newspapers and wrote our own articles in *Triple Jeopardy*.

As much as we were taken with Marxism/Leninism, we were also deeply inspired by and identified with the third world— those nonaligned and underdeveloped nations of the world largely composed of people of color. These included all the countries of Africa and Latin America and most of those in Asia. Mao and Che and Fidel were special to us. From Mao, we learned about criticism and self-criticism, which we employed in our own criticism and self-criticism sessions to help us guard against arrogance, individualism, and excessive liberalism. Che's writing about "the New Man" inspired us to think about the New Woman. His writing projected a vision of what we could become: human beings with a consciousness of justice and truth, new men and new women who were not commodities and did not live with the myth of being self-made.[13]

We rejoiced in books like William H. Hinton's *Fanshen*, which described how the barefoot doctors of China's Cultural Revolution spread out across the country and treated and healed the peasants who had never had access to medical care and how women long oppressed by male dominance in their villages tied up wife beaters and gave them a little of their own medicine. We read nonfiction like *Black Skin, White Masks* by Frantz Fanon, the father of Black psychology, who wrote about how racism destroyed the self-esteem of Black people and how the psyche of white people was filled with stereotypical images of Black and Brown people. We read Engels's *The Origin of the Family, Private Property and the State* and came to understand the role the family played in the acquisition and maintenance of property and property rights, ensuring that wealth would pass from generation to generation, and we learned how the state had evolved into the institution that managed it all. Fanon's *The Wretched of the Earth* educated us about the connection between racism and colonial rule in the United States, the Caribbean, and Africa and led us to understand the need for independence. We read Aimé Césaire's *Discourse on Colonialism*, and Mao's Red Book was one of our bibles.

Our study and our lived experience helped us to shape our views and perspectives. To become a just society, we believed, we must prioritize the concerns and needs of people over the drive for profits. Our struggle focused on the creation of a socialist society. We believed that a capitalist society driven by the profit motive placed us and other women of the third world in the position of "triple jeopardy." Oppressed as workers, as members of the third world, and as women, we were forced to work at marginal and monotonous jobs that paid the lowest wages.

As Alliance members, we did not define ourselves as

communists. From a theoretical point of view, we believed that communism would be the last stage of world socialism. True communism could only come when the whole world was social-ist. Although some members had parents who were members of the party, we also shied away from the term "communism" to distance ourselves from the Soviet Union, both because of its whiteness and its reported repressive policies and programs. The TWWA and its members never distanced themselves from Angela Davis, who was a member of the Communist Party. We celebrated her as a sister and a fellow revolutionary, hoist-ing our banner about her at the Women's March in 1970, and covering her frequently in full-page articles in *Triple Jeopardy.*[14]

Ultimately, the Alliance became a "college" of our own creation. The impact of our readings could be felt throughout our lives. Forty years later, while discussing her thoughts about marriage with me, Brenda declared, "We don't own anyone." Somewhere in her psyche, the socialist principle of nonown-ership had settled. Her statement was clearly a rejection and repudiation of what Engels described as a key aspect of monog-amous marriage: the man's effort to secure his children and his wife as his property.

Praxis

As Marxists, Alliance members believed in the integration of theory and praxis. Praxis—the process of putting theoretical knowledge into practice—was essential to our work, and the integration of theory and praxis meant that the theories we studied would inform our practice and our work; our practice would then, in a recursive fashion, inform the theories. We studied theories about our circumstances and thought about how to resolve the problems in our communities. We tested the theories through our work and changed them as appropri-ate. That led us to debate concepts as we worked. In this way, actions to create social justice would be doubly informed by thoughts and ideas as well as actions in the world.

Our philosophy was an earlier framing of the current saying,

"Think globally; act locally." We believed that our practice should be disciplined and deepened by analysis focused on the particular, local details of our lives and then move to a reflection on the general, global level; having learned and appreciated what was happening at that level, we should then return to the particular, specific factors influencing our lives at home to determine what actions were best to take.

Our vision and our practice were distinguished by an indefatigable belief in our own agency, the sense that women were capable of struggling on their own for their own liberation. This was true of other activists as well. As Fran recalled, "Part of the period was our belief that we could do everything, if we only let ourselves." In families, in organizations, in the struggle overall, we Alliance women were determined to define our own roles.

Committee Meetings

To do our work, we held regular Alliance committee meetings. The Central Committee met to consider policy and oversee the organization. The Newspaper Committee met to assign and select articles, lay out the paper, typeset it at the printer, and plan for distribution. We also had seemingly endless ad hoc meetings to organize events, plan for demonstrations, or do a mass plastering of posters.

We had a Prison Letter Writing Committee and a Committee to Free Lolita Lebrón (the Puerto Rican freedom fighter who had been arrested for entering Congress with guns, calling for the United States to release Puerto Rico from its colonial status) initiated by Ana Celia.

The Committee to Free Lolita Lebrón raised money through activities, including an ad and a letter from Lolita published in *Triple Jeopardy*. Many Alliance women and others from the wider community were involved with the defense committee, including Miriam Colón, founder and director of the Puerto Rican Traveling Theater.

At Hunter College, Ana Celia started the Puerto Rican Women's Workshop as part of the TWWA and provided "three months of weekly three-hour consciousness-raising sessions" for new members there. For two years, *Triple Jeopardy*, along with the Tuesday night meetings, had been the Alliance's main educational outreach tool. The sisters in the Workshop "decided it might be a good idea to try and communicate, through drama, some of the things we had learned about the triple jeopardy that we face as third world women," so they added guerilla theater as method of education and recruitment. They developed a guerrilla theater that became known as La Nueva Mujer. The skits performed had a dual effect. Said one member, "The guerilla theater, more than anything else, has given me a sense of true sisterhood, and working with the women in the group on the skits has really helped me a lot in recognizing the very subtle sexist attitudes that penetrate this society." "For me," said another, "it is a way to act out my beliefs and do something about them, like maybe get people to agree with my ideas."[15] La Nueva Mujer performed fourteen times in 1973 alone.

Regular members also met for criticism and self-criticism sessions, modeled on those in Mao's China. Although Iris Morales, in her book *Through the Eyes of Rebel Women*, describes these sessions among the Young Lords as very

TWWA's bilingual guerrilla theater, La Nueva Mujer.
Photo from the collection of Ana Celia Zentella.

positive, I found them to be rather brutal sessions in which "sisters" focused on telling one another exactly how and why they were totally bourgeois.

My criticisms came in the form of raising critiques about my class background, even though both of my parents were working class. My mother graduated from high school, and my father only completed fourth grade, but they had done relatively well—owning their home and sending me to private Catholic schools. From the perspective of the Alliance's young leftists, this made me "uppity." And foreshadowing the future psychologist in me, I was critiqued for being too "psychologically minded" and not political enough. Brenda recalls criticisms leveled at her for her lack of writing skills after she submitted to *Triple Jeopardy* an article about her time in China. She was also criticized for being too "flippity," changing her mind too often.

Tuesday Night Meetings

The Alliance held open meetings on Tuesday nights at St. Peter's Church. Every other meeting was for women only; the others were open to third world men as well.

In the women-only sessions, we could talk about our concerns in a private space, like the November 2, 1971, meeting on American beauty standards or the Tuesday, January 18, 1972, meeting on white women's liberation and third world women. Two other women-only Tuesday night meetings that year focused on day care and Asian women.

Objections about these women-only meetings were frequently raised by men in the wider community outside TWWA, but Alliance sisters were clear that we wanted to have both closed and open meetings. We wrote in *Triple Jeopardy*,

> Some topics affect women more so than men, i.e., sterilization, abortion, birth control, women's diseases and their treatment, male chauvinism in the home and within organizations, role of women, etc., therefore making it necessary for women to first meet among themselves and discuss and move on the problem and later discuss it and deal with it with men. . . . We do not think in terms of perpetuating chauvinism of ANY kind, which includes female chauvinism. We believe in attacking problems in

the most practical way that we are capable of at the time, until better ways present themselves.[16]

Some men who were concerned about their exclusion critiqued our decision. One man of color wrote to the Alliance from prison, "If your organization is to unite our men and women to wage our struggle for liberation as one, why are men only allowed into your meetings every other week, why the division? . . . Seems to me you are advocating more of this white, ultra-feminine womens [sic] lib. than you are the unity of our Third World men and women for the total liberation of our people."[17]

We printed the brother's letter and our response in *Triple Jeopardy*, but this kind of critique, often coming either from underenlightened men or men with different political analyses, was an ongoing challenge. However, many brothers understood our purpose and supported us.

Our open meetings were either on topics of general interest, such as the meeting called "The War, the Wage Freeze and Third World Workers" and the film *Justice* about the withholding of information by the US media, or topics about which we wanted to encourage conversation between men and women, like "our children" and "femininity and masculinity." We often rued the lack of attendance by men at those open meetings, but as the seventies moved on, many third world organizations, in part because of our efforts, began to recognize women's oppression in society and even in their own organizations. The writer of a *La Raza* article reprinted in *Triple Jeopardy* in 1972 declared, "We must realize that the U.S. system has brainwashed us— in spite of all our shouts of Chicano power we still have strains of white upper-class attitudes that reflect in our ideology" and identified vestiges of the old ideas of sexism and male privilege as part of those attitudes. She acknowledged that "women may have to work on separate projects or services very pertinent for changes for las mujeres."[18]

Despite the critique, some men came, and new sisters joined the Alliance after attending a Tuesday night meeting. Barbara Webb (see portrait on p. 124) was a colleague of mine at Queens

College in New York where we both taught Spanish. I invited her to a Tuesday night meeting, and she immediately joined the Alliance, staying after I left right up to 1977 and working in the core group very closely with Ana Celia and Fran.

Often, we educated ourselves by watching films like *Manos a la Obra: The Story of Operation Bootstrap,*which told the little-known story of the disastrous 1947 United States–sponsored economic development plan for Puerto Rico.[19] Using newsreels, interviews, and little-known government propaganda, the film illustrated how Luis Muñoz Marín's Popular Democratic Party and the US government colluded to move people off their land in an effort to transform Puerto Rico from an agrarian economy to an industrial one. By providing low-cost labor, access to markets, elimination of taxes on profits and imports, and low rental rates, the effort lured businesses to the island and created a so-called economic miracle. Unfortunately, this "miracle" resulted in the diminution of farmland, an increase in pollution, environmental disasters, an increase in the unemployment rate, and a massive migration of rural Puerto Ricans into cities on the island and on the mainland.

In discussions of the film, Alliance sisters came to understand why so many Puerto Ricans had migrated to New York City only to find themselves living in poverty and working in factories, unwelcomed by other citizens who did not understand the reason for this "invasion" from a formerly unknown island off the coast. Here was the history and the source of the exploitation that led to Puerto Rican women living on welfare in the projects or laboring as poorly paid garment workers in lower Manhattan.

We were inspired by other independent films shown at Tuesday meetings. *Black History: Lost, Stolen or Strayed*, which challenged the lies of Black inferiority by detailing some of the achievements of African Americans that had been omitted from textbooks on US history. The 1969 film *Burn*, starring Marlon Brando, was another favorite. The fictional story mirrored events happening all over the colonized world, with colonial power and corrupt politicians vying for control of native populations by means of lies, manipulation, and subterfuge.

Karate

To prepare ourselves for self-defense, we took karate classes at the church where we met; our own sensei came to teach us there. As with much of the Alliance's other progressive work, a karate class was fairly "revolutionary." Although one might find self-defense classes today in almost any college or community, most women in the 1970s did not regularly exercise and rarely studied self-defense. Alliance members did because, like many other activists, we were preparing for a struggle that at the very least meant being able to protect ourselves from the police. Mental preparation was seen as important too, and to strengthen our minds, each karate lesson began with silent meditation.

Triple Jeopardy

An entire dissertation could be written about *Triple Jeopardy* alone. Between 1971 and 1975, the TWWA published sixteen issues of *Triple Jeopardy*, describing its purpose and making an appeal to its readers.

Describing itself as "the ideological organ" of the organization, *Triple Jeopardy* was also the educational arm, and on the East Coast, it was the Alliance's most valuable educational tool. In more than three hundred articles written over a four-year period, *Triple Jeopardy* published on the intersections of race, class, gender, and imperialism in the national and international arena. It is beyond the scope of this book to cover the full depth and breadth of *Triple Jeopardy* and its impact, but two important sources may give the reader a sense of its reach. The *Guardian*, New York City's left-wing publication and the progressive paper with the largest circulation in the United States, named *Triple Jeopardy* the best women's newspaper in the country, and Federal Bureau of Investigation (FBI) files reveal that the organization's agents read and thoroughly reviewed each issue of *Triple Jeopardy*, summarizing each article for their files and taking down the names, phone numbers, and addresses that appeared in the paper.

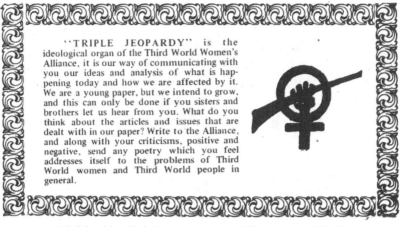

"TRIPLE JEOPARDY" is the ideological organ of the Third World Women's Alliance, it is our way of communicating with you our ideas and analysis of what is happening today and how we are affected by it. We are a young paper, but we intend to grow, and this can only be done if you sisters and brothers let us hear from you. What do you think about the articles and issues that are dealt with in our paper? Write to the Alliance, and along with your criticisms, positive and negative, send any poetry which you feel addresses itself to the problems of Third World women and Third World people in general.

Published in *Triple Jeopardy* 1, no. 2 (November 1971), 2.
Smith College Special Collections, Northampton, MA.

Articles published in *Triple Jeopardy* were focused on exposing and critiquing the triple jeopardy of imperialism, racism, and sexism reflected on the paper's masthead. They also reflected the Alliance platform, speaking to family, employment, sex roles, education services, and self-defense.

Issues of *Triple Jeopardy* appeared on an ad hoc basis. On the front page of the first issue was a drawing of a Latin woman, an Asian woman, and a Black woman, exemplifying the third world women to whom the Alliance was dedicated. This first issue included five articles about the prison system: one about Attica; one about Governor Rockefeller's refusal to meet with the negotiating team for the Attica prisoners who were requesting, among other things, adequate food, water, and shelter (the article, "Rockefeller Asesino," describes his role in what ultimately became a massacre); one about the assassination of George Jackson; one about Patricia Kisha Green, an Alliance member who was seven months pregnant and taken into custody while sitting in the courtroom at her partner's trial; and one calling for women prisoners to unite. There was also a poem from Julia Hervé, Fran's friend in Paris who wrote about

Cover of *Triple Jeopardy* 1, no. 1 (September–October 1971).
Smith College Special Collections, Northampton, MA.

the sons of several New York police officers who had broken into the Bronx Zoo.

An article about anti-war demonstrations ended with the statement, "Third World Women's Alliance calls for participation of all Third World people in the Fall offensive against the war in Indochina. We must lead this offensive and carry it from a simple series of anti-war demonstration to a truly anti-imperialist, anti-racist level."[20]

The first issue also contained pieces of local and national news, as well as an article on female anatomy, picturing and describing the female pelvic and reproductive organs, another on the need for twenty-four-hour free day care, and a column called "Forgotten Women," which looked at "the history of women with special emphasis on Third World Women."[21] A book review reported on Clara Colón's book *Enter Fighting: Today's Woman, a Marxist-Leninist View*. A skills article detailed how to change a fuse, and the "On the Job" column contained an interview with a Maryland factory worker. The second-to-last page announced a rally for Angela Davis Day on September 25, and TWWA's Tuesday night schedule for September and October was printed on the back cover.

Several regular columns were continuing features over the years. The "On the Job" column appeared in eleven of the sixteen issues of *Triple Jeopardy*, refuting the myth that "a woman's place is in the home," stating, "we all know that is a 'so-called' luxury afforded mostly to white middle class women."[22]

One "On the Job" column in the September–October 1973 issue gave an overview of third world women in the workplace, reprinting the text from an Alliance presentation at that year's Conference of Black and Latin Workers in New Jersey and proclaiming, "From the plantations and kitchens and tenant farms of the south to the textile mills in Chicago, New York, and Pennsylvania, Black women have a history as workers."[23]

The story of Puerto Rican women workers was traced from their involvement in the World War II war industry and the increased industrialization and forced migration of Operation Bootstrap and was enhanced by lifting up worker advocates such as Concepción Torres and the Lady's Union of De Tierra. The article ended with the statement, "Third world women because of our history, are a vital and necessary part of the working class and the working class movement today."[24]

"On the Job" columns also covered interviews with individual workers, including a domestic worker, a garment worker, several hospital workers, a secretary, factory workers, and a migrant farm worker. Each column illustrated the ways in which exploitative practices functioned: not getting any days off and no paid holidays or vacation days. "You can't get up to drink water," said one worker. A domestic worker described why she could not quit: "I have to be sponsored back to Trinidad or to another job."[25]

Often, *Triple Jeopardy* contained "how-to" articles describing the skills women needed to become more self-sufficient and competent. The second issue, for example, described how to fix a leaky faucet. In the skills section of the third issue, there was "a list of tools which should be in everyone's tool chest."[26] The final "skills" column was about cooking. In a blunt and humorous style, the author wrote, "Most people look down on cooking when it is actually an art and a necessary skill . . . if neither of your parents could cook you might have starved your ass off."[27] And she followed by providing recipes for piñon and flan.

The newspaper often included book and movie reviews, all with a pro-woman, anti-capitalist, anti-racist perspective. The continuing columns of local, national, and international news briefs covered politics, prisons, racism, striking workers, union activity, and revolutionary leaders around the world as well as the major news emerging from nations in Latin America, Africa, and the Middle East, providing ongoing news of liberation struggles that were not covered by the mainstream press.

One piece invited readers to a conference against racial polarization that was sponsored by rank-and-file workers and Harlem Fight Back in New York City, an organization in which my carpenter brother was very active.

In addition to regular columns, particular subjects were covered in an ongoing way in *Triple Jeopardy*. A favorite subject was Angela Davis, who was covered in three major articles. Her likeness was represented on the February 1972 cover, and several issues published calls to attend rallies to contribute funds for her defense.

Georgette Ioup's articles always kept readers abreast of the difficulties in the Middle East. She introduced us to previously unheard of places, like Oman, and kept an ongoing record of the Palestinian liberation struggles. Her writing often included interviews with women who were involved in liberation efforts in Middle Eastern countries, and this humanized their struggles and strengthened our identification with an international sisterhood of liberation fighters.

Because the health and well-being of Third World women were central concerns, frequent articles were written about our bodies. The book *Our Bodies, Ourselves* was first published in 1970, and our first article on health was a reproduction from that book, including a diagram of women's "pelvic organs" and "reproductive organs." The reproduced article read, "The purpose of this paper is to help us learn more about our own anatomy and physiology, to begin to conquer the ignorance that has crippled us in the past when we have felt we don't know what's happening to us. The information is a weapon without which we cannot begin the collective struggle for control over our own bodies."[28]

Using what we learned from *Our Bodies, Ourselves*, and carefully watching the ways in which capitalism, imperialism, sexism, and racism combined forces to damage our bodies, we began through *Triple Jeopardy* our own campaign to educate ourselves about protecting and taking care of ourselves. We wrote about common vaginal infections, venereal diseases, and sickle cell disease. We documented government attempts to control our bodies and limit our reproductive rights by methods ranging from outlawing birth control to performing sterilizations.

In the early seventies, many of us were getting pregnant and preparing to deliver our babies. *Triple Jeopardy* published a two-page article on "painless childbirth" written by a sister who provided information designed to promote a positive birth

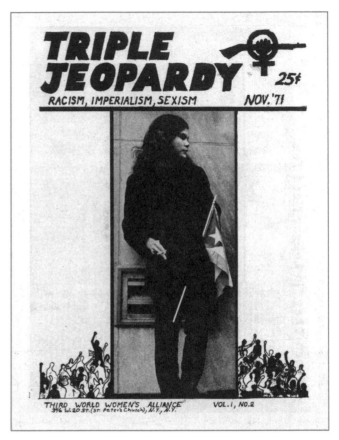

TRIPLE JEOPARDY 25¢

RACISM, IMPERIALISM, SEXISM   NOV. '71

THIRD WORLD WOMEN'S ALLIANCE
346 W. 20 St. (St. Peter's Church), N.Y., N.Y.   VOL. 1, NO. 2

Cover of *Triple Jeopardy* 1, no. 2 (November 1971). Smith College Special Collections, Northampton, MA.

experience for women and described her labor and delivery using the then-new techniques called Lamaze. She summed up her labor and delivery as "an experience we will never forget. My husband and I worked together as a team. Because I had been trained in the Lamaze method, my twelve hours of labor were practically painless."[29] Because of stories like this, Alliance sisters embraced Lamaze as our technique, and some of us also moved away from hospital deliveries to midwife-led birthing centers and then home deliveries.

Most often, the first page of *Triple Jeopardy* featured collages, photographs, or drawings of women from around the world. On one occasion, a photograph of Milagros Pérez graced the cover.

On the front page of our second issue, published in November 1971, Milagros stands with a cigarette in her right hand and a Puerto Rican flag threaded through her jacket as she gazes down reflectively in all her youthful beauty. The only cover which included a man was of the partner described in the article on painless childbirth, and one issue contained pictures of Clifford Glover, a little Black boy who was killed by a policeman in Queens, New York.

We worked at retaining a focus on women. In a note to readers, the *Triple Jeopardy* Collective wrote,

> We feel that as a woman's organization, we should be covering issues that effect [sic] women more. This edition represents our first efforts in this direction. The struggle of third world women in this country for a better life for themselves and their families will begin to get much more coverage in *Triple Jeopardy* this year. In addition, the conditions that we have to face living in a sexist, racist country will be explored in more depth. This does not mean we will stop covering those issues that affect both men and women, but it does mean that we will give priority to those issues that particularly effect [sic] third world women.[30]

With this statement, the Alliance demonstrated its growing comfort with presenting itself as a women's organization, and in the same issue, a call was made to women to send in articles and to keep *Triple Jeopardy* informed about their work.

The previous statement reveals that the Alliance struggled to balance a commitment to "cover a wide variety of subjects including the war in Southeast Asia and the anti-war movement in this country; the prison struggles, the various national struggles around the world and in this country; the fight of third world workers for a better way of life, etc.,"[31] with its commitment to the development of women of color. Looking at the publication from the vantage point of history, the coverage seems exceptionally balanced. The war in Vietnam and protests against it, for example, were covered often from the very first issue of *Triple Jeopardy* through the end of the war, the declaration of the Paris Peace Accords, and the violations of them, alongside articles revealing the abuses of sterilization,

Schedule for January 1972

THIRD WORLD WOMEN'S ALLIANCE TUESDAY SCHEDULE

Tuesday 4   WELFARE MOTHERS

--Conditions that gave rise to the welfare system
--Brief history of wlefare system in 1930's
--What are the present conditions
--Grievances of welfare mothers

Tuesday 11   FEMININITY AND MASCULINITY

-- What do these terms mean?
-- How does the concept of masculinity and femininity affect
   the struggle as a whole?
--What are some of the repercussions? On Women? On Men?
   On Children?

THIS SESSION OPEN TO MEN

Tuesday 18   WHITE WOMEN'S LIBERATION AND THIRD WORLD WOMEN

-- Does sisterhood transcend economic, racial and political
   differences?
-- What is the class basis of most groups and how does it affect
   the white women,s movement?
---Is the movement anti-imperialist?
-- Is the woman question a "class" question, men in one
   class and women in another?
-- Is there any basis for a working coalition with white groups?

Tuesday 25   "JUSTICE"

--Film about prisons and Third World People

THIS SESSION OPEN TO MEN

PLACE: 346 West 20th Street, N.Y.C.
             St. Peter's Church, between 8th and 9th Aves.

TIME: 8:00 P.M. Sharp!

ALL THIRD WORLD PEOPLE WELCOME'

TWWA Tuesday Schedule. Published in *Triple Jeopardy*, 1, no. 3 (January 1972), 17.
Smith College Special Collections, Northampton, MA.

the welfare rights struggles, and our challenges as mothers and workers.

Triple Jeopardy covered news from the Bronx to Guinea-Bissau, from Puerto Rico to South Africa. It presented the struggles in Chile and Vietnam. It examined childcare here and in China and in Cuba, always looking for solutions to the inequities we were experiencing.

Editorials ranged from articulating the role of women in the struggle, to defining the third world, to a conversation with a prisoner who questioned *why* a women's organization, to an articulation of the importance of the radical press, as well as a critique of sexism and how both women and men construct it and respond to it.

We mourned the passing of Amílcar Cabral, founder and secretary-general of the African Party for the Independence of Guinea and Cape Verde (Partido Africano da Independência da Guiné e Cabo Verde; PAIGC), who helped lead Guinea-Bissau to independence.

Poetry was a welcome inclusion. We published the works of some of our brothers, especially poets like Jesús Papoleto Meléndez, my young friend and fellow activist from Latin Action. The centerfold of our third issue included three poems by Papoleto, two of them focused on women. His poem "in a moment" was a beautiful vision of gender relations between activist women in the TWWA and our activist brothers:

> but if
> however
> you cannot wait that moment
> then join me in this movement
> & that will be love.[32]

A different issue had a poem by another fellow activist, Puerto Rican poet Américo Casiano, and we also printed material by and about the Chilean poet Pablo Neruda.

By 1972, there were twenty Alliance members working on the paper, writing, typesetting, doing layout, and handling distribution. For most years, Fran was editor; I served as editor on a couple of issues between 1971 and 1972.

Alliance members were the main writers for *Triple Jeopardy*. Some articles were reprinted from other movement papers. Members of the Communications Committee typeset the newspaper. Individual issues cost $0.25; yearly subscriptions were $3 for individuals and $7.50 for institutions, but *Triple Jeopardy* was also distributed free to anyone who wanted it. Free subscriptions were sent to brothers and sisters in prison. Most issues had a schedule of events on the back cover listing the Alliance's meeting dates for the following month.

Each issue contained photographs or sketches by Alliance women. Chris's work was often represented, along with those of several women whose names are not mentioned because of the absence of bylines and attributions in the early stages of *Triple Jeopardy*. And in what Fran often refers to as the third wave of Alliance membership, Chris was often found leading the editorial work on the paper, assisted by Barbara Webb, Ana Celia Zentella, and Lenore French (see portrait on p. 41).

To encourage the emulation of revolutionary women, stories about women of the third world were an essential component. Consistent with the view that we were part of a worldwide struggle, the articles covered both national and international news. Cuba, the Vietnam War, Pinochet's takeover in Chile, Nixon's visit to China, and the anti-colonial struggles of countries in Africa had a huge influence on us. The obituary of Josina Machel, published in *Triple Jeopardy*, was representative of our commitment to our rallying cry of "Live Like Her," which honored women of the third world.

We were oriented both toward the external third world and the domestic third world (the internal colonies of Blacks, Latinas/os, and Asians in the ghettos of the United States). "Que Viva la Revolución," an article in the January 1972 issue of *Triple Jeopardy* by an Alliance member who had recently returned from the Brigade, described Cuban society as "a workers [*sic*] society" and wrote that women were provided with "a tremendous opportunity for growth that does not exist here in the United States." Day care programs for children and a belief that "everyone should be allowed to develop themselves to their full capacity not only for self-development, but for the

LIVE LIKE HER: JOSINA MACHEL

Obituary of Josina Machel of FRELIMO[33]

It was with great sadness that we of the A.N.C Women's Section heard of the death of Frelimo Comrade Josina Machel. This brave young freedom fighter, wife of President Samora Machel, and mother of a small son, died of an illness in Dar Es Salaam at the age of 25.

It is only right that would be amongst the mourners because of the close and fraternal militant ties we share with the women of Mozambique and the common enemies we face in our struggle side by side with our men.

Her role in the battle as a militant and freedom fighter under arms is a further and clear example of the determination of women the world over to free themselves, their men and children from oppression and exploitation. . . . Josina's death is a great loss not only to the women and people of Mozambique but also the women fighting for freedom in the whole of South Africa, Asia and Latin America.

Her death strengthens the vow we have made to unite with Progressive men and women the world over in the liberation of Southern Africa and the world and continue until the victory. Her spirit will always be with us in the battlefield Mozambique and South Africa and our confrontation with the Enemy, and will determine the tenor of the new society of equality, freedom and happiness in our lifetime." (Statement by the African National Congress Women's section, Dar Es Salaam June 1971; copied from the August 1971 issue of SECHABA.)

FRELIMO is the name of one of the organizations in Mozambique, which is on the east coast of Africa, that is fighting for the liberation of the Mozambique people from their Portuguese colonialist oppressors.

The Third World Women's Alliance shares the sense of loss that the African people have experienced due to the death of Comrade Josina Machel. For us, she stands as a shining example of the ability of all women to function in society on an equal level with their men and make that society strong happy and prosperous for all its people.

development of the whole society" facilitated women's entry into medicine, engineering, and science. Women in Cuba were not discouraged from physical labor for "fear of doing a man's job," and the article called on US women to "realize . . . that we are capable of excelling in any field we choose. We must not allow educators to misguide us; we must not allow employers to shut us out of jobs that anyone can and should perform be it man or women."[34] Columns like "On the Job" covered the experiences of workers, making connections between the oppressive conditions all workers experienced.

Triple Jeopardy turned out to be a rich, informative source of support and perspective for women of color in the 1970s. Members of the Alliance were not the only ones who read *Triple Jeopardy*. Our sisters in the movement read it as well. It drew many women to the Alliance, like Lenore, who took a leave from Harvard University in the spring of 1973 to come to New York. After reading *Triple Jeopardy*, she called Fran to ask if she could write for the paper. Fran thought that knowing the Alliance and being part of its activity were necessary prerequisites to writing for the paper, so she invited Lenore to spend some time with the Alliance. Lenore joined the Alliance and wrote a number of film reviews and other articles for *Triple Jeopardy*. Fran also tasked her with delivering the Alliance's African Liberation Day speech in the spring of 1973.

Even today, *Triple Jeopardy* articles retain the ability to inspire. Eileen Dunn, my student at Mount Holyoke College, researched the newspapers and wrote,

> The most strikingly potent elements of *Triple Jeopardy*, for me, are: the strong female voice that comes out in every article and draws the reader in (more than any verbosely-written article in the *Times* could), the stand against dangerous pitfalls hidden in the terms "pacifism" and "liberalism," the international perspective that actively sought out [sic] to inform and solidify inter-ethnic relations *within* the U.S. by creating a type of global community, and the empowerment of women by urging them to activate and recreate the life that they wanted to live and giving them the tools . . . to do so.[35]

For the first two years of publication, articles written by Alliance members did not carry a byline. We knew we were being surveilled by the FBI, and we did not want to increase our risk of identification and harassment. I wrote several pieces in 1971 and 1972. Fran wrote most, if not all, of the editorials, and many other sisters also authored pieces.

In 1973, bylines began to appear, and in the January–February 1974 issue, the *Triple Jeopardy* Committee was identified:

Editor: Frances M. Beal
Production: Georgette Ioup
Distribution: Maxine Williams Ann Burns, Bernice David, Nydia Muni, Adele Smith, and Barbara Webb

In the next issue, Chris Choy, art editor, was added to the listing. Chris did extensive artwork for the Alliance, even before she was named art editor. It was her habit to sign her drawings on the lower left, but in the early days, she, too, abstained from identifying herself. One particularly detailed sketch appears in *Triple Jeopardy* with an article titled "El Pueblo Vencerá," accompanied by a poem by Victor Jara, the Chilean artist and activist who was tortured and murdered in Chile by the brutal Pinochet regime.[36]

In January–February 1975 and in the final issue of *Triple Jeopardy* in the summer of 1975, foreshadowing the waning of the TWWA and of *Triple Jeopardy*, the phrase "Over-Worked and Under Paid Collective" was added to the listing, along with several new committee member names, including Lenore French and Ana Celia. The latter had written for many issues prior to being listed as part of the Collective.

Although at first written only in English, *Triple Jeopardy* made liberal use of the Spanish expressions then common in movement circles, such as "Hasta la victoria siempre" ("Ever onward to victory") and "Que viva Puerto Rico libre" ("Long live a free Puerto Rico"). The Portuguese phrase "A Luta Continua" ("The struggle continues") was used frequently. In 1973, the

Drawing by Chris Choy and poem by Chilean poet and activist Victor Jara.
Published in *Triple Jeopardy* 4, no. 2. (January–February 1975), 8–9.
Smith College Special Collections, Northampton, MA.

phrase "articulos en español" appeared on the cover, announcing the paper now contained articles in Spanish. The cadre of Latinas writing in Spanish included Ana Celia and Marilyn Aguirre, who often wrote articles in both English and Spanish, as well as Heidy Rodriguez, Miriam E. Gomez, and Gloria Rivera.

All of *Triple Jeopardy*'s coverage supported the Alliance's call for third world women to be "women in our own right"—not unconnected to men or rejecting of men, but undominated by them, not waiting for men or male authority to substantiate our existence or earn our freedoms for us.

The articles provide a history of the fight against imperialism and colonialism, against racism and sexism, but also speak today to the essential ongoing character and power of women to take up the fight for justice, to be both woman and mother, partner and woman in her own right.

Prison Letter Writing Project

The Prison Letter Writing Committee read and responded to letters from brothers in prison. There were occasional columns in *Triple Jeopardy* that listed prisoners' names and addresses and invited readers to write to them. We were writing almost exclusively to brothers. In the early 1970s, the population of women in prison was relatively small compared with the astronomical increase that would occur in the following decades. Nixon initiated his "War on Drugs" in June 1971, and thereafter, the incarceration rate increased slowly but steadily, with most Black men and women imprisoned for the nonviolent crimes of drug use. In addition, many people were imprisoned for their active resistance and calls for change. We often thought of "common criminals" as political prisoners too. We understood criminal activity to be the outgrowth of living in a racist, classist system that put people of color at the bottom of the social ladder. The lack of education, employment, and basic human rights created the conditions from which criminal activity emerged, and we often referred to prisons as "concentration camps" for people of color.

As activists got arrested for their political action, we became informed of the inequities of the criminal justice system and more aware of the harsh realities of prison life and the racism and sexism that pervaded the prisons. High-profile cases like that of the Soledad Brothers, who were accused of the murder of a prison guard in retaliation for the murder of three Black inmates, brought this to our attention, and it came closer to home for the Alliance when our member Kisha was held in custody (although supposedly not arrested) on July 19, 1971, as a material witness because of her alleged involvement with the activities of her partner, Richard Dhoruba Moore of the Black Panther Party.

We began fighting for the rights of prisoners. We paid attention, for example, to the case of Joan (pronounced Jo-Ann) Little.[37] A petty criminal, not a leftist, Joan was a Black woman who went on trial in 1974 in Washington, North Carolina, after murdering a sheriff who had come into her cell with an ice pick and forced her to her knees to perform oral sex on him. She murdered him with the very ice pick he carried as he sat on her bunk with semen dripping down his leg. She was charged with first-degree murder, and the death penalty was an automatic outcome. Her case called together feminist activists, anti–death penalty activists, prison rights activists, and civil rights activists who successfully supported overturning her conviction. Little became the first woman in the United States to be acquitted for using deadly force in a case of sexual assault.

Part of the Alliance's activism was to confront the criminal justice system. We supported the prisoners of the famed Attica uprising, where 85 percent of the prisoners were Puerto Rican and Black, when they took over the prison on September 8, 1971, in both a stand for better conditions (adequate food, water, and shelter for all inmates were some of their demands) and as a reaction to the murder of George Jackson at San Quentin. Jackson had been shot to death by prison officials after serving ten years following a plea of guilty "to a $70 robbery at the suggestion of his court appointed lawyer."[38]

We publicized the inequities of the prison system repeatedly in *Triple Jeopardy* and quoted Jackson in the very first issue: "If I leave here alive, I'll leave nothing behind. They'll never count me among the broken men. . . . They've pushed me over the line from where there can be no retreat. I know that they will not be satisfied until they've pushed me out of this existence all together."[39]

"Live Like Her"

"Live Like Her" was our call to action in the 1970s. It helped us identify and focus on the kind of woman that Alliance activists were determined to be: revolutionary women whose priorities were focused on the liberation of their people, women who understood that women's freedom was inextricably linked to the liberation of the whole. In pursuit of this goal, the ideal models of revolutionary women were identified and celebrated in speeches, articles, and meetings. The first place this phrase appears is in an eponymous article titled "Live Like Her,"[40] which actually was the publication of a speech the Alliance delivered at a rally in DC sponsored by the People's Coalition for Peace and Justice. It names not only one woman but many women in liberation struggles around the world. The Alliance declared, "In China, Cuba, Vietnam and Guinea-Bissau it is assumed that women are a vital part of the revolution, and that no revolution can be or has been successful without them. Of all the revolutions fought thus far, it is from the Vietnamese women that we have been given the best example of what the role of women can be in liberation struggles."[41]

As acknowledged earlier, activism for women's rights by women of color did not begin with the New York City march commemorating the fiftieth anniversary of women's suffrage. Numerous women of color throughout US history have taken up the "woman question." More commonly known, while still underacknowledged, is the role women of color have played historically in the struggle against racism. If we look at the activities of well-known Black women who were involved in anti-racist struggles in the United States, we find that the struggle for women's rights was often part of their struggle as well. Although Black women throughout US history have spoken and written from diverse political experiences, many have focused on the inequities facing Black women. The same was true of other women of color.

"Live Like Her" became our rallying cry, and we conscientiously worked to identify progressive women role models. The women we admired were internationalists, like ourselves. They were anti-imperialist and anti-colonialist freedom fighters. Of the many progressive women Alliance sisters emulated, three examples are offered here: Josina Machel, Lolita Lebrón, and Angela Davis, who are individually profiled in the "Live Like Her" sections in this book.

LIVE LIKE HER: LOLITA LEBRÓN

On March 1, 1954, impeccably dressed in a suit, black heels, and silver earrings, Lolita Lebrón, accompanied by three male compañeros, strode purposefully into the chamber of the US House of Representatives. Within moments, she unfurled a Puerto Rican flag and in an impassioned voice shouted, "Que viva Puerto Rico libre!" Following this clarion call, shots rang out, and the gallery was littered with bullet shells. Five congressmen were wounded. Lebrón, a thin and elegant woman who looked more like a model than a dissident or revolutionary, had walked regally into the Capitol and committed a single audacious act that made her a symbol for third world women and a patriot for the cause of Puerto Rican independence. She wanted freedom for the island, not explicitly by violence but "by any means necessary."

The next day, Lebrón's picture appeared on the front page of the *New York Times*. She was wrapped in a Puerto Rican revolutionary flag and carried in her purse a letter that read, "Before God and the world, my blood claims for the independence of Puerto Rico. My life I give for the freedom of my country. This is a cry for victory in our struggle for independence. . . . The United States of America are betraying the sacred principles of mankind in their continuous subjugation of my country . . . I take responsibility for all."[42]

Lebrón was another symbol of women's strength and commitment to the struggle. Born in Lares, Puerto Rico, the site of the legendary 1868 "Grito de Lares" uprising against Spanish domination and chattel slavery, Lebrón left Puerto Rico for the US mainland in the 1940s. Lares, like other towns in Puerto Rico, had experienced

---

a considerable economic downturn that provided the impetus for the flight of many Puerto Ricans to the US mainland. Lebrón left her homeland hoping for economic improvement and a better life. She settled in New York and found herself in what she described as a ghetto, subject to the poverty and racism that most people of color were subjected to in the forties. She worked as a seamstress. Barely making enough to survive, she soon became an ardent follower of Don Pedro Albizu Campos, a Harvard-educated lawyer who exposed the colonial status of Puerto Rico and called for its independence. When in 1952, Puerto Rico's first elected governor, Luis Muñoz Marín, signed Puerto Rico's commonwealth pact with the United States, Lebrón was convinced that action must be taken. She began to plan the attack on the House of Representatives, carefully plotting each detail involving her and three compatriots, Andres Figueroa Cordero, Irvin Flores Rodríguez, and Rafael Cancel Miranda.

Lebrón was acquitted of the most serious charge: assault with intent to kill. Most of the twenty-nine shots unleashed were aimed at the farthest regions of the chamber rather than the House floor where the chances of congressmen being killed would have been more likely.

At her trial, Lebrón stated, "I didn't come here to kill but to die."[43] On July 8, 1954, Judge Alexander Holtzoff sentenced Lebrón to fifty-seven years in prison. When asked by a reporter about the impact on her children, Lebrón responded, "They need a mother. That's true. But later on, they will need to be free even more."[44] Lebrón also revealed she had sometimes fished for coins in fountains rather than accept public assistance from the country she perceived as her homeland's oppressor. According to Conrad Lynn, who represented Lebrón in her trial, so impassioned and eloquent was Lebrón's account of her life that members of the jury were moved to tears.

Lebrón's life was a compelling call to all dispossessed and oppressed women of color, and the Alliance was honored to announce in 1973 that Lolita had requested membership.[45] Her passion and audaciousness were particularly an inspiration for Latinas, long chafing under the burden of the stereotype of the docile, subservient woman—the limited and constraining notion that seemed to define what it meant to be a woman. Lolita Lebrón's act paved the way for the actions of other Puerto Rican nationalists, as well as female activists of all races and ethnicities.

In honoring these women, we were trying to recognize and remember that they were our foremothers. To remember not just for the sake of remembering but also to remember because there was so much to do. As an Alliance speaker told the massive crowd at the May 1971 March on Washington organized by the People's Coalition for Peace and Justice to protest the United States' increased bombing of North Vietnam, "As third world women we have a job to do. We must recognize our power and our potential. There are no limits."[46]

In the "A Luta Continua: Alliance Women Today" sections throughout this book, you will read the profiles of several women who were members of the Alliance and who have been introduced in this book. It is my hope that one or more of these women will inspire you, that one or more of them will appear as worthy of emulation. I hope you will find, as we did, that if we choose to live like our heroic foremothers, we will certainly construct the world we want to see.

The Alliance educated many women, and many of them became activists through their involvement. I count myself as one. On the East Coast, the TWWA expressed itself as a Marxist, anti-racist, anti-sexist revolutionary organization that followed Chairman Mao's instruction to "serve the people."

As had happened in SNCC, activist women—who in their racial, ethnic, or identity-based organizations were relegated to the cooking or typing or other nonleadership positions—sought out the Alliance. For them, it offered the possibility of full involvement and leadership. Women who didn't work outside the home or were not in school and thus experienced a sense of being tied to housework or the persistent needs of young children came too. The Alliance offered them an end to household isolation by providing mothers with the companionship and support of other women. Childcare was never a problem; women brought their babies along to meetings. We sat and breastfed them, discussed our readings, watched films, and learned together. We came with our own particular experiences of class, race, or gender inequity, and when we came together, we talked and listened to each other and began to understand the connections between our experiences.

Over the six years the Alliance was active in New York, there were three overlapping groups of women who were at the center of organizing: the founders who took the organization from the BWLC of SNCC; the core group who joined after the TWWA took its name; a core group that remained and/or joined between 1973 and 1976.

Half of the founding group left when the decision was made to open the Black Women's Alliance to all women of color. These were women who preferred to belong to an all-Black group. The founding members who stayed included Fran, Yemaya, Stella, Kisha, Affreekka, and Barbara. The second group of women included some founders who remained with the group and others, like Brenda, Barbara, Collette, Ana Celia, Georgette, Nilda, and me. We joined around the time of the March and had a few very active years until disruption was sown by an SNCC member, the partner of an Alliance member, who was said to have been an undercover FBI agent spreading rumors about the Alliance. Trust decreased, and many sisters were disillusioned, leading to an exodus. (I was among those who left at that time.) Several sisters hung on and continued the Alliance work until 1977. The final central core of sisters—Fran, Ana Celia, Barbara, Lenore, Christine, and several others—took the New York Alliance to a higher level of organization and thankfully left good notes and records behind.

A Luta Continua: Alliance Women Today

Georgette Ioup
Professor, Mother, Grandmother, Activist

The Alliance ensured me to a life of passion.
For most of my life has been about the
Palestinian cause. I'm angry about the
injustice—these last colonies.

A Christian Arab, born to a Lebanese father and a Palestinian mother, Georgette Ioup has always been a strong supporter of women's rights. In the era in which she grew up, she felt seriously oppressed in a traditional Middle Eastern home where "men had no respect for women." Even older women in families favored the boys. She recalls that her grandmother was angry that her mother had girls instead of all boys. "She made it clear that I wasn't valued," Georgette said. "She'd take a pear and divide it into two parts. The larger part went to my brother, the smaller one to me. Everything was done that way. Men didn't have to do any work around the house. Once I was reading the comics and my brother wanted them. My grandmother said, 'Let him have it. It's his.'" As a young girl growing up, Georgette felt "unprized. I was resentful. I wanted my fair share."

She began her activism as a founding member of SDS, organizing one of the original thirteen chapters at Wilson College in Pennsylvania, and stayed on until she graduated. Always an intellectual, she believed that one "should organize, not trash and shock. I believed we should try to convince people that we were right." And Georgette demonstrated that commitment by authoring numerous articles for *Triple Jeopardy* that educated us all on the crises in the Middle East and the plight of the Palestinians.

Georgette is now professor emerita at the University of New Orleans, living in the Big Easy where I visited her in September 2006, a little more than a year after Hurricane Katrina. The big X was still on the storm door of her home, and she had just moved back after spending thirteen months in a FEMA trailer—in a compound inhabited by hundreds and hundreds of University of New Orleans faculty and staff—because of the flood that saturated the entire first floor of her home with four inches of water.

Georgette was a member of the Alliance in New York. After moving to Seattle, she was affiliated with the Third World Women's group there that former New York Alliance member Mary Hanley Stone had started. Georgette worked mainly on *Triple Jeopardy*, writing articles while simultaneously engaging in consciousness-raising and reading political texts. Her experience of being undervalued and oppressed as a girl in her family germinated into early advocacy for the liberation of women. Over time, she came to see "how imperialism and colonialism had oppressed the people in the Middle East and how exploited they were for oil."

She became animated as we spoke. "Most of my modern understanding of how the world works came through those educational meetings, through the Alliance. My passion for most of my life has been the Palestinian cause. I'm angry about the injustice!"

Georgette was a professor of linguistics at the University of New Orleans, where the student population dropped from seventeen thousand students prior to Hurricane Katrina to twelve thousand afterward. Her activism has never waned. Whether she is advising Arab student organizations, communicating with editors of the *Times-Picayune*, or helping to work with and establish the Women's Center or the women's studies program, she is always speaking up for the rights of women and of Palestinians. She also works with the American-Arab Anti-Discrimination Committee. Indeed, anywhere in the city where a stand is taken against injustice, it is likely that Georgette Ioup has been at work.

My visit with Georgette in 2006 ended with a trip to St. Basil's Orthodox Church where her family (her son and her brother George and his wife, both professors at the University of New Orleans) sat together as always in a front row. Georgette has always embraced this Eastern Orthodox faith tradition, "even in the most Marxist of times," telling me that to her, "Christianity's emphasis on sharing seems totally compatible with socialism's highest goals."

Yemaya Rice Jones
Mother, Grandmother, Artist, Activist

This was a pivotal time, and we were hyperaware of how important it was for us to define our role in the struggle for equality.

Yemaya Rice Jones connected with SNCC in New York in 1970. There she met Fran Beal and joined the newly formed Black Women's Caucus of SNCC.

Very soon, she said, "We felt a need for us to have our own organization." Everyone was asking, "What was the role of women in the movement? And we felt we need to be defining that. The decision was made, and we started working on becoming the Black Women's Alliance."

Yemaya's strong relationship and identification with women were forged early. "I was not too active in high school, but I went to a rally when the girls were killed in the church in Birmingham," she recalled, referring to the white supremacist terrorist bombing at the 16th Street Baptist Church in Birmingham, Alabama, where four little Black girls were killed on Sunday morning, September 15, 1963.

She became even more active when Martin Luther King Jr. was assassinated in 1968 while she was attending Morristown College in Tennessee. She was president of the student body then and remembered that the demonstrations after the assassination also "turned our campus into a rally and demand for more student rights." As a result, she and ten other activists were expelled. "All of us were women."

Yemaya was a main contributor to the evolution from the Black Women's Alliance to TWWA, and when she spoke with me from her home in St. Croix forty-three years after our time together in the Alliance, she was animated. "So much of the consciousness-raising has served my life and opened my mind. It helped me to raise five really strong women."

"When my girls were growing up, their teachers continually remarked that they knew so much about themselves and their history," Yemaya told me. And the girls themselves (now adults: one in telecommunications, one a physician, one an attorney, one a teacher, and another a physical therapist) often say their mother "treated Black history like a religion that we had to learn."

Yemaya retired from teaching after thirty-four years. All her life, she has been deeply committed to the upliftment of women. For many years, she has been on the board of directors of the Women's Coalition of St. Croix, an organization founded by Audre Lorde and others to help women impacted by violence that has expanded to deal with the violence of issues ranging from breast cancer to racism.

In addition to her political work and her supportive role in nurturing a family with a husband, five daughters, and many grandchildren, Yemaya is a textile designer and a member of the National Association of Fashion and Accessory Designers.

Patricia Romney

Psychologist, Social Justice Consultant, Mother, Grandmother

From each according to his ability, to each according to his need. —Karl Marx

The TWWA profoundly impacted my development and my future work. Always a bit of a late bloomer, I was twenty-six when I joined. I'd had my psychological "encounter" with racism only a few years earlier, working as a teacher in the New York City public schools. Both my students and I were "others" in a school where teachers and administrators were predominantly white and predominantly Jewish. My students were called "monkeys," and I was either invisible to or demeaned by many of my peers.

The Alliance was the first organization in my life where I was accepted and included. The first place where I fully belonged. From the vantage point of inclusion, I was able to look back at my life and look out into the world and see what had happened to me and others like me.

Since my early childhood, I had been discriminated against and excluded because of my race. That was clear.

But I'd had it good. We were not rich by any means, but I'd had a good education, and my family was economically stable—at least until my parents' separation, when my mother had to take on three jobs to afford a place for her and me to live and to pay my high school tuition. My students, my welfare clients, and my cousins growing up had suffered much greater economic deprivation: unsafe homes and neighborhoods, undereducated, not knowing how to read or write, jobless. The politics of the Alliance gave me a frame to understand what I saw and a vision and strategy for working toward equity. In the context of "we," of "belonging," of "sisterhood," I was able to engage in efforts to overturn the racism and class oppression I had experienced and witnessed.

For several years prior to joining the Alliance, disturbed by my parents' ongoing marital conflict, I had wanted to become a psychologist. The experience in the Alliance broadened my view from an individual perspective to a societal one. I wanted more than to help individuals with "problems in living." I wanted to change the systems and structures that enabled those individual and family problems. I entered a clinical program that had a subspeciality in organizational development. My dissertation, "A Search for Space: A Case Study of Institutional Racism and the Colonized Mentality," was an award-winning case study of the Hill Health Center in New Haven where I did my predoctoral internship as a fellow of Yale Medical School.

When I graduated, I became the first "third world therapist" at Mount Holyoke College. I worked with all students but was hired to provide culturally responsive services to students of color whose experiences and challenges were both personal and resulting from racism. Later, as a member of the faculty at Hampshire College and Mount Holyoke, I taught courses that covered my training and my areas of interest: Abnormal Psychology, the Psychology of Oppression, Organizational Psychology, the Psychology of Racism.

I maintained a clinical practice, but over time, I gravitated toward organizational work where I could help bring about systemic change. What was traditionally called "diversity" work was for me always "justice" work. Perhaps my most successful work was right at the beginning as a consultant to a state organization that treated people with developmental disabilities. Although it was early—1995—we focused on class, race, ability, gender, and sexual orientation. With Steven Bradley, an extraordinary leader, I was able to do the most comprehensive work I've ever done, including bringing folks of color into senior leadership; providing educational workshops for close to one thousand staff members; developing mentoring groups for women and people of color; ensuring welcoming spaces for LGBT staff; teaching how rankism and social class impacted the staff; and always, always centering the work on care and respect for the clients and families they served.

Today, I am focused on serving elders and their families in my clinical practice and doing social justice work in my organizational practice. Most recently, my organizational practice has focused on supporting organizations that want to deepen their work around diversity, equity, inclusion, and justice after the murders of George Floyd, Breonna Taylor, and the countless others whose lives have been mercilessly taken.

Combating racism, imperialism, and sexism was the mission of the TWWA. My work has focused on educating people to do that work, as the Alliance educated me. My professional life has been dedicated to helping organizations achieve excellence and equity in schools, colleges, universities, think tanks, and social service agencies by removing the barriers of racism and sexism and working to build truly inclusive classrooms, faculty, board rooms, and workplaces.

I am especially proud of the work I've done over the past eight years to "change the face of the faculty" at leading liberal arts institutions in the northeast and teaching courses for college faculty on Teaching for Inclusive Excellence, a framework that serves to decolonize the curriculum. I felt fortunate to be asked recently to work with a presidential search team at one university to minimize their biases and successfully hire their first Black university president.

When not working, I can be found hosting parties that bring together my multicultural family and reading with my granddaughter, Eva Alejandrina, who at seven is already an activist.

Eva Alejandrina Rosa Chapman at Stonewall 50 – WorldPride NYC 2019. Photo by Imani Romney-Rosa Chapman.

We Were There was sparked by my students' questions and inspired by my Alliance sisters with whom I was able to create my first true organizational home. These bodacious, progressive women are my most important role models and my highest aspiration is to live like them.

Barbara Webb

Professor, Mother, Women's Advocate

I really valued the relationship with these women. I think especially because it was so international.

Everything about Barbara Webb's early background seemed to predict she would someday join the TWWA. She grew up in a Brooklyn neighborhood filled with international families: Irish, Italian, Jewish, West Indian, Cuban. Her parents were strong working-class people with union consciousness. She went to an all-girls high school and then a women's college. She spent a year abroad in Spain where the political activism of the time inspired her. She graduated from college to enter her first teaching position in the SEEK program at Queens College, which was a hotbed of activism but one where male Black nationalism held sway, thus effectively silencing her on the job.

Barbara was impacted and shaped by her race, class, and gender all of her life and over time built a strong international perspective. We taught together in the program at Queens College, and in 1970, when I invited her to attend her first Alliance meeting, she too found a home.

She wrote for *Triple Jeopardy* and participated in solidarity movement meetings, many of them focusing on Black liberation. She made lasting friendships with Georgette Ioup and Ana Celia Zentella, who, like her, would become college professors and lifelong activists.

After her time in the Alliance, Barbara's political work focused on sustaining access and equity in academia, and in the classroom, her teaching focused on cross-cultural comparative perspectives. In her years of teaching Spanish and Afro-Caribbean literature, she made sure that the curriculum remained strongly multicultural. And during her many years of leadership at Hunter College, Queens College, and the CUNY Graduate Center, she worked hard to expand the curriculum, always promoting equity.

Now retired, she worries about the loss of attention to women and women's studies in the academy, noting that the presence and prominence of women's studies programs have diminished, while the economic and other issues that negatively impact women have remained in place. Barbara served as an elected official on the Community Education Council in New York and has continued to bring her commitment and activism to the field of education, honoring the Alliance's call for education to increase knowledge about "the history of third world women and their contributions to the liberation struggle (and) their relation to society."

Ana Celia Zentella
Anthropolitical Linguist, Activist

The students I see really uplifted by my teaching, redirected in some ways by my teaching, are the great joy of my life.

The University of California, San Diego (UCSD) sits on many levels in the rising hills of La Jolla, appearing more like an Ivy League institution than a state university. In her office, Ana Celia Zentella finished a meeting with two colleagues. She introduced me, saying, "Pat is a friend I haven't seen in thirty years. We were both members of a very prescient organization of the 1970s."

We sat and talked about her work and about the TWWA. Ana Celia is a self-described anthropolitical linguist, someone who acknowledges language cannot be divorced from the demographic, socioeconomic, racial, and political realities of its speakers. Her colleagues call her one of the leading Latina scholars in the United States. Language and politics have been Ana Celia's life. Her academic awards are numerous, and the word "excellence" reverberates through them. In fact, New York City's Manhattan Borough president named October 30, 1996, "Doctor Ana Celia Zentella Day," citing "her leading role in building appreciation for language diversity and respect for language rights."

In 2002, she received the National Award of Distinction from the Education Alumni Association of the University of Pennsylvania "for her stellar accomplishments and international reputation for making outstanding contributions to the field of education." And in 2018, the Society for Linguistic Anthropology honored her for Public Outreach and Community Service.

Born in the South Bronx to a Puerto Rican mother and a Mexican father, Ana Celia was bilingual from the time she can remember. Reflecting on this experience, she has written, "I remember the signs in shop windows when I was growing up in the South Bronx in the 1950s: 'Aquí se habla español' ['Spanish spoken here']." Her mother, an activist with an eighth-grade education, worked in the garment industry and was "tough, violent, outspoken. She was very much concerned about justice, and this phrase that she learned, 'your rights.' This is where I got it from. . . . My work . . . is in keeping with that tradition."

Ana Celia told me about her mother's version of Catholicism: "The message of serving the poor and supporting the rights of the community . . . backed up by my years of involvement with the Legion of Mary at St. Athanasius Church, where we visited shut-ins and old-age homes and kids who couldn't make it to religious instruction classes because of mental or physical illnesses, and also the leadership of Liberation Theology in Brazil and Latin America and the Maryknoll missionaries whose magazine came to our home with wonderful examples of selfless activists."

Those early messages and examples led Ana Celia to the Alliance, where for the first time she read political treatises that gave her a basis for more fully understanding what she had seen growing up. In the Alliance, she wrote for *Triple Jeopardy*, led the TWWA Committee to Free Lolita Lebrón, and organized and led a bilingual guerilla theater group, La Nueva Mujer (The New Woman). At Hunter College, where she was teaching, she organized a consciousness-raising group that served as a recruiting vehicle to bring women into the Alliance.

"It was my training in the international perspective and the whole triple jeopardy idea," she recalled of the Alliance's influence on her. Like her focus on language and activism, the "triple jeopardy idea" has remained with her. She taught for thirty-one years at her alma mater, Hunter College, and committed herself to educating the urban poor and working-class students. At UCSD, she has continued her work for women and social justice.

Reviewing her life during our conversation, she said, "There were four causes that I believed in deeply and took some risks for—and went to jail for. Women's rights, especially women's rights to control women's bodies. Affirmative action and equal opportunities for education. An unjust war [in Vietnam]—that was a major, major one. The ethnic studies battle and the issues around free speech and diversity in academia. And that is the one I was arrested for."

Sitting with Ana Celia that summer day at USCD, I found that she worries that the things she has spent her life fighting for are at great risk. She linked the war in Iraq to the Vietnam War. Reflecting on women's rights to control their own bodies, she noted, "They are now trying to turn back *Roe v. Wade*. . . . I'm very concerned about steamrolling over the inequalities, especially in the Black and Puerto Rican community. . . . I think this school [UCSD] should be shut down. It has 216 Black students. The Latino presence is less than one-third of those in the neighboring community. That alone means it's not a public institution."

Thinking about retirement and spending time with her husband (who later died in 2018), her talk turned to "a million things I want to do in my church. With the little children, setting up an after-school program, setting up a kitchen in a very impoverished school in Tijuana." During the COVID-19 and BLM crises of 2020, she helped her church food dispensary and its Faith in Action committee on immigrant issues.

It is noteworthy that Ana Celia's formal résumé and her personal political commitments converge. There is no verisimilitude. There is only lifelong dedication to disenfranchised, underrepresented, underresourced people of color together with a constant focus on women and children. The principles of social justice, deepened by time in the Alliance, seem to be embedded deep in her DNA, as they are with other Alliance members. Quoting "the Liberator," Simón Bolívar, she demonstrates that she is a skilled and strategic activist. Her life exemplifies his words, "Para la campa de batalla la espada, para la salón la flor" ("A sword for the battlefield, a flower for the living room"). In her life and work, Ana Celia has successfully carried both.

PART II

West Coast Organizing

CHAPTER 4

Westward Expansion (1972–1980)

Seattle Third World Women and the Bay Area Chapter

Here there was the major development of quite a few women of color who continue to do social justice work.

—*MARY STONE HANLEY*

In the environment of only women of color, I was able to learn a level of self-confidence and skill I wasn't learning in other places. The Alliance paid attention to developing women of color as political leaders, as activists who had something useful and necessary to say, and as women who could, did, and have made a difference.

—*MELANIE TERVALON*[1]

IN 1971, two Alliance women left New York City for the West Coast. Mary Stone Hanley went to Washington, and Cheryl Johnson went to California.

Seattle Third World Women

Mary Stone headed for the Pacific Northwest, settling in Seattle. I had recruited Mary, an African American sister, while we were both on the Fourth Venceremos Brigade. After the Fourth Brigade, she returned to New York and joined the Alliance, participating for a few months before moving to Seattle. She wanted to take Alliance politics and experience with her and spread its message to other young women.

In Seattle, Mary brought together a group of racially and ethnically diverse women, including Sharon Maeda, Mayumi Tsutakawa, Marcelle Wahba, Evelyn Zakhary, and Kaye Woo. As with the Alliance in New York, the Seattle group took on the demographic aspects of its region—it was largely Asian, with Middle Eastern women being the second-largest grouping. There were a few Native Americans, and Mary was the only African American.

Georgette Ioup, who had been an Alliance member in New York, lived in Seattle between 1975 and 1977 and again in 1979; she worked with Mary to develop the group. Sisters in Seattle met Monday nights for consciousness-raising sessions in which everyone described their family histories and backgrounds and how they got into the organization. Sharon taught them about the history of the Japanese internment camps, where some of their parents had been held, and Georgette educated them about the Middle East and its rich and complicated history.

They assigned political readings, but when they found that most women were not able to complete the readings on time, they decided to read aloud to one another at their meetings. After deciding that they needed education in economic policy and the history of capitalism, they read *Labor and Monopoly Capital* by Harry Braverman. They discussed what they read. The sisters described themselves as a kind of kitchen table "coffee klatch" group that came together to read, study, and discuss. The group maintained contact with New York for at least a year after Mary's move.

The outgrowth of their consciousness-raising and study led to the formation of a campus group at the University of Washington and a community group that worked with Casa de la Raza in the Latin community. For reasons not entirely clear, it was decided that a full-fledged chapter was not the way to go. The Seattle group never became an official part of TWWA, but I include them in this narrative because a group of women led by Mary and joined by Georgette, both Alliance members, did convene to do political education and political work for a number of years. They developed a group of third world women whose activism and ideology closely matched those of the official Alliance chapters, and they are evidence of the activism of women of color that bell hooks suggested was missing at the time. Like other Alliance women, they went on to do important political work: Mayumi edited or coedited four books on Asian American women (*Turning Shadows into Light: Art and Culture of the Northwest's Early Asian/Pacific Community*, *They Painted from Their Hearts: Pioneer Asian American Artists*, *Edge Walking on the Western Rim: New Works by 12 Northwest Writers*, and *The Forbidden Stitch: An Asian American Women's Anthology*), and Sharon became executive director of Pacifica Radio in the 1980s. This account of the Alliance would not be complete without naming them.

The Bay Area Chapter

Like Mary, Cheryl left New York for the West Coast in 1971. She headed to the California Bay Area and sustained communications with the New York Chapter and the Seattle Third World Women's group, as the Bay Area TWWA archives reveal.

The Bay Area Chapter had its roots in Cuba. In early 1971, Cheryl, who had been an Alliance member in New York for less than a year, joined the fourth contingent of the Venceremos Brigade, along with other Alliance sisters, including me. After months of fundraising and political education to finance and prepare for our trip in March, we gathered with people from across the United States to spend two months as participants in the Venceremos Brigade, which that year was dedicated to cutting sugarcane to aid in the Cuban sugar harvest.

Young radicals like Cheryl and I considered this experience exciting. We were assisting in building what the Cubans called the "first free territory in the Americas": a land determined to be free of class distinctions, a country determined to bring equity to its people. In Cuba, housing was free, medical care was free, education was free, and there was full employment. The drug traffic and drug abuse so rampant in the United States, which also had been prevalent in Cuba under Batista, was now nonexistent. Brigadistas from New York were able to meet other young brigadistas from all over the United States as well as people from other countries, who volunteered to come and support Cuba. Among the most memorable experiences for me was meeting the tiny Vietnamese women who seemed so much stronger and worked so much harder than their sisters from the United States.

Cutting sugarcane was arduous, backbreaking work. We brigadistas spent our days in the hot tropical sun, cutting cane

---

LIVE LIKE HER: CARMEN PEREIRA

BOE, Republic of Guinea-Bissau

(TNS) – As vice president of the People's National Assembly and member of the State Council, Carmen Pereira is the highest-ranking woman official of the new Republic of Guinea-Bissau.

She is also one of the most experienced members of the African Party for the Iindependence of Guinea-Bissau and Cape Verde (PAIGC). In her long record of struggle, Pereira has held a wide range of posts.

Her first activity was curing the wounded fighters in the areas close to the Senegal border. At the same time, she worked as a seamstress and used her wages to buy medical supplies.

Her three young children are studying in Cuba. She says she hopes to see them become active members of the PAIGC.

Asked about her main activities as president, she replied, "With the creation of the People's National Assembly we plan to reorganize the women's movement. The party had to dissolve the women's organization at one point due to lack of cadres."

Women take part in all areas of activity of the party, she pointed out. There are women on the municipal and regional committees, they are political commissars; they work in health, education, agriculture and the people's militia.

"As you have seen," she told me, "there are a large number of women who are members of the National Assembly. We are leaders, we work with the men and there is no inequality.[2]

heavily laden with soot in fields that had been burned prior to cutting to allow for more efficient harvesting. Our hands throbbed from wielding the heavy, unfamiliar machetes; our backs ached from stooping low to clutch the stalks close to the ground; and our forearms grew sore from swinging the machetes to cut the cane stalk at ground level, close to the roots. But nights brought exhilarating and informative cultural and political events where we learned about Cuban culture and the successes of the Cuban revolution, and we also organized ourselves into panels to speak to our fellow brigadistas about political issues. Coming from different organizations and political affiliations on the left and from places all across the United States, we wanted to share our thinking with one another and engage in political dialogue.

On weekends and for two weeks at the end of our time in Cuba, we toured the country. We visited hospitals where humane care was provided for those with mental illness. At one mental hospital we visited, patients regularly spent time outdoors growing vegetable gardens and raising chickens rather than being locked in closed psychiatric wards. We took a trip to Varadero Beach, one of the most beautiful beaches in the world, where workers were able to vacation in a place they could not have afforded to stay before the revolution. We visited the Bay of Pigs and learned that the Cubans called it Playa Girón, and we learned that, like the name, the Cuban story differed from the North American story. Cubans spoke of an attempted invasion of its sovereign nation, while the United States spoke of an effort to "free" Cuba. Brigadistas also visited former mansions that had been abandoned by rich Cubans who fled to the United States during the early days of the revolution. These mansions had been turned into schools when the Cuban government established universal free education and began to turn around the illiteracy rate that plagued Cuba. By the end of the Cuban Literacy Campaign, which began in 1961, 96 percent of Cubans were literate, making Cuba the country with the highest literacy rate in South America; virtually every primary school–aged child was in school.

I had traveled to Cuba with Joaquín. Cheryl, while cutting sugarcane, attending lectures, and traveling across the island, met and fell in love with a towering, bear-sized young man whom everyone called Smokey. He was a Bay Area activist and a red-diaper baby (a child of parents oriented toward socialism or communism). Smokey identified as Black but, like Fran, he was biracial—the child of a white Jewish mother and an African American father. It was the norm in the spirit of those "Black is beautiful days" to simply identify as Black in order to build unity and erase the color hierarchy that had arisen during the enslavement of Africans in the Americas. Smokey and Cheryl's relationship blossomed quickly, and when Cheryl returned to New York in May, she began to make preparations to move to California to be with Smokey.

It did not take her long. Four months later, in August 1971, she made the move. Young, vibrant, more than ready to change herself and the world, Cheryl provided what would become a history-making opportunity to expand the Alliance to the West Coast. Having met many people from California while in Cuba, Cheryl found the Bay Area's Venceremos Brigade organizing committee to be a useful way to connect with activists and with women of color whom she hoped to recruit to begin a TWWA chapter in California. A captivating powerhouse of energy and organization, Cheryl knew how to build relationships and how to organize. She'd done this in her earlier years while on the Kappa court, an African American fraternity in New York City for which she'd helped organize parties and other social events. The politics of these two organizations were dramatically different, but some of the skills required were similar.

Cheryl's decision to form an Alliance chapter in the Bay Area was well thought out. She had discussed this with the sisters in New York and had received both the go-ahead and a promise of support. She had been a new but very active member of the Alliance in New York before joining the Brigade, but her full talent had yet to be discovered. Cheryl was drawn to the Bay Area by love, but she was a virtuoso community organizer, and it did not take her long to establish a chapter there.

Outreach

Many early attendees at Alliance gatherings were members of the Venceremos Brigade. Regional organizing for the Brigade led groups to develop a deep sense of camaraderie and cohesiveness before leaving for Cuba, and in Cuba, they were organized into cadres by city/area of origin. This facilitated Cheryl's organizing. Members from the Bay Area Venceremos Brigade knew each other, and as Cheryl had met and developed relationships with several of them, she had a ready pool of recruits.

Cheryl invited sisters to come to her house—the collective on Oceanview Avenue in Oakland, where she lived with Melanie Tervalon, their partners, and a few other activists—to crochet or knit. And then they would talk. Miriam Ching Yoon Louie (see portrait on p. 172) recalls lots of laughter and sisters moving back and forth between personal stories and political analyses. She also remembered that the narrative content was interspersed with singing, often songs made famous by the group Sweet Honey in the Rock. The invitees were all young, in their late teens and early twenties, and they were all progressive. If they had not met one another in Cuba, they knew each other from political rallies or meetings of the Bay Area Organizing Committee of the Venceremos Brigade.

The political talk began fairly quickly and went deep. This was fortunate because some like Michelle Mouton (see portrait on p. 188), a young African American woman who had been an activist since high school, had no interest in handicrafts. She told the other sisters directly, "If it doesn't get beyond knitting, hey, it's not for me."[3] But soon Michelle came to see that the knitting was merely a "subterfuge for talking about other things." The knitting circles evolved into informal rap sessions. They talked about Cuba, international liberation struggles, Palestine and Zionism, Chile, the Black Panthers, police brutality in the East Bay, and anything else that had to do with trouble in their communities and progressive political ideas about how to solve those problems.

Their own experiences as women in the movement were also

an important part of the dialogue. Zelma Toro (see portrait on p. 196) was concerned about male chauvinism in her political work. She had not been in Cuba but was working in the struggle to resist the takeover of the International Hotel in San Francisco, where many immigrant Filipino workers lived. As she shared with me when I interviewed her, she found this experience frustrating. "It was really fucking hard to try to get your voice heard. You'd be shouted down or you'd say something and then some guy would get up and say the exact same thing you just said and he'd get acknowledged. You know. You were like, 'Fuck. I just said that. Why is it more important from this guy?'"[4]

Melanie Tervalon (see portrait on p. 192), who had met Cheryl in Cuba and was heavily engaged in political work after dropping out of Radcliffe College, also came to the meetings. Melanie got started in her activism as a tenth grader through her volunteer work with the SCLC in Philadelphia. She and Cheryl became fast friends and co-organizers. When Melanie was on the Brigade's national committee, she found, "I was the only woman in leadership fighting with them about who was going to chair the meeting and struggling to get to rotate the role of meeting chair. With the Third World Women's Alliance it was clear that it was about women learning and sharing skills. Different people chaired meetings. Different people figured how long parts of the meeting would be. The word facilitation wasn't in common use, but we were being taught all those teeny steps that make it possible to take people from one level to the next."

Vicki Alexander (see portrait on p. 164) was in medical school at the time, but after meeting some of the sisters in the Marxist study group her husband led, she came too. Concha Delgado (see portrait on p. 170) was living in the big house in the Bay Area and was invited to join. Rebecca Carrillo (see portrait on p. 167) heard about the Alliance through friends and joined because she "liked the idea of dealing with the intersection with race and the issues with women, particularly when it came to domestic violence and reproductive rights. That kind of drew me."[5]

Linda Burnham worked on the Campaign to Free Angela Davis for a long time and with the Venceremos Brigade where she met Cheryl and Smokey. She went to Cuba with the fifth and sixth brigades and soon after Cheryl invited her to an Alliance meeting. Linda was already committed to women's issues. She attended abortion rights rallies in San Francisco and other activities related to women but felt that "white feminists had no conception of how race functions in America," so the invitation to join the Alliance allowed her to bring together her concerns about women and racism. When I interviewed Linda, she recalled, "Addressing issues of racism, sexism, and us functioning in the world in one organization was attractive to me. It was also important that I could then have strong social ties with some really nice people."[6] And as in New York, little by little, more and more women came.

There was something magical about being together. Yes, politics was important to all of them, crucial even. Without the politics, they would not have been together. But there was something else, something empowering and enlivening. They were meeting in one another's living rooms. They were working together in various organizations. They were dating brothers who knew each other, and they were living in small collectives of four or five people. And when they were together, they felt a commonality, a shared experience, just as the New York TWWA members felt when they walked down Fifth Avenue together on August 26, 1970.

As Zelma put it in my interview with her, "Ray [her compañero at the time] and I started going to their parties at an old house they had on Alvarado Street and that's where I met the Third World Alliance. Because that's where these fabulous women got together to cook, sing, hang out. I was just like . . . who *are* these dynamite women? Who are these dynamite *women*?! . . . The International Hotel activists I met were from the old Communist Party but also from the Filipino Democratic Union. Those were the only people that I was really dealing with, in terms of political, community stuff, but then here I meet *these women*!"

Building a Chapter

The women who came together in those early days of 1971 and 1972 felt the Alliance was a place for *them*, and as they worked together, they made a place for themselves in the movement where they could meet their goals and serve the needs of their communities. From their very first official meeting on September 25, 1971, they worked steadfastly to build a chapter and ultimately an organization that would play a leading role for women of color in the movement.

Like their New York sisters, Bay Area Alliance members focused on two directions: internally, on the development of Alliance members and the organization, and externally, on social change at community, national, and international levels. Although the work in these areas often overlapped and was at times difficult to differentiate, for the purpose of a clearer story, I will talk about these two facets of the work separately.

Internal Work

The Alliance's internal work involved political education, recruiting women, educating members, and endless efforts to develop both the correct political line and the best organizational structure. Although the political line was under constant refinement, the archives show that the key point articulated was that

> imperialism is the major enemy. As Third World Women, we know from experience that racism and sexism exist. But we also know that it is not just a question of sexual inequity and injustice or just a question of racial injustice. We see clearly that these are manifestations of a deeper root cause. Therefore, we see ourselves as a part of the larger anti-imperialist movement in this country.

The meetings began to move from Cheryl's house to other women's homes. Miriam's house was a particular favorite: women sat at the large round wooden table that's still in her kitchen and talked and planned while eating the sumptuous

Chinese and Korean delicacies Miriam prepared. In addition to her culinary skills, Miriam showed acumen as a brilliant activist and organizer, and she swiftly came to play a key leadership role.

As in New York, at the meetings, women found something they hadn't realized they had been missing: a group of women who were committed to developing political analysis, political activity, and friendship. They found a sisterhood. Early members recruited their friends and family. There were many Black sisters, and on the West Coast, the Latinas were mainly Chicanas. There were Filipinas and Japanese women in addition to the Chinese women who had been active in New York City. Before long, the Alliance became the hub of intense activity for third world women in the Bay Area.

According to Lucas Daumont, founder of Latin Action in New York and leader and cofounder of the Venceremos Brigade, who had moved to California during this time, Cheryl had "a kind of vision and an absolutely on-target intuition."[7] As the women came together, the Alliance grew and began to draw in women who were not affiliated with the left—for example, the women of the Price family (see Ann-Ellice [Price] Parker's portrait on p. 190). In the large extended Price family, membership in the Alliance became an informal but real expectation.

September to December 1971 was designated the first period of the recruitment phase. Cheryl's goals were to have weekly consciousness-raising sessions covering only women's issues and to recruit four or five women to form a decision-making body. After the "informal rap sessions" of the fall of 1971, membership was by invitation, and a core group developed that became the leadership of the Alliance. The chapter was first listed on the front page of *Triple Jeopardy* in the November–December 1972 issue with a post office address in Berkeley. Slowly, women who came to the Wednesday night consciousness-raising sessions and wanted to get more involved formed an "intermediate level" of membership.

The consciousness-raising sessions grew to include expanded topics as diverse as political prisoners, liberation struggles in developing countries, and infant nutrition as well as crocheting.

To join the Alliance in California, a woman had to commit to some kind of project in the community. Because many of the interested women were affiliated with other movement organizations, the core leadership group decided to bring them into the fold by declaring that their outside political work would be their project for the Alliance. Miriam, for example, continued her work with Korean and Chinese community organizations. Concha worked with the Farm Workers' Union.

This dual focus—on women and on people from one's own ethnic group—was easy conceptually but difficult in practice. From Miriam's point of view, this was "the privilege and the burden of triple jeopardy. That we women of color serve as bridges to so many movements, but it burns us out if we don't manage it."[8] Although it was difficult, she managed it, believing that "there are certain things that the Alliance could accomplish and then there are certain things the Alliance couldn't accomplish. You had to go to other places to take care of business with that."

By 1973, there were twenty-five women in general membership meetings. Sisterhood was one factor that drew women to the Alliance, and the *uniqueness* of that sisterhood was equally compelling. Miriam identified the Alliance as a "cross-racial organization." The Alliance, she said,

> gave you an opportunity to work with amazing sisters from so many places. Being in the Alliance gave me a chance to work with the descendants of slaves. Being in the Alliance gave me the opportunity to work with people who used to *be* the Southwest. People that *are* the Americas. And then being with me, sisters got to tap into some stuff from across the ocean.

Meetings also focused on the sisters' own development as women and as members of an important women's organization. A consciousness-raising session on February 28, 1973, for example, was about the division of labor in the home. The Alliance upheld the position that the "doble jornada" ("double duty of women") was not in the interest of women or their partners and families. They determined that sharing household and childcare responsibilities was a must.

As the group came together, there were also contradictions and difficulties. The year 1973 marked the outbreak of "antagonistic contradictions" between straight and lesbian sisters in the Bay Area. Lesbian members felt that much of the discussion of the woman question was oriented toward heterosexual sisters. The year before, the Bay Area TWWA had been challenged to develop a position on homosexuality. At the time, the sisters seemed not to remember or honor the Alliance platform, written by the New York Chapter, that had a progressive, open position in this regard. It read, "Whether homosexuality is societal or genetic in origin, it exists in the Third World community. The oppression and dehumanizing ostracism that homosexuals face must be rejected and their right to exist as dignified human beings must be defended."

The core group in the Bay Area took the position that a political position on "homosexuality" was not a priority for the Alliance. The unfortunate result of this position was that lesbian sisters withdrew from the organization, and the feelings around this ruined many friendships and precluded the intersectional work and fight against homophobia and heterosexism that might have occurred.

March of 1973 ushered in a period of intense political education. Members read all manner of works on leadership, and the crocheting sessions became routinely paired with watching political films. One 1974 meeting, for example, involved crocheting and watching *A Luta Continua* (*The Struggle Continues*), a film about the Mozambican fight for independence from the Portuguese. The sisters also educated themselves through presentations from numerous internal and external presenters who shared their knowledge about political and social systems in other countries—China, the Philippines, North and South Korea—and about the situation of farm workers in the United States.

Part of the political education included sisters also reading (and selling and distributing) copies of *Triple Jeopardy* that were shipped to them from New York. They read the literature and then wrote papers of their own, on topics as diverse as security and consciousness-raising, that they distributed to their membership. They read radical underground newspapers of all kinds, including the local Black Panther newspaper, as well as important newspapers on the national scene, like *Rising Up Angry*, a Chicago movement newspaper published by a young white leftist group of the same name.

They read and discussed material of all kinds from the socialist/communist canon. Sisters read "Afro-Americans," the first article from Mao Tse-Tung's "People of the World Unite." They read "The Role of Women in the Struggle," which was compiled by Alliance members. They read the pamphlets "Where Do Correct Ideas Come From" by Mao and "The Woman Question Is a Class Question" by Lê Duân. General Alliance committee meetings continued with a series of programs tying woman's problems to the larger struggle, such as women in the labor movement, childcare, and the effects of cutbacks.

They read many papers by Mao, including "Oppose Book Worship," which encouraged readers to investigate issues on their own and to explore their own methods of resolution rather than believing that a book would hold the answers to their problems. They read "Combat Liberalism," which encouraged them to wage ideological struggle—that is, to struggle with ideas rather than settle on easy and nonsubstantial resolutions made just for the sake of peace. They read "On Practice,"[9] which reminded them of Lenin's statement that "Marxism is not a dogma but a guide to action." They read articles written and distributed by members of the Venceremos Brigade on the oppression of women and on commitment. They read *20 Enemy Forces within a Revolutionary Organization That Must Be Combatted* by James Forman.

Along with readings in the socialist/communist canon, Bay Area members also did their homework about women of color. As women's studies and ethnic studies programs did not yet exist, the sisters did their own research. To learn about Asian women's history, they focused on Chinese and Japanese women's history "as examples of the two earlier arrivals in order to not become too scattered."[10]

All of the readings were consciously and explicitly connected to the work of the Alliance both internally and externally. For example, a reading and discussion of the article "Combat

Liberalism" were integrated into an examination of the relationships between the Internal Education Committee, the Political Education Committee, and the Newsletter Committee.

The Alliance also read and studied in conjunction with other groups. For example, members read and studied *Das Kapital* in a group sponsored by the Venceremos Brigade and attended, on an individual voluntary basis, meetings of the Asia Information Group, Korea Committee, Kalayaan, African Support Committee, and the Black Scholar.

In conjunction with study, the efforts to consolidate the Alliance were ongoing. As early as the beginning of 1972, the Alliance began to concentrate on chapter formation. Recruitment continued mostly through personal contact, and during that year, committees began to form including the Health Committee; the Internal Education Committee, cochaired by Linda, and its two subcommittees, the Newsletter Subcommittee for Internal Communication and the Political Education Subcommittee; and the Cultural Committee, which Miriam cochaired. The Family Development Committee, of which Cheryl was the cochair, set up a system of childcare that included outings each month for the older children and developed permanent staffing for a childcare center where Alliance women did shifts as well. The Principles Committee worked mainly on developing Alliance principles by reading and summarizing important progressive literature like Clara Zetkin's article "Lenin on the Woman Question." When the Alliance considered changing its structure, as it did on a fairly regular basis, the Reconstitution Committee met, and the Ad Hoc Committee took up any issue that didn't have a designated committee. A Fundraising Committee arranged bake sales, tag sales, and anything else that would raise money. The Coordinating Committee (early on known as the core group) oversaw it all.

By the end of 1972, "extensive discussions were held in New York about the possibility of recognizing the Bay Area as an official chapter. It was agreed based on the practice and development in the Bay Area that this was the logical road to follow."[11] Cheryl and the core group had accomplished their goals. The Bay Area TWWA Alliance was added to the cover of *Triple Jeopardy* at the end of 1972.[12]

The Alliance held regular retreats, beginning in 1973, to focus on internal issues designed to strengthen it. From the end of January through March 1973, the "intensive retreat" involved weekly political education in which sisters worked to define the organization and develop short-term goals. They also discussed and attempted to clarify their relationships with other movement organizations. During this period, their only work was consciousness-raising sessions and internal political education.

In January 1973, the Bay Area branch sent a report covering the previous year's work to the head chapter in New York and mentioned our sister group in Seattle. The report took the form of reflection on the last year of chapter formation. As would become the norm for all the work on the Bay Area Alliance, this report was serious, detailed, and written in the spirit of criticism and self-criticism. The Bay Area leadership noted their own tendency to focus on personal problems and warned against seeing criticism/self-criticism sessions as opportunities for confessions or condemnations. "It is our hope to keep politics in command in pushing the revolutionary struggle forward."[13]

Following the retreat in 1973 came a period of consolidation. The Program Committee met to decide what programs were to be held. The Newspaper Committee worked as an adjunct to the *Triple Jeopardy* Committee in New York, writing articles and giving feedback on articles written in New York, as well as evaluating the newspaper's content, writing style, and perspective. They began to consider a West Coast newsletter covering events in the Bay Area, and they also developed distribution plans. The Political Education Committee was intent on developing "systematic" political education.

By the second half of the year, in a general membership meeting attended by twenty-five women, the Bay Area Chapter was discussing what had been accomplished in the consolidation months. They gave an update on membership status and a short presentation on the history of the Alliance in the Bay Area. They also presented ideas for the future and began to plan another retreat in July to take a look again at membership status and the relationship with the New York Chapter, as well as the group of women who were organizing in Seattle. Relationships with both continued, but the Bay Area was beginning to become more and more prominent.

In the March–April 1974 issue of *Triple Jeopardy*, the address of the chapter no longer appeared on the masthead, although there is no mention of that omission.

By 1975, Nixon had resigned, and the Vietnam War was all but over. The Alliance continued its work on behalf of third world women and communities and began to draft a proposal to reconstitute the organization, even while sisters were pregnant and becoming young mothers. Cheryl's son Robeson, for example, was born on February 25, 1975. Ann-Ellice joined that year, seeing Alliance membership as an entrée to joining the Venceremos Brigade.

Seeking to deepen and widen their outreach into the community, to work to educate women of color, they developed a set of four principles that were presented at the January 29, 1975, meeting.[14] Having explored and studied the topic of cadre in the last year, the first principle they identified was to avoid creating "a small, close-knit group with a scarcity of ideas."[15] Rather than preaching Marxism-Leninism, they wanted to "develop consciousness around Marxism-Leninism as the philosophy that operates in the interest of the people."[16] Their second principle was to make the first principle more specific through concrete examples. The third principle was to promote understanding that racism is rooted in the economic structure of society, and the fourth principle was to avoid emphasis on individualism.

In 1977, in the midst of the internal work of the organization as well as the rallies that were an ongoing aspect of movement work, the Health Education Committee offered workshops, and the Internal Education Committee undertook an intensive political education program that lasted several months. They explored the "women question," the women's movement, Asian American women's history, and Latina and Black women's history in the United States.

As in New York, political study and political work went hand in hand. Nothing was done without examining the principles that supported the action. It was necessary to examine the complex and saturated interconnections between economics, gender, and race. Members reviewed principles of unity and important articles from Marxist literature. Their study continued to be propelled by pressing questions: What factors generated the situation they found themselves in as women of color? Why were they so disadvantaged economically and politically? How were their reproductive capacities being politicized and controlled? What was their role as an organization of women of color?

Rejecting an idealist perspective, they always framed questions in terms of materialism. They held that women were not oppressed simply because of human nature: "Women are not oppressed because men think them inferior, but . . . the idea that women are inferior is generated and regenerated by the objective fact of their oppression."[17] They acknowledged that "until recently women in our society did not find equal protection under the law,"[18] and that "in most religions, women are seen as inferior beings. And in many cultural manifestations, women are depicted in a degrading way that denies their full stature as human beings."[19] They asserted that it was not ideas but rather "the actual life processes of society (how we produce, sustain, and reproduce ourselves as human beings in society)"[20] that created the oppression of women. They urged activists to look to "women's position and role in the family and women's position and role in social production."[21] If they did, they would understand that marriage has been a property relation. They would understand that "economic dependence and a severely restricted sphere of activity are at the root of women's inferior position within the bourgeois marriage."[22] Women, they asserted, "have operated in the shrunken arena of kitchen, bedroom, and nursery. We have been partners in an unequal relationship."[23] They noted, "It is a great step forward for humanity in general and women especially to gain control of reproduction."[24] But they also commented, "Then social institutions become more involved in regulating this area of our lives."[25] Echoing Engels, they determined that historically, women's bodies and lives were controlled and regulated to control property, secure wealth, and track and control inheritance.

They also asserted the importance of seeing women as workers: "The oppression of women is a reality that must be dealt with, but from the perspective of working people. This is the only perspective that is fully in accord with our history from the first day we set foot on these shores, all the way to the present."[26]

In addition to the four principles by which they operated internally, the Bay Area Chapter developed principles of unity, stating the basis on which they worked together and naming the criteria they would use in deciding which other organizations they would work with. The principles were (1) solidarity with working people around the world, (2) acknowledgment of struggles and victories of women, (3) linking the woman question to the larger struggles of our peoples, and (4) working in the spirit of study, struggle, criticism, and self-criticism.

They wrote numerous papers that ranged from the theoretical to the practical. In addition to papers on the "woman question," they crafted papers on how to chair a meeting and how to produce an event. They wrote regular letters to sisters affiliated with the Alliance to keep them updated about Alliance happenings. They wrote letters of critique to other organizations. They wrote analyses breaking down their work into stages, periods, etc. They kept careful logs of all of their decisions, as well as their intentions.

They took note of their criticism and self-criticism sessions for use in plotting the course ahead. For example, in January 1973, they noted that they hadn't foreseen that their two-week recess would impact their recruitment efforts and vowed in the future to designate someone to take responsibility for mail and other issues that came up during recesses and retreats.

External Work

While all of the internal meetings and study efforts were going on, the Alliance was deeply involved in community work and collaborations with other organizations. Sisters also traveled to Cuba, Vietnam, and China to study and participate in the life of socialist societies. Work outside the organization began early, even as the chapter was being formed. The Bay

Area Alliance, like their sisters in New York, wrote to brothers in prison, most notably the San Quentin Six. Committees of the Alliance met with other organizations, including the Mime Troupe, Agbayani Work Brigade, the Association of Vietnamese Patriots in the U.S., the African Liberation Committee, Concilio de Mujeres: La Razón Mestiza, Katipunan ng mga Demokratikong Pilipino (KDP), known in English as the Union of Democratic Filipinos, and many others. The Alliance also developed explicit partnerships and collaborations with other movement organizations.

Some were groups to which sisters belonged, such as the Asian Student Union, or to which friends and partners belonged. There was collaboration with the Panthers Health Clinic, with which Alliance sisters who were in medical school were especially involved. They worked with the San Francisco Citizens Council for Criminal Justice and with Council member Edison Uno, a Nisei civil rights leader who worked to educate the public about the injustice of the forced removal and confinement of 120,000 people of Japanese descent during World War II. In 1973, the partnership prepared a position paper titled "Introduction to Legal Attacks on New Prison Construction in California: Legal Memorandum Panthers Health Clinic."

Other partner organizations included the Asia Information Group, the Korea Committee, Kalayaan, the African Support Committee, Black Scholar, TEACH, the *Guardian* (an independent radical newsweekly published in New York), Empleo Por Unidad in Berkeley, and Committee for Solidarity with the Korean People. They covered all parts of the Bay Area and all ethnic identities representing the third world.

In August 1973, a work brigade of Alliance women traveled to Delano, California, to support the United Farm Workers in building the Agbayani Retirement Village for retired Filipino farmworkers. At the end of October, the Alliance held an educational potluck with a slideshow about the Agbayani work project.

The Alliance worked on the Inmates Communications Project and the Women's Jail Coalition in San Francisco. This work focused on prisoners' grievances and requests for more medical personnel subsequent to the deaths of two diabetic prisoners who had accidentally been given overdoses of their medicines. In addition, they fought the practice of withholding medicines for punitive reasons. As a result of the work, the San Bruno prison achieved visiting rights for minor children, although conditions were still bad for the children to witness, and women were still not allowed to speak Spanish in the jail.

Ongoing Alliance work against the war was a central part of external activity. In 1973, the Alliance was hard at work on anti-war activities. Although all parties in the Vietnam War had signed the Paris Peace Accords, the fighting continued. The Asian members of the Alliance found that this state of affairs affected them in "a very visceral way," according to Miriam, "because you had victims being shown on TV, bombings, the impact, the destruction, the Napalm . . . and it's like you see people that look like family members being treated that way."

The sisters began to consider why so many of the speakers at anti-war rallies and marches were white, and Miriam recalled thinking, "When this war impacts people like us as Asian people, like the large numbers of Black and Brown men that are going into this thing, our thing was to get out our perspective as [a show of] solidarity." And this they did. At anti-war and other rallies, Alliance members became known for their catchy, innovative chants and the way they moved to them—not just walking but dancing to the chants whether they were marching down a street or standing on a sound truck. Miriam noted that the chanting and dancing enlivened many an anti-war rally and brought a "different voice to the anti-war movement."[27]

The Alliance worked in support of the activist film collective Third World Newsreel and developed a women's group at Laney Junior College. It continued meetings with the African Liberation Support Committee and in May, members delivered a speech at the celebration of the eighty-third birthday of Ho Chi Minh. In the summer of 1973, in addition to a co-op flea market bake sale on July 4 to raise money for its many projects, the Alliance put together a display for the Remembrance of the Moncada attack that initiated the Cuban people's revolution against Batista, sponsored by the 26th of July Organizing Committee.

In August 1973, the Alliance sent a speaker to a forum supporting third world workers' struggles in the United States, joining speakers from the United Farm Workers union, the Farah Strike Support Committee, and Filipino American activists from Kalayaan.

In 1975, the Alliance and other movement activists participated in the interorganizational Committee to Free Lolita Lebrón. As a result of these activities, Alliance memberships had doubled in size by 1976[28] and the *Third World Women's Alliance Bay Area Newsletter* began to publish, printing four times that year.

In this period, the Alliance also became active in the struggle for affirmative action, an initiative born in the 1960s in challenges against school segregation based on race. Rulings at that time referred to an "affirmative duty" to desegregate. The law stated, "Even in the absence of past discrimination, a recipient in administering a program may take affirmative action to overcome the effects of conditions which resulted in limiting participation by persons of a particular race, color, or national origin."[29] Following this, many other laws and regulations were enacted allowing "race-conscious" methods to increase opportunities for those who had previously experienced discrimination.

Affirmative action, a program that had been designed to rectify historic discrimination against people of color, was particularly controversial in the mid-1970s. Support for the policy among progressives had risen all over the country in response to a claim made by Allan Bakke, who had twice been denied admission to University of California, Davis School of Medicine and blamed affirmative action.

In 1977, the Alliance became active in the affirmative action struggle and participated in an anti-Bakke rally, where Miriam delivered a speech in support of affirmative action in her customary inspiring and provocative manner. She recalls looking out at the crowd during that demonstration in Delores Park and seeing the Alliance dressed in red with gold armbands. It was, she remarked, "just a powerful bunch of women, a really powerful bunch of women."

The Bakke case was close to the hearts of Alliance women in the Bay Area. African American member Vicki Alexander had graduated from UC San Francisco School of Medicine in 1974, and Melanie Tervalon was a medical student at UC San Francisco at the time that Bakke brought his case. Alliance members spoke and demonstrated in support of affirmative action and against the claims of Bakke. At the 1977 rally prior to the Supreme Court decision, Alliance sisters proudly performed their newest chant: "Little Allan Bakke / thinks he's kind of cocky / says he's not a racist but that is a lie! / So rise sisters rise open up your eyes. / Put your hands on your hips and give the man some lip."[30]

Activists on the left across the country were waging a battle to ensure that affirmative action continued, and the Alliance was there. The Bakke case was one of the first in what developed into decades-long attacks on affirmative action, and by 1996, Proposition 209 effectively ended affirmative action in California. But not without a fight.

In 1979, while many of the social movements were beginning to wane, the Alliance continued its work, paying attention to the issues of the day, including the swelling worldwide opposition to apartheid. On March 8, 1979, members protested apartheid by picketing in front of the South African Consulate.

The praxis of the Alliance reached its highest expression in the Bay Area Chapter. Committees had a tangible, observable impact and specific projects were long-lived. Por los Niños (For the Children), an outgrowth of the Alliance's Family Development Committee, for example, developed a highly intricate cooperative system that provided childcare twenty-four hours a day, seven days a week to ensure that sisters could be active in the political process. Members of several organizations helped with the childcare that the Alliance provided.

The Coalition to Fight Infant Mortality (CFIM), a committee on which Melanie, Barbara Morita (see portrait on p. 174), Vicki, and other sisters served, involved numerous women who were not explicitly members of the TWWA. Members organized in low-income housing projects in Oakland and at places like the Eastmont Mall. And the largest organizing project of all, with an impact far beyond the organization, was International Women's Day (IWD).

Writing

In April 1980, CFIM published its first newsletter, an eight-page booklet filled with cartoons and drawings of babies and mothers. The newsletter described the health crisis for poor women and women of color in Oakland. In accessible, engaging prose, the Coalition asked some hard questions: How is it that twenty-six out of every one thousand babies born to mothers in our community die before they reach their first birthday? What causes East Oakland babies to die at a rate twice that of the national average and seven times that of nearby (but wealthy) Piedmont? How is it that several third world countries, including Jamaica, Thailand, Jordan, and Hong Kong, have lower infant mortality rates than East Oakland?[31]

In a proactive, informed way, the writers described "a program that works"[32] at San Francisco General and asked readers to join them to help fight infant mortality in Alameda County. In one single article, readers were introduced to concrete numbers, graphics that would elicit their mothering instincts, a description of the horrors of infant mortality in their community, and an example of how things could be better. Implicit in it all was the idea that if you joined the Coalition, you could help change the situation.

The CFIM newsletter was published in two separate editions, in English and in Spanish. In July 1980, the second newsletter appeared with an endearing mother and child rendering on the masthead. CFIM informed the community and brought women into the movement. As Alliance member Melanie remarked, "For me, I'm happiest when there is some theoretical idea that I believe in that gets turned into some practice that get tested and turned into a useful idea in people's lives to make our lives better."

Writing was an important part of the Alliance's political work. Members wrote to educate themselves and to educate sisters and brothers in the third world community. They wrote articles about healthcare, about women in the struggle, about their own phases of organizational development. They wrote the speeches that they gave at various rallies.

One noteworthy piece of writing that went to the heart of their existence and their work was their own articulation of the answer to the "woman question." In October 1977, they wrote a paper "to articulate the need for a third world women's organization . . . not in order to justify our organizational life . . . but to clarify for ourselves some of the theoretical issues involved in the woman question."[33]

Again, they posed the following questions: "In what ways are women oppressed? How can women fight oppression? What is the common history of the oppression of third world women? Why should third world women organize?"[34] And truly, as if they were speaking to themselves, they wrote that they found "a more developed way of asking that most basic of all questions having to do with the condition of women."[35] They posed the questions essential to dialectical and historical materialists by exploring the material basis of women's oppression—that is, that "women are not oppressed because men think they are inferior, but the idea that women are inferior is generated and regenerated by the objective fact of their oppression."[36]

Genius Organizers

In the nine years the Alliance existed in the Bay Area, members developed incalculable activities, initiatives, educational enterprises, and coalitions. Cheryl began it all. The first meeting took place one month after she moved from New York to California, at a time when others might still have been unpacking.

That was Cheryl! Always purposeful. Always thinking ahead. Always prepared. Always documenting and always planning for the next step, the next event. Always beginning with the end in mind. And the sisters who joined her in the Alliance, becoming leaders and sustaining members, were essentially the same. They were highly political, highly intelligent, organized women who were community leaders, UC Berkeley students, teachers, medical students, nursing students, public health students, and law students.

Their self-evaluation was both verbal and written. The written documentation gave them material to evaluate and reevaluate, to preserve a history of the organization for posterity. The sisters of the Bay Area Chapter were planners, analysts, and integrators of theory and practice. Every event was planned, structured, and evaluated, leading to clear recommendations for the next event's structure. Even committee work and structure were evaluated and analyzed deeply, leading to the reshaping of future events based on the findings. Elements of the evaluation were: who participated in the committee, what was the quality of the participation, how could participation be improved, and how did committees interact with one another.

If we want to learn from these sisters, we should take notice of how they diligently preserved records; did intense, detailed planning; reviewed and re-reviewed; evaluated; and focused on outreach, always going wider and wider. They wrote detailed meeting agendas, maintained and addressed financial reports, included political readings, and always sought new knowledge. All of this was fed by their strong connection with one another. They sang while they marched, partied together, and watched one another's children.

They were young, between the ages of eighteen and thirty, with most in their early twenties. They were in school or "between" school. Melanie had dropped out. Cheryl had left her teaching job to go to California. Miriam dropped out of college shortly after the Third World Strike at UC Berkeley when she and her fellow students were trying to create a Third World College and their activism led them into the community. Vicki was in medical school, but she was one of only a handful of women there and felt so alienated by her classmates' emphasis on making big money that she actively sought a relationship with other like-minded women who would be supportive.

Some of them were young mothers, like Ann-Ellice and Delores Price, who wanted simply to keep their minds active and have something to relate to outside of the dishes and diapers. Their partners were activists as well. Miriam met

Melvin Louie in her Chemistry 1B class at Berkeley. Melanie met Lucas Daumont through her work on the Brigade. Vicki's former husband, Harry Chong, was an expert on Marxism and a leader of the progressive left in the Bay Area. Zelma and Ray Toro were dating and close to Michelle and Juan Fuentes. They got married and participated in one another's weddings. Lucas recalled Teresa Guerrero's wedding—"All of these women went, and they sang in chorus in celebration." It was an organization that had found a way to blend family and the political into a "thing." Doing political work and having fun. And then the babies started to come, and the sisters began to take care of one another, to support one another as mothers.

They were like any other young people, but the context created by time and place was one of deep activism. All of them were working to make the world a better place, as they felt called to do after the experiences of Vietnam and the violent racism and imperialism of the sixties. They were driven to study and work using the principles, theories, and practices used by many young activists of their time. They made choices based on their analyses, and they set up programs to effectuate change.

The End of TWWA and the Beginning of the Alliance Against Women's Oppression

The TWWA organized the community, drawing more and more women of color into its incubator, especially through IWD celebrations, which will be described in the next chapter. And as they worked, like the master organizers and master activists they were, they documented and critiqued and reformulated, integrating theory and practice in a manner worthy of the movement's highest intention.

This approach was emblematic of everything the Bay Area Alliance did: ask the important questions, generate the facts, mobilize support, and take action. And then another evolution took place.

At IWD 1980, the Bay Area Alliance presented a summary of its history, which they wrote before they transitioned into the Alliance Against Women's Oppression, an organization in which white women and women of color joined together. It high-lighted three central themes. The first was the "Importance of Grasping the Centrality of Party Line."[37] The Alliance asserted that "everyone who participates in the political arena from the left to the right does so off of some kind of political perspec-tive, some kind of opinion of what is a problem in the society, what is the cause of the problem, and what should be done to minimize or do away with the problem." They concluded that the TWWA had "groped around for some eight years without being conscious of political line" and that they had over this time worked with "vague politics." The conclusion was that the members wanted and needed to "hold ourselves accountable to sum up what seem to be the most advanced lines current in the movement, critique and interact with these lines, struggling to formulate the view that most closely captures our political reality and goals, and use this analysis to guide our work."

Their second theme was "Struggle to Transform from Spon-taneous to a More Conscious Class Force." The history of this theme in the Alliance, as they saw it, was that the organization initially arose spontaneously as part of the "mass movements of the '60s and early '70s" and needed to develop into a more conscious class force. They needed to transform themselves by becoming more conscious of their "more strategic interests as a class."

"Grasping Lessons from TWWA History as a Microcosm of the History of the U.S. Movement" was a third theme. Concluding that "our history holds lessons not only for ourselves, but also for the broader movement," the Alliance focused on the need to do a summary of the trends and demarcations within the anti-racist movement, the development of revolutionary nation-alism as an ideology and its impact on the movement, the need to sum up trends in the women's movement, and so on.

The history of the Alliance that the Bay Area sisters gener-ated at this time covered four periods. The first, TWWA–New York (1968–1977), relayed the history of the Alliance from its inception within SNCC to its demise in 1977. They noted that the early political line of TWWA–New York was a posi-tive advance over the thinking of the time because it "targeted imperialism rather than men or whites as the enemy." The early political line also "stressed the commonalities and basis for unity of Third World women" and asserted the perspective that "the organizing of Third World women and addressing the problem of sexism would be an asset rather than divisive to the overall struggle."

Their critique of the New York Chapter's ideology and practice was that we had "failed to consistently specify the relation between imperialism, racism, and sexism and identify which would be the principle focus of the organization." "Sometimes, imperialism is projected as central," they wrote, "at other times all three 'isms' were listed co-equally." They also critiqued New York for "individualism on the part of leading activists and failure to develop collective leadership." They summarized that TWWA–New York likely dissolved because it was not a strong collective and wasn't able to deepen its political line. They reported, "Failing to reorient itself to the new period [the ebb] in the movement, the TWWA–New York eventually folds in 1977."

The analysis divided the Bay Area period into three stages: Formation of TWWA–Bay Area to Transformation into Mass Activist Organization (1971–1976), Activist Transformation to Identifying the Need to Develop Revolutionary Political Line (1977–1979), and Current Transformation to Unite on the Revolutionary Political Line (1979–present).

They believed initial work in the first phase of organizational formation in the Bay Area constituted "a step backward in comparison to TWWA–New York" because of the crochet lessons and "tendencies toward self-cultivation and small group mentality." The organization at that time, the Alliance declared, was seen "as a haven for the development of TW women in isolation from the pressures of the larger movement." The paper recognized the success of the Alliance in expanding its membership and its initial base, but declared, "It degenerated into a political sorority!"

The second phase (1977–1979) of transforming to a more activist stance saved the Alliance from dissolution, the paper asserted, through holding "itself accountable to the needs of the broader movement." This allowed it to do the external work of a mass activist organization like work with the National Committee to Overturn the Bakke Decision, Southern Africa Solidarity, and Oakland's CFIM.

After working on the organization's main shortcoming—the alienation from the mass movement—the contradiction that appeared was the "lack of a leading line to guide our intervention in the mass campaigns." The Alliance needed to "pay attention to line struggle" in order to correct "serious right errors in our practice, the flourishing of anti-left lines, demoralization, shelving the question of revolution and the remnants of incorrect lines being reproduced in the work."

The Alliance was in the middle of the last phase of the development addressed in the paper. Members had completed the first stage of transformation to unite on a revolutionary political line. They had completed a political history; they were beginning to focus on the struggle against women's oppression, which had always been a part of their work; they were getting ready to take step three, "the transformation of the racial composition of the TWWA in accordance with the principle that composition is determined by unity on political line." The Alliance finally concluded that it had begun to "put the whole over the part, the needs of the movement over organizational and individual interests, to objectify our subjectivity and to deepen our class orientation."

In another paper, "Deepen the Working Class Orientation of the Women's Movement," also presented at the IWD celebration in 1980, the Alliance spelled out in greater detail the conditions women faced and women's potential as a revolutionary force, the impact of the lack of revolutionary line, and their responsibility around the question of women's oppression. The paper's orientation to women and to the working-class struggle was made clear. "We are convinced," they wrote, "that through our unity to take up the struggle against women's oppression and to transform women into a mighty revolutionary force we will have a profoundly positive impact on the women's movement in particular and the overall people's struggle for revolutionary change and will advance these struggles closer to victory."

These efforts were part of the party-building movement

of the era, and after almost a year of study and discussion, the members of the Bay Area Chapter of the Alliance made a decision to merge with white women and gay women into an organization called the Alliance Against Women's Oppression (AAWO), a group profoundly focused on women's oppression nationally and internationally. Despite the Alliance's carefully articulated presentation at IWD 1980, the organization's decision was not uncontroversial and did not reflect all members' perspectives.

Cheryl was deeply hurt. She was part of the group that felt they needed to maintain the TWWA as an organization when, as she recalls, the proposal came to integrate "feminists" into the body. She had started the Alliance in California, yet she was not asked to be in the leadership of AAWO. The group moving forward was an intellectual one and strongly oriented to theory, and reflecting on it years later, Cheryl felt she "didn't have the intellectual knowledge that some of them did." She recalled, "I didn't at that time have the writing skills or the intellectual skills. I'm the organizer. I get things done. Most of the people of color had gone to Ivy League colleges. I went to college at night. I didn't have the intellectual acumen that others in the movement had, and it didn't bother me until the shift [to AAWO]." In addition, since she had just earned her bachelor's in 1979, was deeply involved in promoting affirmative action in her job at the Legal Aid Society of Alameda County, and was well positioned in the Bay Area Black community, she didn't move on to the AAWO.

Ann-Ellice also stopped when the TWWA evolved into the AAWO. As she recalled, "Life went in another direction. I was no longer doing that work in that form. I was hit with the AIDS epidemic and did work on women's reproductive rights and HIV."

These differences did not all occur in that moment. Women's experiences had been changing as "the line" was developed; Barbara recalls with some bitterness the way Alliance sisters accused her of being "careerist." Other sisters remember being similarly chastised because of what was considered excessive interest in their careers. Pushed beyond their comfort zones, either because of the highly intellectual discourse or because of a heightening Marxist orientation or feelings of solidarity and membership as a group of women of color, some sisters left the organization at the time of the transition.

But it wasn't all bad. Miriam recalls, "We went through a very careful process about the transformation . . . a several months process in two stages—one to sum up the work that we had in the Third World Women's Alliance, and then the second thing was to figure out the political perspective of the group going forward. And I think we cleaned up our act in terms of anti-lesbian politics that had existed in the Third World Women's Alliance."

Vicki also saw benefits. Reflecting on the transition, she said in my interview with her, "Through that process of analysis, we came to understand that all white women were not the same. That there were some white women that had consciousness around race, that if you were talking to them and did not see the color of their skin, that you would not even know they were white, necessarily."

White women had been coming to the IWD celebrations in greater numbers and, as Zelma told me, they "began beating down our doors." Things were beginning to change despite some of the negative history with white women in the movement, such as the time that the Alliance sent out an action alert to a white women's organization and had it returned to them by women who had corrected all the grammar and punctuation. The organization was beginning to turn toward a more racially inclusive look at women.

As the seventies progressed, everything changed. As the personal is political, so is the political personal. The issues on the world scene had changed, and what many women saw as personal decisions—wanting to spend time with their kids, needing to earn a living, planning to go to graduate school—were decisions that hinged on a political reality. The days of this era of activism were coming to an end. Age also had something to do with it. These women were turning thirty, and their lives were changing. Still, the impact of the times and their experience in the TWWA remained.

Some, like Miriam and Linda, continued on, working with

the AAWO for many years, authoring several Marxist papers about women's oppression. As they worked together intensively and grew even closer, they determined that there was still a need for an organization for women of color. Together, they cofounded the Women of Color Resource Center (WCRC) in Oakland to "carry the best of the politics into the new era." The WCRC continued until 2009, serving as a resource to scholars and working with women of color throughout the region. A great deal of effort was put into organizing and cataloging the archives of the TWWA, which were transferred to Smith College when the WCRC closed.

By some accounts, the decision to merge with white women was deemed an error. Looking back during my interview with him, Ric Ricard believed that AAWO "raised the political level higher than where most women were at."[38] AAWO apparently reflected where the leaders were politically, not where the women were. Perhaps, too, the language of the Alliance shifted to a high-level intellectual/socialist vocabulary that was not only obfuscating for many women but also devoid of a sense of the people, the human side of revolution. In that shift, TWWA lost its base of working-class women.

These contradictions were not the only ones the Alliance found itself struggling with. There had been the matter of attention to the issues of oppression among lesbians, as well as ongoing disagreements about "what reflects a class line in a women's organization." To be sure, in this period, many other things were taking place. The sixties and seventies era of leftist political activity was coming to an end. The left had been infiltrated, the United States was still intact, and the children of the Alliance were growing up. Ric, husband of Alliance member Jeanette Ricard, recalled, "Jeanette would have stayed involved. Of course, she became a mother, too, but this whole ideological thrust of moving upward and leftward left folk out."

The Bay Area Alliance thus concluded nine strong years of activism. As in New York, there were no membership cards and no formal membership arrangements, but certainly, between 1971 and 1980, scores of women were affiliated with the Alliance, and hundreds of others had some connection to its work through its many outreach programs.

A Luta Continua: Alliance Women Today

Vicki Alexander
Physician, Activist, Mother, Grandmother

The Third World Women's Alliance was a safe space to encourage women to become politically active around the three isms—class, race, and sex.

In a large three-story house in the Maxwell Park section of Oakland, California, Dr. Vicki Alexander lives with a bunch of multilingual and multiracial international women student boarders from Mills College. Her daughter, Maya, and her granddaughter live there too.

Vicki was in the first class at UCSF Medical School that benefited from affirmative action, one of twenty-nine African Americans and even fewer women among more than 120 students. When I asked what led her to join the Alliance, her quick response was "alienation in medical school." Her alienation, she explained, was not just about her minority status: "I was sort of appalled because I was brought up to think that people should serve people and that if you wanted to be a doctor, you would serve people, not serve yourself." She was discouraged by her peers' conversations about what they wanted to be and how much they wanted to earn.

She graduated in 1974 and did her internship and residency at UCSF, deciding after her third-year obstetrics clerkship that she "loved it; loved being there for the women and supporting them. Holding their hands."

Vicki has spent her personal and professional life surrounded by women. She joined the TWWA in 1972 to help combat the alienation she felt at school. "Maybe I can do something with a women's group and keep myself oriented," Vicki recalled thinking. "I might be able to have a contribution with women's health." She was active in the Alliance's CFIM, engaging in what became a lifelong commitment to health equity and justice.

The daughter of a shoemaker and a union organizer with roots in the Communist Party, Vicki retained a focus on poverty and social class. And coming from a multiracial family with roots in the civil rights movement, she paid close attention to race. These were constant issues for Vicki throughout her medical career.

Vicki is the founder and chair of the board of Healthy Black Families, Inc. During Black History Month in February 2011 and Women's History Month in March 2011, the City of Berkeley twice honored Vicki for founding the city's Black Infant Health Program. Announcing her award, Carole Kennerly, former council woman and vice mayor of Berkeley, began, "South and West Berkeley [where the BIH program is located] has a history of being the part of our city that has suffered so much in terms of allocations of resources. One of the manifestations has been low birth weight among many African American infants. She's the kind of physician we dream of," said Kennerly. "She's concerned about the inequalities in our society. She works tirelessly to serve children and families."

Linda Burnham

Activist, Organizer, Writer, Cofounder of the WCRC

The Third World Women's Alliance is the foundation for my outlook up until today.

Perhaps no member of TWWA has retained a greater focus on the intersections of race, class, and gender than Linda Burnham. She was born a "red-diaper" baby in Brooklyn to Dorothy Challenor Burnham, a microbiologist, and Louis Burnham, a journalist. Both of her parents joined the Communist Party in the 1930s at the height of the Depression. Dorothy and Louis lived in Birmingham in the 1940s, leading the Southern Negro Youth Congress and raising their family. When the family returned to New York in the late 1940s, her father edited *Freedom* newspaper, working closely with Paul Robeson, its publisher. Dorothy became a leader in Women for Racial and Economic Equality. In our last conversation, Linda reported her mother "was on family Zoom yesterday. She will be 106 in March. We'll celebrate this summer on the Vineyard."

Linda began her activism as a teenager and has engaged in left politics ever since. She joined the TWWA in the early 1970s, doing "political education work—coalition work with other organizations, singing, going to rallies and demonstrations, working closely with the Venceremos Brigade," and "being a speaker about some key Alliance issues for women of color." From Linda's perspective, "The Alliance's greatest contribution was its insistence on creating that vantage point, that analysis for women of color whose concerns, outlooks, needs were not being addressed." Reflecting on the women's movement of the seventies, she offered the thought, "Most white feminists had no conception of how race functions in America. Even if they wanted to address it, they didn't have the capacity. . . . It's not accurate to identify the white women's movement as monolithic. It wasn't, but none of those organizations were able to articulate issues they had no experience with and would not know how to address if they wanted to."

After working with the Alliance for seven years, Linda transitioned to the AAWO along with other TWWA members. Never losing her focus on women of color, she and Miriam Louie cofounded the WCRC in Oakland, California, which ran from 1990 to 2010. As executive director for eighteen years, Linda helped create a vibrant connection between activists and scholars by focusing on the political issues affecting women of color.

In the early 1980s, she frequently contributed to *Line of March*, a Marxist journal, and was a member of its editorial board, cowriting special issues on feminism and racism. Linda led a women of color delegation to the United Nations Third World Conference on Women in Nairobi, Kenya, in 1985; the United Nations Fourth World Conference on Women in Beijing in 1995; and the United Nations Conference Against Racism and Xenophobia in Durban, South Africa, in 2001.

In 2005, she was one of a thousand women nominated for the Nobel Peace Prize. She won the Twink Frey Social Activist Fellowship at the University of Michigan, Ann Arbor, in 2008.

As national research director for the National Domestic Workers

Alliance from 2010 to 2017, Linda led research projects that documented the living and working conditions of domestic workers throughout the United States. Her work in this domain directly exemplifies the platform of the TWWA. In 1970, the Alliance platform named domestic workers as prime objects of exploitation, and in 1974, Viola Mitchell, founder of the California Homemakers Association, spoke about that same issue at the first IWD celebration in Oakland in 1974.

Linda's four grandparents emigrated from Barbados in the first decade of the twentieth century. Her grandmother worked as a nanny. The long-standing confluence of race, class, gender, and global issues is both personal and political for Linda.

Known for her incisive analysis and political commentary, Linda continues her lifelong activism in projects focused on long-term strategy and political education. And she writes and writes and writes.

Rebecca Carrillo

Teacher, Organizer, Mother, Grandmother

I never gave up the fact that our work was good, and I was going to continue to fight back.

In the South Valley outside of Albuquerque, New Mexico, near the almost dry Rio Grande River, Rebecca Carrillo lives on a small property with a ranch-style entrance. Her husband, Alberto Martinet, another activist, recently passed away. This is horse country for some wealthy millionaire families, but for most folks, many of them Mexican immigrants, this is a life of rural poverty and underresourced schools.

"This area surprises people because it is so beautiful. Many people think of this area as a ghetto, which is ridiculous," Rebecca said. "Alberto and I came to New Mexico to experience something different from the Bay Area, and perhaps be able to buy some land. This is a state with statistics always being compared to Mississippi. We wanted a new experience, to meet new people, learn new traditions, and to be able to contribute."

Rebecca and I are long-time compañeras. We were both on the Fourth Venceremos Brigade to Cuba in 1971, where we spent two months cutting sugarcane. We both named our sons Maceo, after

Antonio Maceo, El Titán de Bronce, who led his group of warriors, "the Mambises," to revolt over enslavement in Cuba. During our conversation, I discovered that Rebecca had been very busy since I last saw her in Cuba, and her astute analytical mind and progressive politics were still robust.

Continuing her political activism after the Alliance came to an end, Rebecca worked in the ethnic studies department at San Francisco State and Jesse Jackson's Rainbow Coalition, and joined with others in the Central America solidarity movement. During this busy period, Latinos Unidos and Somos Hermanas were also formed and were organizing fact-finding missions to El Salvador and Nicaragua with a collective of teachers, artists, union reps, and community organizations, and they organized a women-only brigade to meet with Central American women who were experiencing the ravages of war.

Aside from raising her son and now being closely involved with her granddaughter, Rebecca has been intimately involved in the public schools since moving to New Mexico in 1996. We talked about the state of education in New Mexico and the inequities of schooling. She retired from teaching at Rio Grande High School in 2010, but her analysis and commitment are still strong. "Rio Grande is basically overwhelmed in the numbers of children in need of good services. . . . You have 60 percent of English-language learners that basically don't have the support and the infrastructure of bilingual programs like they should have," she said. She carefully watched the challenges and debacles of public education, working to make a difference as a member of the teachers' union.

Rebecca declared she is not as active as she used to be: "If I was younger, I probably would have done a dissertation on the classic institutionalized racism in this school district." It is clear that she is an inveterate activist. We talked about her mentoring of young teachers and the work on sustainability and cultural heritage that she does with her son. "When I work with these young people, I am the oldest person there."

She speaks widely and has participated in workshops on the No Child Left Behind legislation, which is full of "lots of rules and no funding to actually improve learning." Through the visionary work of *Rethinking Schools* magazine, Rebecca has tracked the textbook industry's involvement in schools and its investment in the privatization of public education. She is outraged by the industry, "which tests everything that is happening with students" but notes that in New Mexico, "when tests are too expensive, they tinker with old and obsolete tests to make them appear relevant."

Rio Grande, the high school where she taught, had been the center of controversy in the years before Rebecca retired, with new administrators brought in from out of state to try to "clean up" the schools by wiping out schedules and creative curriculum, ignoring teacher input, and generally failing to improve education in the South Valley. "In the last seven or eight years, we had maybe six or seven principals," Rebecca said. Solutions included bringing in new regimes and pouring in new money, but with little attempt to engage and build with existing teachers or the community.

In her teaching, Rebecca often developed challenging lesson plans, like reading *Animal Farm*, to educate and motivate her students. "*Animal Farm* and the principle of Democracy, I thought, this will be a tough one because of the vocabulary. I struggled with how to update it," Rebecca recalled. "And then I thought it is perfect for [the Arab Spring in] Egypt and perfect for the democratic rights that our school is trying to achieve." During the *Animal Farm* lesson plan, Rebecca and her students would discuss at length how "people who are under the gun or oppressed or poor get fed up." "They want to fight back. That is what is happening to these animals [in *Animal Farm*]," she said. "What happens to people when they are in these conditions day in and day out, when they see sad things happening in their community or they can't provide for their families. . . . I had the kids throwing out ideas back and forth." Rebecca's work exemplified the best kind of teaching, and the principal of the high school seemed to acknowledge that she was enlightening her students and simultaneously empowering them.

Referring to the prerevolutionary politics of the 1960s and 1970s, she said, "I see myself as definitely progressive. That is not even a question. How I look at revolution is I would sure like to have one here in the United States. I will tell you that much."

In the meantime, she collaborates with her son Maceo, a Cornell graduate, who works on sustainability. Querencia Institute and the Jardines del Bosque Project are two of his efforts that she integrated at her high school. Working together with various partners around the city, these projects have provided stipends for summer programs for young people around sustaining land, water, and food. To these efforts, Rebecca brings "the whole collective work spirit type of thing . . . that concept of working with a group that can share, give, organize, and be accountable."

She credits her knowledge of experience and organizing to her work with the Alliance. "You have to make your contact," she said. "You got to know who your key contact is. That person will get you ten or fifteen other contacts." She teaches about the importance of going out into the community. "Go where people are at and meet who they are, and you have to find the people who are doing it and just connect with them, just sit down and figure out where they are coming from."

With the light that has been shed on police brutality since the murder of George Floyd in the summer of 2020, Rebecca has shifted her activism to using social media and electoral newsletters. She, like other Alliance sisters, is an elder now, and in the time of COVID-19, she said, "I've been staying inside. Along with working on a memoir, I've been consulting with younger people doing police brutality work and anti-racism stuff, dealing with old colonial stuff, like the split between Chicanos and Hispanics, which never seems to die."

"I do see myself responsible to future generations," she declares. "That doesn't go away."

Concha Delgado Gaitán

Professor, Author, Community Leader

With the Third World Women's Alliance . . .
I was able to stay focused on the community
and what the empowering aspects were,
and to understand how structurally and
economically the pieces fit.

Concha Delgado Gaitán was born in Chihuahua, Mexico, right on the border of El Paso, Texas. Her first exposure to political groups was in college, where she had "some dissatisfaction with some of the real radical Latin organizations. It was not a comfortable place for me to be politicized because of the level of militancy and [their being] very ethnocentric. I was raised in very diverse communities . . . so I was exposed to many different groups."

She began her professional life as an elementary school teacher and quickly rose to become the first female public-school principal in the district. This happened so early in her career, she says she was "still a baby." While she taught, became an administrator, and went on to earn a PhD at Stanford University, she did political work with Brown Beret affiliations, the United Farm Workers, and with the TWWA. Concha was involved with the Alliance's childcare and healthcare initiatives and very deeply engaged in studying the political and economic texts that would later inform all of her work. The Alliance helped her "break the barriers and stereotypes about women of color" and to understand what class distribution and wealth meant in the global sphere.

The connection to other women of color was what drew Concha to the Alliance: "I think it was just a loud statement about the potential of third world women—the strength, the potential, the intelligence, the creativity that women in our communities have," she said. "It was animating and inspiring. It gave me this amazing perspective on the world landscape and what poverty was, how it happened, and what our role was in eliminating it." Empowerment became the watchword of her career.

Since her days with TWWA, Concha has continued her pursuit of social justice by uniting the principles of study and praxis that she learned so well in the Alliance. She has taught at the University of California, where she rose to the rank of full professor as an educational anthropologist and won the University of California's President's Recognition Award for research leading to improvement in education. Other accolades include a lifetime achievement award from the American Anthropological Association and the Pearl Chase Award from the University of California for research contributing to community development. She has written and published ten books and over sixty essays and scholarly articles.

Today, Concha writes, lectures, and continues her community work. She has also turned her attention to women's health because "we as women were raised with two different messages. On the one hand, you are supposed to be a trailblazer and have all this responsibility to your community, but on the other hand, there was no real support for keeping us healthy." Research on aging has also become an important pursuit. Perhaps because of the important relationships she had with people in the Alliance, her work on aging focuses on "friendships and relationships," those things that "only get a few pages in the many books about aging."

Miriam Ching Yoon Louie
Activist, Speaker, Organizer, Writer,
Cofounder of the WCRC

This is the privilege and the burden of triple jeopardy. We women of color serve as bridges to so many movements.

Miriam Ching Yoon Louie is a community organizer, speaker, author, and cofounder of the WCRC, which was based in Oakland, California. We sat at the table in her kitchen for our interview. The round oak table was a cherished memory for the women of the Bay Area Chapter of TWWA. Meetings there were accompanied by sumptuous Korean and Chinese delicacies that nourished their conversations.

At that table thirty years later, Miriam interviewed me first, cursing without inhibition and going deep into Korean history and her own family story. She gave sage advice to my young research assistant and asked us probing questions. She was in command of the interview.

Salty and brilliant, Miriam has spent her life serving the people. She is perpetually busy—organizing, delivering keynote addresses, writing, publishing, and now spending more and more time trying "to figure out what Miriam needs to do."

Miriam's mother was Korean and her father Chinese. She met her Chinese American husband and life partner, Belvin Louie, more than forty years ago in her Chemistry 1B class at UC Berkeley. They worked together on the Third World Strike at Berkeley, the student activist events that generated the birth of the ethnic studies departments there and nationwide. The Berkeley students of 1968 had hoped for "something bigger"; they wanted a Third World College that would have been a "lot more liberation-oriented, very community-oriented." The ethnic studies departments changed the landscape of academia, and most of those students ultimately "went into the community and founded different political organizations."

Miriam was one of those students. At age eighteen, she joined the First Venceremos Brigade, traveling to Cuba in 1969 to cut sugarcane and help build schools, hospitals, and apartments. She was a key contributor to the Alliance. She also worked with the Asian Immigrant Women Advocates, volunteered with Fuerza Unida, and cofounded the WCRC in 1990. She has worked on BRIDGE, an education project of the National Network for Immigrant and Refugee Rights. She was a key leader in the Somos Hermanas delegation of eighteen US women to Nicaragua in 1984.

Her nonfiction writing centers on activism and progressive politics. *Sweatshop Warriors: Immigrant Women Workers Take On the Global Factory*, published in 2001, tells the story of the Chinese, Mexican, and Korean immigrants who led the anti-sweatshop movement in California. Her best-known article, an outgrowth of Alliance intersectional politics, is "It's Never Ever Boring: Triple Jeopardy from the Korean Side." She has written for *Ms.* magazine, *The Nation*, and *Amerasia Journal*. With her youthful spirit, she also jams with younger poets at various venues.

Miriam associates her writing with her time in the Alliance: "I learned how to write speeches and leaflets and all the rest of the stuff you do in learning how to chair a meeting, organizing demonstrations. . . . And then I did newsletters at my Asian Community Social Service jobs and organizing jobs." Miriam later included fiction in her repertoire and published *Not Contagious—Only Cancer*. "It's still writing," she says, "so the skills that I've acquired go into this. It's like you are learning a new instrument yet you play another instrument, so you can use some of what you've learned from your other instrument in this thing, and it's interesting."

Miriam brings her commitment, endless energy, and quick wit to her work. At an IWD event in 2002, she began, "On this beautiful, fragile International Women's Day I offer the warmest of greetings to you. First, from my Korean diaspora identity as one of Bush's 'Axis of Evil' peoples. Second, from my Chinese diaspora side peoples with undocumented immigrants and low-wage workers. Third, from my colored girl membership in the rainbow warrior women's movement for peace and justice."

For five decades, Miriam has dedicated her life to advancing social movements—"women of color, immigrant women workers, grassroots Asian communities, and other kindred troublemakers." These are the women, she eloquently states, "without whose labor, love, sweat, and tears we would not even exist on this planet. They serve as the tree shakers who knock down the fruit, the piñata-busters who break open the goodies—of economic democracy, gender justice, and human rights—for all of us."

Barbara Morita
First Responder and Mother

My core values are serving the underserved and the importance of communities.

Growing up as a young Japanese American girl, Barbara Morita knew she didn't fit in. "I was never 100 percent American. . . . I always knew that I was different, even though I thought, 'I have light skin and dark eyes and straight black hair, which is the same as this young man over here . . . but he's not called a name that I'm called.'" Her father was an engineer and had a good income, but as a child, she still watched "doors be slammed on my father's face" because he was Japanese. For her, "that was painful, but I didn't know what to do," and she saw that kind of treatment "eat away at him."

She experienced sexual harassment as a young woman "in public places where men would come over and actually touch my hair and my shoulder and say, 'Come with me,' because I reminded them of their Mama-san from World War II."

She found her time with the Alliance helpful. "Being able to share, especially when we started working more with the women's movement. That it's not just, 'Aren't you oversensitive?' To talk with another sister who says, 'If I hear that again I'm going to scream.'" And with racism, "You just know you don't have to explain it again, that we know that what she said was racist, and we don't have to re-explain that racism exists."

Barbara's travels as a first responder and emergency preparedness coordinator for Alameda County's Health Consortium have taken her worldwide. Her core values have shaped her work and her family, and her background of activism helps her "to frame" everything she does. She and her team were the second team at the Super Dome when Katrina struck, and she also served at the World Trade Center after 9/11. She saw how poverty and limited resources impacted so many in New

Orleans. From her perspective, "In the United States, as you purchase healthcare, you also purchase safety," and she is aware of how safety is diminished for so many. She has seen societies that she believes function better in disasters. She mentions that "during an equivalent hurricane [Hurricane Dennis in July 2005], Cuba lost six people and the hurricane went right up the middle of Cuba. The United States evacuated three hundred thousand people. Cuba evacuated six hundred thousand people, and they were able to do it with very meager resources." They were able to do this, she says, "because of the way they are organized."

She has seen the democratic socialism of Sweden and the safety net it provides for people. People there don't "live in fear . . . but it's not the same in the United States. You lose your job; you're worried you're going to end up on the streets; you're going to be robbed. You know all of these horrible things are going to happen to you, and you live with that tension and that fear." Sweden has a social security system that supports people. Even an unemployed friend of hers gets enough to rent a small apartment and pay for food. "It's much more humane."

During our interview, she reflects on Bhutan, where "instead of a gross national product they have a national happiness product. It's wild that the success of their country is based upon happiness." Barbara retired from the disaster medical team in 2018. "So, when COVID hit, I was climbing the walls since I had never 'sat out' a major disaster before, and my team was going out on missions. I have settled into doing a lot of volunteer hours with the Food Bank of Contra Costa County—in the warehouse and community distributions. At my age," she says, "it is probably a good compromise."

CHAPTER 5

International Women's Day

International Women's Day is our day. Our success will be a victory for Third World women and for all working people.

—*DELORES PRICE*

MORE THAN ANY other activity, International Women's Day (IWD) epitomized the spirit of TWWA in the Bay Area. Without exception, former members of the Alliance, their families, participants on the left, and the larger women's community in the Bay Area remembered IWD. Each time I spoke with someone about IWD, her face conveyed a sense of deep satisfaction as she recalled the events with unmitigated enthusiasm and pride.

In fact, of the many actions that the Bay Area Alliance engaged in, IWD is the clearest and most compelling in the hearts and minds of former members. It spoke most vibrantly to their commitment to build a community of activist women of color linked solidly to their families and dedicated to liberation.

Becky Carrillo had gone to Cuba with Cheryl Johnson and me. She was introduced to the Alliance there, and had begun to read *Triple Jeopardy* when she returned to California. She was working for the Brigade and trying to finish college and was at first too busy to work with the Alliance, but the IWD celebrations drew her in.

Ann-Ellice Parker saw those celebrations as "the primary focus of the Third World Women's Alliance. We had committee work as well, but International Women's Day celebrations were a huge to-do. They taught me how to do large events, taught me how to organize based on common interests and common goals, provided me with the skills that allowed me to join the work world far more than a liberal arts degree."[1]

Concha Delgado, a young activist member of the Alliance, recalled the celebrations clearly:

> There was an enormous amount of work for us in organizing . . . there was so much detail and care in providing for the children. People were training the volunteers and taking that much care in providing snacks and making sure the children were going to be comfortable. That they would be safe and all of the details that are important when children are concerned . . . and for the express purpose of freeing the women to be present at the event. I remember always being impressed by that. The men were also brought into the fold, which was important. It was a very powerful statement about how it wasn't just by women, for women, but that it was really a family-oriented emphasis.[2]

Nancy Wong, who joined the TWWA while doing community service at UC Berkeley, remembers IWD as "the main event" of the Alliance,[3] and Cheryl described it as our "signature work." Cheryl noted that it brought out the Asian, Hispanic, and African American communities, and led Alliance women to be "incredibly empowered" as women. "That's probably where I developed the most," she said. "I was always in the middle of it. It reached so many people. All levels of people. All kinds of folk. It reached the broadest base, active or not." Melanie Tervalon said it was "a great recruiting vehicle" and was quick to add, "and you know it was that kind of celebratory event where you had a chance to recognize people that had been in the struggle for a long time."

IWD has both national and international origins—each founded on the socialist labor movements for women's rights in the early twentieth century in North America and Europe. The Socialist Party of America declared the first National Woman's Day on February 28, 1909, to honor the women who took part in the 1908 garment workers' strike in New York

City—fifteen thousand women garment workers had demonstrated at Union Square demanding better wages and improved working conditions. They were mostly immigrants, many of whom spoke only Yiddish. Many of them were teenagers who worked thirteen-hour days, seven days a week, and had a half-hour for lunch.

That demonstration inspired a strike of several hundred workers the next fall, and on November 22, Local 25 of the International Ladies' Garment Workers' Union also voted to strike, which quickly increased the number of strikers to thousands. The strike lasted three months, becoming known as the "Uprising of the 20,000." The women's demands were accommodated gradually, and women finally and ultimately won higher wages and a fifty-three-hour workweek.

An "international" day was proposed first in 1910 at a Socialist International meeting in Copenhagen, Denmark, to commemorate the women's rights movement and to press for universal suffrage for women. A hundred women from seventeen countries unanimously passed the proposal. Acknowledgment of the day quickly grew worldwide after the declaration of the socialist parties in Europe and America. The first celebrations outside of the United States were held on March 19, 1911, in Denmark, Austria, Germany, and Switzerland. "More than one million men and women attended IWD rallies campaigning for women's rights to work, vote, be trained, to hold public office and end discrimination."[4]

One week after the March 19 celebrations, an unforgettable event seared IWD into the consciousness of workers and women's rights advocates across the United States. A fire broke out at the Triangle Shirtwaist Company sweatshop located on the eighth, ninth, and tenth floors of the Asch Building at 23–29 Washington Place, an unregulated and unsafe tenement in New York City. One hundred forty-six workers died, in great part because of the bosses' decision to routinely keep the fire escape doors locked. Ninety percent of the workers were women, most of them immigrants, largely Italian and Jewish. The oppressive and unsafe conditions under which they toiled highlighted the discrimination women endured, and the Triangle Fire, the need for improved working conditions, and adequate labor legislation became the focus of subsequent IWD commemorations, in which women demanded workplace safety regulations and memorialized those who had died in the horrific fire.

The IWD commemorations pushed women's issues to the forefront of nations' political agendas and became part of the protests against World War I. Russian women observed their first IWD on the last Sunday in February 1914, and in other European countries, women held anti-war rallies to express their solidarity with the day.

In 1917, women textile workers in Petrograd (now Leningrad) stormed the streets protesting their working conditions and conducted a strike for "Bread and Peace." Czar Nicholas II abdicated days after, and the provisional government gave women the right to vote. In 1928, the first Australian IWD rally organized by the militant women's movement called for equal pay for equal work, an eight-hour day, the end of piecework, and annual holidays with full pay.

IWD celebrations spread around the world. On the fiftieth anniversary of the day in 1960, 729 delegates from seventy-three countries met in Copenhagen and adopted a declaration in support of the rights of women. Finally, on March 8, 1975, the United Nations held its first observance of IWD. The Alliance was part of the groundswell and made a memorable contribution to raising awareness of IWD and its meaning. In the fall of 1973, the Alliance developed an IWD subcommittee cochaired by Cheryl Perry and Vicki Alexander to plan for its first celebration in 1974. They wanted a sponsoring group that would extend beyond the Alliance, and they convened a meeting of women they knew. About twenty-five women attended, embraced the concept, and a group calling itself the Third World Women's Committee to Celebrate International Women's Day formed. They developed the following guiding principles: "1. Solidarity with working peoples. 2. Acknowledgement of the women's struggle as an integral part of the people's struggle. 3. Recognition of the leading role women have played in the movement for social change."[5]

Miriam Ching Louie, an experienced organizer who had

planned many events for the Venceremos Brigade, attended that first meeting. She quickly became a committee leader and worked on the initial celebration, which took place at the Black Panther Party Learning Center in East Oakland. She recalls an "amazing event" with "a great program."

From the very first celebration, there was huge community involvement in IWD programs. That first year, there were thirty-nine "task sign-up sheets" for publicity, programming, fundraising, shopping, and cooking. An ethnically and racially diverse group that included surnames like Emelia, Yohida, Jackson, Hernandez, Tactqui, Hopkinds, Aztlan, and Steinberg signed up. The list also included men's names: Luis, José, Anthony, Westley, David. The sisters had done a good deal of groundwork inside and outside the movement. They even received a letter of support from Congressman Ronald V. Dellums stating, "Through such organizations as the Third World Women's Committee to Celebrate Women's Day and the recognition of our role in building a better society through the celebration, we will make great strides toward our goals as women and as Third World people."[6] This and other messages of solidarity were read at the event.

The TWWA speech at the end of the celebration ended with the injunction, "We women have got to be bold. . . . We must come forward to articulate our ideas and take on greater positions of responsibility. There is a Chinese saying that 'Women hold up half of heaven.' Our participation is crucial in the struggle to better the conditions of our people. . . . THE PRESENT IS STRUGGLE. THE FUTURE IS OURS! LONG LIVE INTERNATIONAL WOMEN'S DAY."

By every measure, the first IWD celebration in the Bay Area was a huge success. Hundreds turned out, but as Delores commented at the time, "The success of our work is measured less by the hundreds of people who attended the event, than it is by the spirit of collective accomplishment which prevailed during the celebration and the eagerness with which we approach the work."

The *Black Panther* covered the event on the first page of its March 16 issue that year with the headline "International

Women's Day Celebrated." Below it was a picture of Cheryl Perry sporting a huge Afro and a very satisfied smile. The article reported that six hundred people packed the Community Learning Center where the event was held.

Each year following, on March 8, or a convenient day close to it, the Alliance mounted a major community event to celebrate IWD. The emphasis on supporting workers, especially women, was a recurrent theme from the very first celebration, at which Miriam spoke about the philosophy of the larger Third World Women's Committee. Other speakers included Viola Mitchell, founder of the California Homemakers Association, who talked about the effort to gain collective bargaining rights for domestic workers in California; Sister Doan Thi Nam Huu of the Union of Vietnamese in the United States; and a striker from the Farah Company, who spoke about their struggle against the Texas-based company, which at the time was the nation's largest manufacturer of boys' and men's pants. The workers were trying to organize a union to support them against the bosses' use of speed-up techniques and other harsh practices. The Farah Strike Support Committees had four organizing points. The first named the Farah strikes as "an important battle in the overall struggle of the working class." The second identified them as "an important battle in the Chicano people's struggle against national oppression." The third let it be known that Chicana women made up nearly 85 percent of the striking workforce and that one of the strikers' demands was for paid maternity leave. The fourth stated, "The strike was also important in the battle against runaway shops and unionization of the Southwest."[7]

Janice Cobb did a poetry reading at the first celebration, and Sister Johnnie Tillman, welfare rights activist, spoke about the welfare rights struggle. The celebration ended in song with a chorus comprising all the women in the organizing committee singing "The Rising of the World's People."

Based on the success of the 1974 celebration, the sisters began to prepare for the following year's event. On February 13, 1975, Cheryl and Miriam wrote a letter on TWWA stationery to their "comrades," announcing, "We're halfway through the work for International Women's Day and the momentum is building fast for our celebration. We must look closely at this year's efforts at outreach, because each has pushed forward the work immensely. The TWWC is now preparing for the third outreach activity which all our committees are being asked to support materially."[8]

Delores delivered another presentation at what became an annual preparatory potluck dinner. Describing the work of the IWD Third World Women's Committee, she asked attendees to spend a night in discussion about IWD.

The specific goal of the potluck was to recruit folks who would be active in the development of IWD 1975, with the long-term goals of educating third world communities and bringing women into the movement. In Delores's words,

> As Third World women we have been oppressed along with our men by racism—and we recognize the necessity to wholeheartedly embrace the struggle against our racial subjugation. As working women, we are faced with a shrinking job market and rapidly rising prices—and we recognize the necessity to expose and combat the fundamental inequities that create these conditions. As women, some of the issues that concern us most are adequate child care and education for our youth, maternal and child health care, training for skills that have been denied us, and employment and wages based on ability rather than sex—and we recognize the necessity to make our brothers more aware of the particular concerns of women and involve them in this aspect of our common struggle.[9]

Delores explained to the attendees, "The idea for a third world celebration of International Women's Day grew out of discussion within an organization called the Third World Women's Alliance. These sisters had participated in many anti-imperialist coalitions and support activities for working people's struggles." She recalled, "In 1973 the Alliance began to see the need for directly addressing the women's question. It was felt that International Women's Day would be a good focal point for involving third world women in learning about our history and speaking out about the issues that affect us most

TWWA Bay Area poster for International Women's Day by Chicano artist and activist Juan Fuentes.

deeply." In a call to action and participation, she concluded with the rallying cry, "International Women's Day is our day. Our success will be a victory for Third World women and for all working people. Will you join us?"[10]

The IWD celebrations were grand, with each year's event bigger than the one before. Up to 50 percent of Alliance members were involved in planning, executing, and debriefing. Many individuals and organizations—both leftist and main-stream, including elected officials like Rep. Ronald V. Dellums and Berkeley City Councilwoman Ying Lee Kelley—endorsed the event. And the participants became increasingly varied, from organizations and communities as diverse as the California Association of Community Health Workers, the KDP (Union of Democratic Filipinos), and the Presbyterian caucus. Over time, many white women activists also participated in the celebra-tions. In some years, latecomers to the events were informed that there was "standing room only." Besides the *Black Panther*, the San Jose paper *In Struggle* and the *Guardian* covered the 1974 event.

Each celebration was unique, but all followed a similar pattern. There was food—participants especially liked Renata Tervalon's (see portrait on p. 195) Louisiana gumbo. There were skits. And almost always, Michelle's husband, the gifted artist Juan Fuentes, would create a special poster. There were songs, invariably including the "Internationale." Leticia Wadsworth was the song leader, just as she was at marches and demonstrations. She would compose songs, and at every IWD celebration, committee members would sing at the end with their children on stage. "Leticia led the singing, and she didn't even have to look," Miriam remembers. "All of our voices came in behind her."

There were vendors, picture takers, and speakers at the cele-brations. Belvin Louie (Miriam's husband), Ray Toro (Zelma's husband), and other brothers acted as security guards. Will-ing brothers took over childcare for the day and brought the children into the big hall to join their mothers and aunts on stage for the finale, which was filled with singing and danc-ing. Parents came, especially mothers. Mrs. Price—Delores's mother and Ann-Ellice's mother-in-law—met Vicki Alexander's mother and the two became friends. Families gathered as whole units—grandparents, parents, and children. The head of the Communist Party in the Bay Area proclaimed that these IWD celebrations were the place to go; there was no other.

The Alliance was the first organization to bring IWD to communities of color and to the progressive community in the Bay Area. These were legendary celebrations, and in the Bay Area in the 1970s, the Alliance and IWD were almost synonymous.

The skits performed each year focused on issues that were crucial to the Alliance's analysis and organizing efforts. They were based on the Cuban plays about integrating women into the revolution and on works by contemporary street theater groups like Teatro Campesino and the San Francisco Mime troupe. These skits stood in sharp contrast to the portrayals of family life seen on television in the 1970s. Family life as portrayed in *The Brady Bunch* and *The Partridge Family* was largely fun and games, and although the Black family in *Good Times* gave a face to low-income families, the representation did not inspire a call to action.

IWD skits were about the hard realities of life—and were a great recruiting tool. Year after year, IWD drew more and more women to the Alliance, and they learned about the history and meaning of the day. Here is one example from the Alliance archives.

AT HOME

Things are kind of chaotic. Nobody listening to each other but everybody yelling.

Ma walks in, takes off coat, and starts looking at bills.

BOY: What's for dinner?
MA: I just got home.
BOY: (disappointed): God, I'm hungry.
MA: (annoyed): I just got home.
PA: Hi.
MA: Don't ask. I just got home.

(MA starts preparing dinner; phone is ringing)

PA: (loudly): Isn't dinner ready yet?

MA: I told you I just got home. I got off late from work.

BOY: (yelling from other room): How come dinner's not ready yet?

MA: (doesn't answer; cooks faster, banging pots around, etc.)

PA: What's wrong with you? Now what you got to complain about?

MA: Nothing. I'm just tired. Do you want rice or potatoes with chicken?

PA: Chicken. Again.

MA: Listen. You want this or not? I'm in a hurry. I have to go to a meeting tonight.

PA: Meeting. What meeting? What for?

MA: Don't look at me like I'm crazy. It's a serious meeting about the telephone company.

PA: Well, I have one, too.

MA: So, we both go. If it's important we go. We both work, don't we? We both pay the bills, don't we? So, both meetings are important. Right? Right.

NEIGHBOR: (enters): Hey, man. What's happening? I didn't mean to bust up anything between you and your lady.

PA: Oh, she's just tripping. Women.

NEIGHBOR: About what?

PA: Her job. Something about some stupid meeting.

NEIGHBOR: Yeah, I heard about it. Mel's going, too. It looks real serious. The supervisors are giving them a hard time.

PA: She doesn't need to work anyway. She'll go off to this meeting and be back so late she'll be tired. And I'll end up with cornflakes in the morning.

NEIGHBOR: Hey, what kind of attitude is that? Her job is important. Man, when she brings home that bread you dig it. And she takes care of you and the family, too.

PA: Hey, man. Has women's lib gotten to you?

NEIGHBOR: Look, when Mel lost her job, we were hurting for a while. I realized then that she was contributing equally. And these ladies really get pushed around. Not because they don't do the work, but because they're women, and not white at that.

PA: I guess I do take her a little for granted.

NEIGHBOR: You guess? Brother, I know you do. You're taught to think you're indispensable, and sometimes that big head doesn't think too straight.

Skits like this that dealt with workers' struggles and the empowerment of women while exposing male chauvinism and the doble jornada were a crucial component of every IWD celebration. The Alliance intentionally set out to address some backward, anti-women attitudes, reminding audiences that women worked and that housework was not only women's work. Ma in the skit needed to be able to attend an evening meeting concerning her job, just as Pa could. The partners and spouses of Alliance members played the male roles in these skits and were often booed when portraying male chauvinists. Not only were the brothers supportive good sports but also getting involved and stepping into those roles helped them "reflect and learn," as Marty Price recalls.[11] For them, it was all about becoming new men.

The Alliance in the Bay Area was the backbone of the passionate planning, organizing, and celebrating of IWD. As Delores put it in one of her organizing speeches, "The need for third world women to organize and work together with other segments of the population to build a strong, progressive movement for social change is clear. We see our work on International Women's Day as part of this process."

A Luta Continua: Alliance Women Today

Michelle Mouton
Community Organizer, Patroness of the Arts, Mother, Grandmother

We were making connections that I don't think a lot of other people were making at the time. There were all these alliances that were being made, and we took that and ran with it.

I met with Michelle in July 2011 in her beautiful home in the Bayview Section of San Francisco. Although she calls her neighborhood "the hood," her gorgeous home sits on a spacious street that looks for all intents and purposes like a grand boulevard. Her house, easily the most beautiful on the block, is the home of an artist—hand-placed tiles, hand-painted designs on the pink stucco façade, and a gate designed by her husband, the renowned printmaker Juan Fuentes.

Her hospitality is a mélange of New Orleans Creole "bienvenu" and Mexican "mi casa es tu casa." She is dressed in a long black skirt, a Mexican print blouse, and a Guatemalan head wrap. Over the days I spent with her, the outfits change to represent other parts of the world: Cambodian tops, Egyptian caftans, cotton in all forms. She finds them "more affordable" and "forgivable to all figures. You let them out when you're pregnant, take them in after."

If cooking counted as a revolutionary act, Michelle Mouton would be among our greatest heroes. The sister burns. There are no other words for it. She is the kind of cook and hostess whose door is always open and whose home is a place where people linger for days and weeks as yet another meal is lovingly prepared from the freshest ingredients.

When I asked if she still considers herself an activist, Michelle answered in the affirmative. She proudly spoke of her "straight job" at UCSF and of all that it had afforded her family—healthcare and other benefits are invaluable, as is the opportunity it provides Juan to do his creative work as an artist. They have been together for more than thirty years, and no one is a bigger supporter of Juan than his wife. Everything about her—her dress, her home, her family, her work—speaks of culture and community. She is no less an activist today than she was thirty years ago.

Aside from working a full-time job, Michelle organizes and supports Consejo Gráfico, "an independent network of print workshops that has formed to advance the legacy and viability of Latino printmaking in the United States." Her latest activism has centered on her neighborhood. Finding themselves living on a street where drug deals and debris coexisted, and where shootings and overflowing sewers were common-place, Michelle and her neighbors decided to advocate for better living conditions. Their advocacy led the city to plant over twenty trees on the block, realign traffic lanes, repave the road, and install permeable pavers so the sewer system would not back up. Streetlights were also placed to deter nighttime crime. "Our neighbors have worked hard to realize the dreams that are beyond many people's imaginations. This is where we live, and we're reclaiming our street," Michelle said.

Like the activist she has been since high school when, at age sixteen, she was one of the youngest members of the Venceremos Brigade, Michelle is fiery. She speaks her mind publicly and vociferously. She reveals that she occasionally mouths a faux pas, catching herself more and more as she ages. She does not suffer fools lightly, and she offers analysis rooted in solid data. She does not overly value rank or station. She values work in the interest of the people. She is an activist who is of the community, and she still lives in its heart.

Shirley Nakao

Attorney, Community Activist

People have to mobilize for change to happen.

Shirley Nakao retired in 2008 from her years of working as an attorney in the public sector. I interviewed her in her home in the Oakland Hills surrounded by her mother's collection of Japanese dolls.

Shirley joined the Alliance while working at the Legal Aid Society of Alameda County, and she particularly remembers IWD as the height of Alliance organizing and celebrating. During her years with the Alliance, she was also very involved with the Venceremos Brigade, making three trips to Cuba, in 1983, 1984, and 1985.

After the Alliance, she continued her political work as an attorney, participating in the struggle to maintain affirmative action rights in the face of opposition by Allan Bakke and others. She also worked as an attorney for disability rights. "I still believe I'm a leftist," she says. "I still believe in core socialist thoughts. There are aspects of socialism that would better this country. The worst aspects of capitalism put us into the 2007 recession. We didn't have enough regulation of banks; it was free-reign capitalism—organizations without concern for people. On the other hand, we have the most potential to do good, given certain aspects of our constitution, like our commitment to freedom. In communist countries, they ban books and squelch ideas and here we allow free thought and that is important for change."

Shirley remembers the Alliance fondly and is still inspired by the women each time she meets with them. She was a coproducer of *Of Civil Wrongs and Rights: The Fred Korematsu Story*, which won two Emmys.

Ann-Ellice Parker

Minister, Death Midwife

The Alliance taught me the value of community. It remains a stable value for me.

Ann-Ellice Parker joined the TWWA following all the other female members of the family into which she married. It was basically expected. "We were products of our times," she recalls. "The whole world was making discoveries. The war, the anti-war movement, and the peace movement impacted us. We had a group consciousness. We were united in changing the world." Her membership in the Alliance was also an entrée into the Venceremos Brigade, and going to Cuba to support the revolution was another thing that members of the Price family did. Although she joined as expected, what Ann-Ellice gained from the Alliance motivated her to stay involved.

Ann-Ellice's "main portal into the larger world" was the Alliance when she was a young mother with the luxury of being able to stay home and take care of her young children. In the Alliance, Ann-Ellice found women who were sensitive and motivated and doing intellectual work as well as taking care of their babies. What inspired her was "sitting in those meetings, hashing out how we felt about abortion, how to make the Alliance more of a people's alliance."

Ann-Ellice stayed in the Alliance until things began to change. "We had families and needed to make a living," she said. Then she recalls being "hit with the AIDS epidemic. My people, women of color, were most at risk, and then HIV and AIDS descended on our community like a plague. I was literally in the war for the first two years working as a health educator, a lobbyist. And I did needle exchange work in a program funded by NIH." She stayed in this work for twelve years until AIDS became "a manageable disease."

Today, Ann-Ellice's work is still founded on the "basic idea of equality that drew us together; these things still motivate me today," she says. She continues to work in the same communities and doesn't feel there is any loss of her political ideals, although her mind and heart have turned to the spiritual. Aside from her job as a paralegal for a life scientist whose efforts are directed toward new ways of fighting disease, her vocation now is largely in the area of spiritual practice. She is a licensed practitioner in the Church of Religious Science, preaching regularly to a congregation that includes Alliance members. She is also a licensed yoga practitioner.

Ann-Ellice's newest venture is an end-of-life practice in Berkeley. She is a death midwife who works to "empower and re-empower families around end-of-life and death and dying issues." She believes that death and dying are a sacred time and that people have to open themselves up to the possibility of transformation. True to her political origins, the word "empowerment" finds its way into her current practice. Reflecting on her experience with the Alliance, she defines it as "invigorating exhilaration," a time when she learned deeply about the value of community.

Melanie Tervalon

Pediatrician, Consultant, Teacher/Trainer, Social Activist, Mother, Grandmother

Many of the dreams I continue to follow were birthed and followed as a result of the Third World Women's Alliance.

I meet with Melanie Tervalon in the kitchen of her 1922 wood-frame house in Oakland, California. The table and chairs are circa 1955. The original sink and cabinets are still there, although a new floor has been laid. Her home is an oasis of peace, with its calming blue walls, bright light, and artwork. There is beauty everywhere—flowers, colors, and a sense of openness.

Little in this home is new. There is no hint of the McMansions of Melanie's era. There is no indication of wealth, nothing that boasts of the nationally renowned physician she has become. No "Dr. Tervalon" message on the answering machine. No "Dr." on the mailbox. There is no television. The enclosed deck on the back of the house contains her "craft" studio where she paints and illustrates quotations that she places around her house. This is the house her children were raised in and where her ninety-year-old mother passed away while Melanie provided end-of-life care.

Although her house is traditional, Melanie looks different now. Gone is the huge Afro she achieved by "untaming" her hair with the help of harsh detergents. She wears her hair natural, long, and gray, neither dyed nor permed. Her look bespeaks the naturalness that is typical of the California Bay Area. In the Alliance, Melanie's work focused on Black infant mortality in the Bay Area. She was a brigadista traveling to Cuba for the Fourth Venceremos Brigade, where she cut sugarcane and was a frequent speaker on behalf of the brigadistas.

Melanie has continued to carry the banner she lifted during her time in the Alliance. She graduated from medical school and later earned her MPH from UC Berkeley. She is a pediatrician, consultant, and teacher, with faculty affiliations at UCSF's School of Medicine and UC Berkeley's School of Public Health. She has lived in Oakland for the last thirty-six years as a pediatrician in a predominantly Black community known for its high rates of crime and infant mortality, contributing much as a solid member.

Her credentials are extensive. From 1992 through 1998, she provided direct patient care and instruction to pediatric interns and residents at Children's Hospital Oakland. In April 1994, under her direction, the Multicultural Curriculum Program was created at the hospital based on a teaching partnership, which places community scholarship and leadership at the center of healthcare education and practice. From 1998 to 1999, she was the senior adviser of special projects in the Office of the President at the California Endowment. She has worked at UC Davis at one of ninety centers nationwide focused on the relationships between nutrition, new gene research, and health disparities. In 2000, as a School of Medicine faculty member at UCSF, she was co-coordinator of faculty work on integrating issues of culture, community, and behavior into the curriculum redesign.

She received a Pew Fellowship in health policy studies at the Institute of Health Policy Studies, UCSF, under the mentorship of Dr. Philip Lee. As a consultant, she has guided leaders and teams from ideas to products as a project director and facilitator, crafted funding initiatives, written position papers, and provided expert knowledge in public health, pediatrics, and culture in health.

In 1998, while at Children's Hospital Oakland, she coauthored the article "Cultural Humility Versus Cultural Competence: A Critical Distinction in Defining Physician Training Outcomes in Multicultural Education," which shifted thinking about cultural knowledge in medicine and beyond. Melanie served as director of the Office of Cultural Competency at Kaiser Permanente in Oakland from 2007 to 2009 and from 2009 to 2011 as an associate director for Policy Link's health team. From 2010 to 2013, Melanie served as professor of human values at Children's Hospital and Research Center in Oakland, working with medical interns to center their care in the principles of cultural humility.

Since then, Melanie has focused on presenting nationally and internationally on cultural humility while continuing the work of training practitioners from many disciplines to use the principles and practices of cultural humility in their work. Along with Jann Murray-Garcia, MD, MPH, Melanie is completing a text that traces the origins of the cultural humility concept and illustrates how its principles become actions in the work to respect the voice and experience of patients fully and to engage in mutually beneficial partnerships as a way forward to equity and justice.

Most of her speeches, like the one she delivered at her graduation from medical school, receive standing ovations. Her life's work has been dedicated to inclusion and social justice in healthcare.

Since her diagnosis of multiple myeloma in 2016 and subsequent stem cell transplant, Melanie described an even deeper dimension of understanding the Black woman patient experience "now being the patient, the vulnerable one, in the doctor-patient relationship."

Melanie's work has never been about the accolades, nor the touting of personal or professional accomplishments. It has always been about achieving the goals of the Alliance: to end racism, sexism, and the oppression and disadvantage of class status. As a testimony to that, she presented at the 2006 "Isms Conference: Privilege, Bias, and Oppression: Addressing Barriers to Eliminating Health Disparities within Health Organizations." She believes deeply that racism trumps class in the disadvantage of medical patients.

During our interview, at certain moments, her blue eyes turned steely, and her teeth and jaw set. It is not about being nice—her stance is about justice and about telling it like it is. Melanie has lived the vision of the Alliance, bringing together community and family and engaging in an ongoing quest for justice for women and children. She was one of the founders of the Harriet Tubman Critical Mass Health Conductors, a community-based initiative to bring health and well-being to Black citizens of the Bay Area by educating and enrolling them as community health conductors. This movement has had a wide base of support, so much so that when I had dinner at Le Cheval with a friend in Oakland in 2007, he proudly announced, "I am health conductor 294." As this work spreads throughout the Bay Area, you can be sure that Melanie Tervalon will be keeping count.

Renata Tervalon
Mother, Family Bridge Builder, Singer

All the knowledge I gained in the Alliance I poured into my son because as I learned in the Alliance, culture is passed down via women.

Renata Tervalon has been an activist since she was a child, starting with her work as a peer tutor for the SCLC, tutoring students in math and helping them get their homework done. She was the baby of the Alliance, moving to California in 1977 at age twenty-one to start a new life with the support of her older sister, Melanie, who had relocated to the Bay Area a few years before. The Alliance had not developed its childcare program, so she began her work by watching the kids, helping the sisters "to figure out how to take care of all these little babies they had."

Renata's next and ongoing Alliance project was reproductive rights, working to support *Roe v. Wade* and a women's right to choose. She was also involved in cultural work, singing and leading chants at rallies and IWD gatherings. She transitioned to the AAWO and was on its steering committee.

She worked with AAWO until her son, Keith, was born in 1987. From that point on, "all the knowledge that I gained in the Alliance I poured into that boy." She got an MA in interdisciplinary computer science and continued her political work through her position as program manager for diversity at APL, Ltd. As head of its Diversity Council, she began meetings by announcing her political viewpoint, which was, of course, also the truth. "Racism and sexism are alive in Amerikkka, and we are *working* in the belly."

For many years, she was active in electoral politics, "walking the flatlands" of Oakland as a volunteer with Oakland Rising when her niece Esperanza Tervalon was its executive director. She enrolled voters and let those with arrest records know they had a right to vote.

Renata is the founder of Cane River Gumbo Company and currently works for Salesforce as senior technical curriculum developer. Her newest project is the creation of a series of Black dolls representing the men and women who have been getting shot by the police: Oscar Grant, Trayvon Martin, Sandra Bland, Eric Garner, Alton Sterling. "In 2015, there were 208 Black men and women who have been killed by police violence," she tells me. "Philando Castile was the 136th so far in 2016."

Her greatest joy now is her singing.

Zelma Toro
Mother, Grandmother, Childcare Administrator, Culture Bearer

A woman's place is in the struggle.*

I picked up Zelma at her home in the Mission District of San Francisco, and we drove to Michelle Mouton's house in Bayview for our interview. She was dressed in her huipil and was happy to explain its significance. "It's a blouse that Indigenous women wear throughout Latin America, in particular Mexico and Guatemala," she told me. "Girls weave the fabric and embroider designs that identify which community they come from. It's a blouse that girls wear throughout their lives. That's why there are two sets of pleats at the shoulder—when they grow into womanhood, they let out the pleats. In some huipils that I have, there are cut slits in the pleats where women would breastfeed their babies, then sew up the slits later. I love these blouses. They all tell the story of a woman's life from girlhood to motherhood to elder still wearing the huipil that she made."

Undeniably, Zelma represented this history well, as I found out over several days as she talked about her girlhood in New York; her years in California as an activist, a mother, and a wife; and her perspective on what it all has meant to her.

Zelma was raised in New York City in a Puerto Rican family. Her parents were independentistas, and her father lost his job because of his activities in support of Puerto Rican independence. That experience led them to caution her about becoming involved in leftist political work and, in fact, they prohibited her involvement, saying, "You don't know what it's like for the FBI to come to your house and to go to your employers and tell them to fire you."

---

*Words printed on a TWWA banner sewn by Zelma Toro, now in the archives of the Lesbian and Gay Historical Society in San Francisco.

As might be expected given the activism of the 1960s and 1970s and Zelma's psychological loyalty to her family, she did not take up the mantle of activism until she moved to the Bay Area. One of her first activities was to support the immigrant worker tenants of the International Hotel. Mostly Filipino, the workers protested the closing and planned razing of the residence hotel that was home for most of them. After months of protests, those who lived there were ultimately dislodged, as the San Francisco police invaded the hotel on horseback and drove the tenants out.

This loss did not stop Zelma. She had a strong women's consciousness because of her mother's experience and cogent advice, and when she met the women of the Alliance, she quickly became involved in the organization. She was very active with IWD commemorations and continued to do outreach work in San Francisco communities of color. She worked on reproductive rights and access to abortion through Somos Hermanas. She raised consciousness around the role of women in the struggles in Central America, also connecting and working with Salvadorian and Nicaraguan sisters who came up to California. She talked about this time as a "golden opportunity to work with women who were at the forefront of the struggle. There was a tendency in the support groups to dominate and put in American values. We realized that they were at the forefront of their struggles. We wanted to show respect, develop solidarity."

Today, Zelma is active with the California Childcare Resource and Referral Network. As with her work with the ACLU in California, she brings her Alliance expertise. "Through working with Alliance sisters, you got to know the line, what work style was expected out of you, how to put together a program that reflects your goals," she recalls. Today, she brings those skills to everything she does.

Nancy Hing Wong
Mother, Grandmother, Activist,
Community Attorney

Joining the Alliance really changed my life.

The daughter of immigrant tenant farmers, Nancy Wong joined TWWA during her senior year at UC Berkeley. Nancy grew up in Suisun Valley in an immigrant family struggling to make ends meet and adapt to life in the United States. Her father came to the United States first and his wife twenty years after they were married in China; her father was twice incarcerated at Angel Island Immigration Station, and at first her mother was prevented from immigrating to the United States by the Chinese Exclusion Act.

In their early years in the United States, the Wongs were so poor that the older daughter, ten years Nancy's senior, was sent to live with relatives in Oakland. Nancy and her brother had to work on the farm after school and during vacations, picking apricots, plums, peaches, pears, and walnuts. Nancy's mother wanted her first child born in America to be a boy and was disappointed with both daughters' births. Nancy recalls being instructed as a child, "When you're a child, you have to obey your father. And when you grow up to be a woman, you have to obey your husband. And after you have children, you will obey your son." Nancy wrote, "Working hard and getting good grades in school was my road to freedom from that nonsense."

Nancy got into UC Berkeley and became an Asian American studies major, signing up for the program the year it was initiated. She joined the Alliance during her senior year, encouraged by her professors. In the Alliance, she found wonderful women who became her teachers and mentors. The Alliance assigned her to help with a Kwanzaa celebration at Berkeley, and there her political education began. The politics and the activities she participated in, as well as her work on the Health Committee, gave her a framework to understand her own circumstances. In joining the Coalition to Fight Infant Mortality, Nancy recalled, "I learned that the struggle was not only about me and my community but about all poor people who did not have access to affordable healthcare." Today, that coalition's early work has given rise to a network of community health clinics throughout Alameda County.

Nancy continues her fight on behalf of poor people. As an attorney, she has represented children and parents in the foster care system for over two decades. "The bottom line," she says, "is that America does not prioritize children as a precious part of our society, and all you have to do is to work within the foster care system to see how poorly these children are treated."

From 2015 to 2020, Nancy battled the outgoing administration on behalf of immigrants. Summing up that work, Nancy said, "The attacks on immigrants have been fierce, relentless, and professional. We must meet these attacks with the same ferocity, persistence, and profession- alism. I will always stand with my peeps and work for poor people until the day I die." Through it all, she credits the Alliance: "It helped uplift me from this feeling like my family or I was personally responsible for our poverty. In the Alliance, I had this epiphany that has been my life's compass."

PART III

Alliance Legacy

CHAPTER 6

Third World Women's Alliance Collaborators

To see these women come together and do something that was educational to a lot of us brothers helped me to move beyond the nationalism, and think broader, and fight the chauvinism.

—*RIC RICARD*

THE ALLIANCE, both on the East Coast and the West Coast, had relationships with numerous organizations. We collaborated on liberation issues and joined in "fronts" to maximize our overall influence.

Many Alliance members were also members of other organizations or worked with other organizations. We learned about the Women's International League for Peace and Freedom's work in support of ending the war. From the Venceremos work brigades to Cuba, we were educated about the accomplishments of the Cuban revolution—free education, free healthcare, and full employment, among other successes. We worked with Latin Union, the Young Lords, El Comité, I Wor Kuen (IWK), and many union activists. And we were part of coalitions, including the November 4th Committee (1972) against the war in Vietnam, the Third World Front Against Imperialism, and many others, bringing our politics to the fore and demonstrating through our actions and participation that women were indeed active and leading participants in the movement. Although it is impossible to document, I believe that the Alliance leadership positively influenced women in the organizations with which we worked.

We traveled to Canada and across the United States to attend conferences and work with activists, both domestic and international. To help advance liberation around the world, Alliance women traveled to China and Cuba to observe and participate in the development of socialist societies. In both countries, our members studied the role of women and the welfare of children, focusing on women's integration into the work of the nation and the free day care that socialism had constructed to help them do that successfully.

As Alliance sisters traveled, they wrote about their experiences for *Triple Jeopardy*. In "Puerto Rican Woman Visits China," Genoveva Clemente extolled the equality of gender opportunity in work, stating, "All over China women can be seen working alongside men and doing all kinds of jobs . . . half of China's doctors are women. . . . We saw women working in the fields, driving buses, trucks, bulldozers, wielding picks on road gangs."[1] The article celebrates the end of feudalism in China but also acknowledges the work still to be done in equal pay, diversifying the Central Committee, and helping men's attitudes to develop further.

Organizing and Demonstrating

We worked with other groups to support progressive organizations and people. One of our positions was to support the passage of the Equal Rights Amendment to affirm that women and men have equal rights under the law. First proposed in 1923 and raised again in 2018 by publications as different as *Mother Jones* and *Forbes* magazines, the US amendment that declares "rights may not be denied or abridged on the basis of sex" has still not been ratified.

We stood and demonstrated with the Young Lords Party at the United Nations to protest the colonization of Puerto Rico on October 30, 1970; at anti-apartheid marches; at the Women's March on Fifth Avenue; and at Washington, DC, demonstrations for justice. Everywhere we went, we dressed for revolution. Our "uniform" consisted of green fatigue pants, T-shirts, and green army jackets, maybe topped with a blue peacoat in winter. Alternately, we wore farmers' jeans with a bib and a T-shirt or turtleneck. T-shirts had become universal attire by then. It seemed every organization silk-screened its name, logo, or other important slogans—like "People before profits," "A woman's place is in the house and in the Senate," and "ERA now"—onto the front or back of the shirts.

Our shoes were combat boots, work boots as they are called now—the kind usually worn by construction workers. They were orange-brown with metal tips and long, strong laces with hard ties and hard rubber-ridged soles. This was the active-wear of the day. We needed sturdy, flat shoes to move furniture, clean parks, cut sugarcane in the fields of Cuba, and run from the police or fight if we had to. I spent the winter of 1971 in Cuba cutting sugarcane in the town of Aguacate, and the front of my left boot had two half-inch cuts where my machete had grazed it as I bent low, my left hand grabbing the burned stalks of sugarcane as close to the ground as possible, while my right hand swung the machete hard and low to cut the stalks at the exact point where they rose out of the earth. It was incredibly hard work, and I was very proud of those shoes!

We were involved in the major political issues of the day, participating in demonstrations and speaking at rallies decrying the war abroad and the rape and plunder of our home communities at the hands of drug dealers, the police, and the draft board. We pressed for the decolonization of Puerto Rico, shouting, "Despierta Boricua. Defiende lo tuyo" and "Dare to Struggle. Dare to Win." We provided support to members of the United Auto Workers Union at the Ford plant in Rahway, New Jersey, traveling over to the plant to pass out fliers to workers, criticizing racism in the union, and promoting Black union leadership. We joined with the Black Workers Congress, the Young Lords Party, Asian Coalition, Puerto Rican Revolutionary Workers, and Vietnam Vets Against the War.

We had an ongoing supportive relationship with the Garment Workers' Union and with the Drug, Hospital, and Health Care Employees Union–District 1119, both progressive workers' unions in New York City, and just before the New York Chapter of the Alliance disbanded, the Alliance gave a speech at a July 4, 1977, rally to support affirmative action.

In 1974, perhaps inspired by the Bay Area Chapter, we held a celebration of IWD at our office.

Latin Union/Unión Latina was one group with which some of us were particularly close, and their members joined us when we studied dialectical materialism with Jim Former at TWWA offices in Manhattan.

In the early seventies, a heroin epidemic was sweeping across the inner cities of America where low income, joblessness, and poor housing offered up ready victims. Many veterans were returning from Vietnam with addictions, and the Bronx was burning.

Latin Action, a precursor of Latin Union, began organizing there. We organized youth in efforts to clean up their neighborhoods and sweep up the burned-out lots, and we met in the basement of buildings and talked to the kids. We educated them, asking questions about their circumstances, helping them to see the larger picture, making friends, building community, being there for them. We encouraged their art. Helped them to kick drugs. Let them live with Latin Action members when they needed a home, sometimes bringing the youth into our own homes to detox. We helped them to get into college, instilling pride in their Puerto Rican heritage. Concha Mendoza, Zorina Costello, Joaquín Rosa, Jesús Papoleto Meléndez, Ramón Zapata, and I were a part of that early group.

Later, the group moved its work to the West Side where some of the members were living and changed their name to Latin Union. They opened a storefront and provided services for Latin folks in the community who were mostly new Dominican immigrants. They offered English classes and helped prepare neighborhood youth to pass their GEDs. Dr. Pat Salomon, a white, Jewish pediatrician and activist, would come at night after her work at her clinic to provide the injections the children needed to get enrolled in school. The new immigrants did not have their own doctors and were intimidated by the health centers. They knew little English, and Latin Union members spoke to them in Spanish, got to know them and their families, and helped them to feel safe.

Emulating the barefoot doctors of China, Pat trained some of the members to use otoscopes so they could go into the community and check for ear infections. When they required more medical attention, she would refer patients to her brother, Dr. Mort Salomon, at Montefiore Hospital in the Bronx.

Latin Union also worked with teenagers. While political education was always part of the work, a major impetus was to keep them away from heroin use. They would take the kids up to Pat's farm in upstate New York and expose them to new experiences. Ernesto Guadalupe, who had just gotten clean himself after coming out of the treatment program at Daytop Village, worked with them. Joaquín remembers, "They had never seen big supermarkets with rows and rows of food. Out of their element, they would spend the night looking up at the stars."[2] On Saturday mornings, a Latin Union member would bring their parents up, and the country atmosphere would inspire sharing about their years back in the Dominican Republic. "They would let their hair loose and walk around in freedom. The kids started talking with their parents from a different perspective. A whole new respect for parents evolved."

Latin Union also did work with housing in the neighborhood. They organized rent strikes, got the youth jobs with Manpower, and helped them to learn skills to repair their own homes. José Acevedo, Lucas Daumont (who later married Melanie Tervalon), and Tom Beato, Brenda's husband, were part of the Latin Union period.

Mainly through Latin Union, around 1970, the Alliance became acquainted with El Comité on the West Side of Manhattan, the community-based organization protesting so-called urban renewal programs that were replacing low-income housing with high-rise developments.

The Black Panther Party was another organization the TWWA was close with and one that we emulated in many ways, producing a newspaper as they did and coming out with a platform as they had done. We agreed with them on the responsibility to defend our community and, like them, we wanted "All Power to the People!" Several of our members dated men who were Panthers, and Kisha married a Panther. We participated with them in many coalitions.

On the West Coast, sisters were also close to the Panther organization and held one of their IWD celebrations at Panther Headquarters. TWWA sisters who were physicians provided medical care to the Panthers, and the Panthers had a strong partnership with Alliance sisters who worked on the infant and maternal mortality rate in Oakland. Together, they "went to the County Board of Supervisors and changed how the county's hospital handled pregnant and birthing women when they came to the hospital for care."[3]

On the East Coast, we had strong relations with the Young Lords Party. In her book *Through the Eyes of Rebel Women*, Iris Morales wrote, "In the early days of the Young Lords Organization (YLO), the women members were practically invisible. . . . Women were not treated as equals in the Young Lords Organization, and the struggle for gender equality began then."[4] But over time, because of the leadership of Iris and other women in the organization, the Lords, like the Panthers, began to make good use of women's leadership. Our Alliance sister, Milagros, joined the Young Lords Party because of their emphasis on community work.

We were with the Young Lords on October 30, 1970, during the march to the United Nations, yelling "¡Despierta Boricua, defiende lo tuyo!" with the loudest of them and demanding an end to the colonial status of Puerto Rico and the release of Puerto Rican political prisoners. In *Through the Eyes of Rebel Women*, Morales stated that "the women in the Young Lords were faithful and avid readers" of *Triple Jeopardy*.[5]

We marched with the Lords in the streets to protest the killings at Attica. And we marched with them and Latin Action when chased by the police at the People's Church in Harlem, which they had occupied.

The Venceremos Brigade was probably TWWA's closest organizational ally. Like the Brigade, we were committed to showing our solidarity with the Cuban revolution by helping them to accomplish their sugar harvest goals. The added bonus was the time provided to witness the successes of the Cuban revolution. Many Alliance sisters participated in the Third, Fourth, Fifth, and Sixth Venceremos Brigades and became active on both the East and West Coast Brigade committees to ensure that the Brigade would continue. Melanie joined the National Committee for the Brigade. West Coast sisters were very instrumental in organizing a group of children, los vencerimitos, to visit Cuba and several children of Alliance sisters participated.

We connected with the Puerto Rican Socialist Party, the proindependence group, at many events, and one of the members wrote articles for *Triple Jeopardy*. Several Alliance sisters were with them and twenty thousand other people at the proindependence rally at Madison Square Garden on October 27, 1974.

We were close allies with IWK, a radical Marxist Asian American group from Chinatown in New York City. Like the Lords, the Panthers, and us, they had a platform and published a newspaper. We worked with them on several coalitions, especially the Third World Front Against Imperialism, a mass organization of people who defined themselves as descendants of the peoples from Africa, Asia, Latin America, the Middle East, and the original people of North America.

The united Front came together to support our sisters and brothers struggling against the US invasion of Southeast Asia. Along with the TWWA, the Front was composed of IWK, Asian Americans for Action, Asian Coalition, Asian Women's Coalition, Black Organization of Students at Rutgers, Black Panther Party, Black Workers Council, El Comité, the Republic of New Africa, SNCC, Third World Youth Movement, and Unión Latina. The goal of the Front was, ultimately, "the defeat of imperialism throughout the Third World. We are comprised of various community organizations and interested individuals whose energies are channeled towards one main objective—organizing in our communities so that our people might help in taking an active role in supporting Third World peoples struggles for self-determination, which in itself is a just struggle against imperialism."[6]

Bay Area TWWA Brothers

One of the most noteworthy aspects of the Bay Area TWWA was its emphasis on children and families, but the story of the Bay Area Chapter could not be told without writing about the brothers who stood in solidarity with the women. These brothers were among the Alliance's closest allies.

Men of color on the West Coast who were in relationships with Alliance sisters were fellow activists and dubbed themselves "the brothers of the Third World Women's Alliance." (Although Linda pointed out, "We jokingly called them the auxiliary.") Frederick Douglass Perry (Smokey), Lucas Daumont, Belvin Louie, Ric Ricard, Bob Wing, Barry Burnham, and Ray and Marty Price were among those active and supportive men. Although most of the male partners and husbands of New York Alliance members were supportive, the more collective, communal spirit of the Bay Area Chapter made California men's support more visible and cohesive.

In 2008, I interviewed Marty, Lucas, Ric, and Fred, all of whom had been married to Alliance sisters. I wondered what they remembered and how they had been impacted by their partners' and wives' participation in the Alliance.

The group interview with Marty, Lucas, and Ric began with them joking about their childcare duties. "Women had meetings and we'd be watching the kids," Marty recalled. But quickly their comments turned more serious. They said their support of the work of Alliance sisters evoked "a sense of being in an important moment of history."

For these brothers, the Alliance was "a kind of political center" for the movement in the Bay Area, a center that served many functions. They recognized the value it had in helping those who were stay-at-home mothers have "a place to get away with other sisters and talk about stuff they were doing." It was a relief from the daily chores and isolation of being at home with young children. These brothers did not see the Alliance as separatist or destructive. Most of them were also involved in political work, and often, their partners and wives worked alongside them in organizations like the Venceremos Brigade and the Third World Strike at Berkeley, as well as with the Alliance.

Certainly, male chauvinism was prevalent, but they thought it had decreased, especially after their experience in Cuba. They'd worked in the cane fields, on construction sites, and in orchards picking fruit with women from the United States and other countries. They saw how hard the women worked and how committed they were, and brothers respected this. Reading works like Ernesto Che Guevara's *Socialism and Man in Cuba*, which called for a new consciousness, a partnership of men and women in building a society freed of inequality and devoid of a caste system, also helped. Che and his partner, Tania, who was undercover with him in Bolivia, were role models of activism and exemplified a moral and ethical framework to which they aspired. The Cuban revolution itself espoused freedom for women and named them as fellow revolutionaries, and this profoundly influenced the thinking of progressive men and women in the United States.

And yes, often when the sisters had meetings, the brothers would be watching the children, and at other times, brothers would organize something and just take a bunch of the kids on a "field trip." Two benefits of their involvement with the children stood out to them as we talked that day in Oakland. First, the brothers became very closely involved with their children. Unlike many of their own fathers, these men bathed and toilet-trained their children, changed diapers, and wiped noses. This gave them a full appreciation of what had been called "women's work" in their own formative years. The second advantage they named was that the children grew close with other Alliance children, and their political sensibilities were shaped early in their lives as they played and learned together.

During our interview, the men spoke frankly, admitting that despite their readings and experiences, some of the brothers still retained vestiges of chauvinism and sexism when they joined the movement. At the fiftieth anniversary of the women's suffrage march on Fifth Avenue in 1970, Lucas recalled that he had to restrain and retrain his eyes from focusing on women's breasts, which had been his habit until that day. "My eyes used to stay between the neck and the knees. On that day I looked up above the breasts. There was so much humanity on the streets."

And as had happened with Lucas, over time, the men's attitudes changed. Part of Ric's growth was "looking at women of colors as sisters." "Their growth was a beautiful thing," he said. "My responsibility as a brother was to do what I needed to do as a brother, to walk the talk." According to Ric, the Alliance helped to bring him to the place where he could unequivocally say, "I support sisters."

In talking with these brothers, I reflected on what I saw as a definite progression from the early days of SNCC. The work and leadership of Alliance women had changed attitudes. Marty was quick to point out, however, that this progression didn't mean that sexism did not exist. He remains convinced "that men are intrinsically chauvinist in a patriarchal society." But through participation in Alliance activities, many of the men were educated about women's strengths and came to recognize their own biases and exploitative behavior. With their new awareness, they worked hard to remake themselves. These, indeed, were a different kind of men.

For some of them, the difference began before the Alliance. As mentioned earlier, some were red-diaper babies. They were radicals who, according to Lucas, had "left political organizations and were building our own cadres more autonomously." And the Alliance had a well-developed political position that helped to keep them on track.

The brothers reflected on the family-building benefits of the Alliance. Marty said, "The Third World Women's Alliance brought my wife closer to her mother. Vicki Alexander's mom and my mom met at an Alliance event. For me as a man, we were very proud of these sisters. They were able to forge the organization and keep it together. All of these powerful women! Diana Gong, a Third World Women's Alliance member, became the first Asian woman to drive a BART train. There were a lot of firsts."

The men praised the Alliance's work extensively. Marty called the experience "one of the periods of my life that I'm most proud of. What our women did; what our children were involved in! And in some ways, the effect of the Alliance was long-lasting. The thing is that most of these women have carried the ethic, and they brought it into other things. All of the women went on to have some kind of impact on their work. Our kids all found each other, ideologically and simpatico-wise. Our kids all went to the World Youth Festival in Cuba. Our sons are feminists. That's a leap. We didn't even have the language for that then. Personalization of involvement is what the Alliance brought— what you wanted for you and your kids."

The involvement with, and care of, children was real and had its challenges for men who at first were not experienced in dealing with children. During my interview with Miriam Ching Louie, she recalled a time when there was a meeting at the Women's Building in Berkeley. A boyfriend of one of the women was in charge of childcare. "To our credit, we always had childcare for all of our activities. This time the kids just took over; they got into some paint; they just painted the whole place." The sisters emerged from their general meeting to find children with paint all over their bodies and all over the room. The children's work was so comprehensive that they had to pay the Women's Center to have the room repainted.

This kind of thing was a rare, albeit funny mishap. Many other events went very smoothly with the brothers and fathers involved, but they were on a learning curve in the 1970s. And it was not all about childcare. There was a lot to learn about children and women as equal members of a movement to change the world.

Women are often said to be the bearers of culture for their families, and the brothers understood that "culture moves before the body politic moves." Ric spoke about "the beauty" that he found within the Alliance, and how it helped him move beyond his own nationalism. "While on the one hand I maintained a nationalist perspective, on the other hand, I developed an internationalist perspective. To see these women come together and do something that was educational to a lot of us brothers helped me to move beyond the nationalism and think broader and fight the chauvinism. I remember when that came out of me. Seeing these strong women . . . carry on with their lives and to see the girl children do well. . . . The girls that came up under these women have something to stand on."

Reflecting on the Alliance's recruitment of Black women, Marty said, "Some of us came from church, and that gives you access to the Black community. For all women of color, they broke down the racial stuff. The message was 'be proud of what you are,' but they moved the analysis to a slightly higher level in a class society." When the Alliance came to an end, the brothers missed having their wives involved. They "missed the opportunity for us to be together as men of color, to be together in a political way with our partners and with our children."

By the end of the interview, I was contemplating how early on these men had defied the prevalent stereotype about men and especially men of color. Many of these brothers growing up in low-income and single-parent families had to learn to cook and do their own laundry. Childcare may have been new to them, but they threw themselves into that work too, with a vigor and a commitment common among progressive men. They were brothers indeed!

CHAPTER 7

Reflecting Back/Looking Forward

No one can win the war individually. It takes the wisdom of the elders and young people's energy.

—JOHN LEGEND, COMMON, AND RHYMEFEST[1]

IT IS NOW forty years since TWWA ceased to do political work as an organization. In this chapter, I reflect on how we responded to injustice in the seventies and the import this may have for women of color and our communities today. The reflections and viewpoints are mine. Some Alliance sisters may agree with my conclusions; others will not. And, as differences always did, this will hopefully inspire us toward more careful analysis.

Almost all of my Alliance sisters, as you've read throughout this book, vigorously object to being characterized as feminists. As Michelle Mouton put it, "I never considered myself a feminist, none of us did." Yet, I placed the Alliance in the second wave of feminism, and I am able, I believe, to justify that decision.

As I thought about the Alliance in the context of life in the United States in the second decade of the twenty-first century, I remembered the way that questions framed our studies in the seventies. We explored the "woman question" and asked if women could "take a leadership role in the struggle." I remembered the exhaustive list of questions Gwen Patton compiled when she was gathering Black women for the SNCC conference meeting. I thought, also, of the questions young women ask me today when I talk about this project: "Where are the women now? What did they do after the movement?" "How did you achieve unity between women of different races and ethnicities?" "How did men of color respond to you?" The centrality of questions in Alliance thinking and organizing led me to lay out the second section to respond to some of the key questions women have asked me. The final section comprises my concluding thoughts.

How Did the TWWA Come to an End?

Every movement, like the human life cycle itself, like the history of civilizations, has its beginning, its middle, and its end. By the mid-1970s, the spirit of revolution that had been in the air began to dissipate, dampening perhaps because some victories were won. The war in Vietnam ended with an American withdrawal; Tricky Dicky Nixon was driven out of office; former colonies achieved their independence. The free breakfast program started by the Black Panthers became a federally funded program in all schools by 1975; women gained greater access to colleges and the world of work.

As the movement faded, the Alliance, too, came to an end. Alliance members had children to raise and professions to pursue. I left the Alliance in 1974 when I enrolled in graduate school. By then I had a husband and a twenty-one-month-old baby, and I was working full time. Still wanting to learn and to be an activist changemaker, I wrote in my application to graduate school that I wanted to study the mechanisms of change at two levels: the level of the individual and that of social systems.

I was accepted into two clinical psychology programs: one at Teachers College, Columbia University, and the other at City University of New York, Graduate Center. Eschewing the elite environment of Columbia University, I enrolled in the latter, an institution that was closer to the people and included an organizational studies program focused on the study of authority and authoritarianism.

On the East Coast, the Alliance fell prey to internal rivalries, possibly seeded or exacerbated by infiltration. As it did with so many other organizations, the FBI likely infiltrated the Alliance on the East Coast (there is an FBI file on the Alliance),[2] causing dissension among its members. People began to wonder who was or wasn't an agent. While there is still no concrete evidence of infiltration, the FBI files do show that it followed the Alliance's activities. Much information in the files is redacted, but there was a clear emphasis on the analysis of the articles in *Triple Jeopardy*.

On the West Coast, the Alliance evolved into the AAWO, a Marxist organization that included white women and had a progressive acceptance of lesbians. Some Bay Area Alliance members fell away at that time for reasons described in chapter 6; others continued until the AAWO dissolved.

Linda Burnham and Miriam Ching Louie continued their activism on many fronts and also founded the WCRC, which for some twenty years carried the spirit and history of the Alliance forward, engaging in community organizing, educating women, sponsoring IWD celebrations, and serving as a resource for women of color in the Bay Area. Their website contained a wealth of resources for scholar-activists. The Alliance archives were housed there, and a project looking at Alliance history produced the DVD *Paving the Way: A Teaching Guide to the Third World Women's Alliance.* Were it not for mismanagement by second-generation leadership, the Alliance would likely still exist today.

Was the TWWA a Feminist Organization?

Young women of color who equate the term feminism with white women still ask this question. I hope I have demonstrated throughout this book that we were indeed feminists.

Linda described her perspective on "feminism" in a 2005 interview with Loretta Ross:

> When I'm working around a particular issue, I'm not necessarily looking for people to, you know, adopt my whole world outlook

and whole brand of politics and become a feminist or any of that. I'm looking for some movement around whatever the particular issue is . . . whatever the particular women's rights issue is—whether that be, you know, how women of color experience homelessness or what reproductive rights issues look like for women and for women of color, or what the welfare system looks like for women and women of color . . . so in that sense it's not kind of an abstract fight about a feminist worldview.[3]

In 1983, three years after the Bay Area Alliance joined with white women and became the AAWO, Alice Walker, in her book *In Search of Our Mothers' Gardens: Womanist Prose*, wrote about the term "womanist." She defined it as "a black feminist or feminist of color," "committed to the wholeness and well-being of entire people, male and female," and "someone who is not a separatist except periodically for health."[4]

Walker might well have been speaking for TWWA. Long before she defined "womanism" this way, Alliance women lived it. Surely the historic activism of women of color in the 1970s and earlier had an influence on the development of the new term.

Scholars like Kimberly Springer[5] and Becky Thompson[6] have looked back on the work we did and defined it and us as feminist, even though many of us eschewed the term. They came upon the work of the National Black Feminist Organization, founded in 1973 (three years after the TWWA evolved from the Black Women's Alliance) to combat racism, classism, sexism, homophobia, and lesbophobia. They took note of the work by the Combahee River Collective, a Black, lesbian, and socialist women's organization that began meeting in Boston in 1974. They examined the work of women of color across the globe— women who were involved in development efforts, women who protested their lack of education or their restriction, women who were "reading *Lolita* in Tehran"—and they defined the work as feminist.

The concept of triple jeopardy identified sexism as one of the factors that oppressed women of color. If feminism is about dismantling sexism, then yes, we were feminist. In 1981, in *This Bridge Called My Back*, Barbara Smith wrote, "Feminism is the political theory and practice to free all women: women of color, working-class women, poor women, physically challenged women, lesbians, old women, as well as white economically privileged heterosexual women."[7] By this definition, we in the Alliance were feminists. We focused on women of color, working-class women, poor women; we saw ourselves as different from economically privileged women. We stood for women's rights.

Also in 1981, bell hooks wrote in *Ain't I a Woman*, "Feminism is a commitment to eradicating the ideology of domination that permeates Western culture on various levels—sex, race, and class, to name a few—and a commitment to reorganizing United States society, so that the self-development of people can take precedence over imperialism, economic expansion, and material desires."[8] By that definition, we were most certainly feminists.

In 2014, Nigerian writer Chimamanda Ngozi Adichie wrote *We Should All Be Feminists*, a book detailing her experiences with sexism and what she has witnessed in the treatment of girls and women. She ends it with her own definition of feminism: "A feminist is a man or a woman who says, Yes, there's a problem with gender as it is today and we must fix it, we must do better. *All* of us, women and men, must do better."[9]

When the Alliance marched down Fifth Avenue in New York and when Alliance members stood on the stage each year at IWD celebrations in California with their children, we were announcing ourselves to the world as feminists, third world feminists. We were part of the surge of activism that inspired the term "third world feminism."

Women in the Alliance were third world feminists before the concept of third world feminism had been developed, influenced by national and international movements: Palestinian rights efforts,[10] the Black liberation struggle, the struggle in Guinea-Bissau and other African liberation movements, Asian liberation struggles, the struggle for Latino rights in the United States, and an end to Puerto Rican colonization.

Yes, we were feminists. And as the pages of *Triple Jeopardy* and our other activities show, we were more: We were womanists, internationalists, anti-racist activists, and leftists. We were community builders and border crossers. And once again, yes, we were feminists.

What Held You Together across So Many Identities? What Made It Work?

There were many variables. Unquestionably, "revolution was in the air," and we were carried along by that groundswell. The era in which our movement took root was a compelling time to be a young activist. The fight for freedom and self-definition was happening on the world stage as colonized nations asserted their rights to be autonomous and self-ruling and to determine their own destiny. Linda thinks the political context of the times made it possible. "It was the movement of the third world and the thinking about how third world nations should come together against US hegemony. That's the background. That we might have something to talk about and we did."

As we talked, we saw that a synchronicity was occurring between what was happening in the world and in our own lives. As Concha Delgado put it, "I think there was always a common thread that we would maintain; we would focus on topics that would cut across all of our communities." We were young women who had experienced the "isms" in our everyday lives, and we were outraged. There was Georgette Ioup, whose brothers always came first; Vicki Alexander, isolated in medical school; Fran Beal, who lost her friend to abortion; me, discriminated against as the only Black child in my classes throughout my Catholic school education; Christine Choy, whose name was changed, country lost, family left behind; Stella Holmes Hughes, raised in poverty with a mentally ill mother; Brenda Boho Beato, whose capability and vision exceeded the options she had been presented with; Ana Celia Zentella, who witnessed poverty and discrimination in the Bronx; and Yemaya Rice Jones, who was expelled from school for raising a voice against segregation.

Collectively, we watched our brothers go off to war while rich white men, like Donald Trump, evaded the draft, and we saw our leaders shot and killed, even the most nonviolent among them, like Martin Luther King Jr. We determined that we would not die like sheep. These conversations led to our coming together in what Linda described as "a big step forward in the progressive movement in the US."

Of course, not everyone in the seventies went in the direction we did. Perhaps it was a matter of character for us or our family backgrounds. Perhaps Alliance members were a set of young women with a propensity to revolt rather than accommodate, to protest rather than acquiesce. That would certainly be true of this writer, who was born chronologically in the silent generation but has few personal characteristics in common with that birth era. Perhaps we were a set of women who came from more troubled or broken or poorer families. My own extended family was torn apart by the shattering breakup of my parents. There was a range of economic backgrounds in the Alliance. Some of us were certainly less privileged than many of our peers, but many were more privileged than others. Perhaps we simply were introduced to a way of thinking about the world that made sense to us as we searched for understanding. Some sisters, like Linda and Fran, because of family background, were more educated about resistance.

We were border crossers. We were mixed in so many ways, individually and collectively. I was a Black woman of mixed racial heritage, growing up in an extended West Indian family whose members came from different islands and spoke different languages. My father began teaching me Spanish at an early age, and my Cuban aunt and her sisters had a profound impact on me. My family was working class, the men mostly carpenters and the women maids and waitresses, and later office workers. Yet after the age of eight, I was raised in an Italian and Irish community in the Bronx. The plight of those economically less fortunate was emphasized in my home, and although colorism was definitely alive in some of my family members, I was never taught to think about racism. As a result, when I encountered racism outside of the home, I was shocked and unprepared. And then in my first jobs out of college, I saw the poverty and economic and cultural oppression of my Puerto

Rican students in PS 50 and of my Black and Puerto Rican clients in the Department of Welfare in New York City!

Miriam Ching Yoon Louie, who is Korean and Chinese, feels strongly that it was our progressive politics that brought us together and held us together. "Because you know . . . there's a thin layer of people that will do all of that . . . most of the people maybe are in the ethnic-specific groups but there's always a thin layer. . . . And I think it is the progressive politics that allows that to happen."

Ana Celia stressed unity as the key that brought us together. "There was a tremendous sense of the importance of that unity," she says. Ana Celia grew up in the Bronx where "Black women had always been a part of my life. This was my community. That's what growing up Puerto Rican in the Bronx was."

Becky Carrillo believes that most of us were already politicized and that we came together out of a need to share, "to collectivize and to broaden our horizons." For her, "womenness" was also central. "The whole thing around women, your aunts or your grandmothers. They get together, and they talk all kinds of stuff, and it came together on a higher level. All of that kind of stuff that human beings need, we were able to do that with sisters. A lot of the secondary issues were not important when you thought about what was happening with the South African women or the Palestinian women."

Maybe we were systems thinkers—a group of people who were ahead of our time. We did identify as part of the vanguard. We were asserting our identities as Latin and Asian when the Black liberation and women's liberation movements were the most frequently identified. We were supporting gay and lesbian issues in New York before it was "safe" to do so. We kept connecting concepts and people: Marxism with people of color, Marxism with women, Latinas with Asians, Blacks with Latinas, Marxism with Maoism, domestic issues with international issues. We kept our brothers and our families very close. We kept our languages together, too, publishing bilingual Spanish-English newspapers in the 1970s.

As for identity, it is important to remember that the Alliance was not an identity-focused organization. We were sisters in an international movement for justice. It was never about iden-tity, per se; it was about common oppression. We believed the common oppression we shared as women of color went beyond anything that any one of us had known as individuals or as specific races or ethnicities.

Our struggle for women's equality was another unifier. We stood for women's right to determine their own lives and our responsibility to participate fully in the struggle for justice. We stood for economic justice and the removal of genocidal drugs from our communities. We stood for peace and an end to war. We stood for an end to the racism that affected us all collec-tively. We saw the connections! Ultimately, as I mentioned in the introduction, we saw ourselves as a political category—a group of women oppressed by race, class, and gender. And this was the fundamental root of our unity.

Many factors contributed to our coming together and staying together. The era explains it; our personal and political expe-riences of discrimination because of gender, race, ethnicity, or economics explains it; a theory that helped us understand explains it. And as I look back with my psychologist's lens, I believe the concepts identified in relational-cultural theory (RCT) offer an understanding as well.

In 1976, Dr. Jean Baker Miller, a white psychiatrist, published *Toward a New Psychology of Women*, exploring the dynamics of dominance and subordination in relationships. She wrote about power—"power over" and "power with"—and she asserted that women were more likely than men to be able to engage in relationships characterized by "power with," having power with one another, power through one another.[11] She characterized the psychology of women as being centered in relationships and connection, and elsewhere she defined connection as "an interaction between two or more people that is mutually empathic and mutually empowering."[12] This is exactly how Alliance members experienced one another.

When we spoke, Lenore French reflected, "I love that it was led by women. I just loved it. It was like doing work as a politi-cal activist with your best friends. The Alliance was this group of powerhouse women—unapologetic and super focused." I can hear Melanie Tervalon's words about her first meeting with Cheryl Johnson when she was on the Fourth Brigade in Cuba: "I arrived late one evening . . . and I found Cheryl sitting at a table. I was fascinated by her. She had an immediate warmth, and conversational ability that told me we would be friends." I remember Zelma Toro's words when she met the Alliance sisters in California: "These *dynamite* women!" she exclaimed. Miriam said, "To me, it was a privilege; it was really a privilege and an opportunity to work with sisters so closely and to make such enduring friendships for so long." And as for me, I see the New York members huddled together in front of the illustrated vagina posted on the wall at a consciousness-raising session. I remember that feeling I had on Fifth Avenue on August 26, 1970. Connection and power!

Yes, RCT and the "five good things" that Dr. Miller conceptualized as emerging from growth-fostering relationships explain the psychology of Alliance women—a sense of zest or well-being that comes from connecting with another person or other persons; the ability and motivation to take action in the relationship, as well as other situations; increased knowledge of oneself and the other person(s); an increased sense of worth; and a desire for more connections beyond the particular one.[13] These were all values we shared and behaviors in which we engaged.

And the concept of mutual empathy as Miller described it, "the capacity to feel and think something similar to the feelings and thoughts of another person," was also a factor.[14] Fran's statement that "even though there were some particularities to Black women's oppression and some particularities to Puerto Rican women, the idea of dealing with a gender and a racial similarity at the same time was more unifying than the fact that we had some particular cultural aspects."

We must also consider the importance of our role models. Both Miller[15] and Patricia Hill Collins[16] wrote about "controlling images," those images that define who and what we are, what is acceptable and what isn't, what people can and can't do. These images exert a powerful influence on how we act and how we construct relationships. In the Alliance, with our mantra to "live

like her," we created images of strong women leaders and revolutionaries based on the future idea of who we wanted to be in
relation to our communities. The WCRC DVD *Paving the Way*
reports that "by building relations with women's organizations
in other countries and educating communities of color about
the issues they tackled, TWWA establishes that U.S. women of
color had a particular role to play in the 'global sisterhood.'"

A final thought from *Triple Jeopardy* is perhaps the best
response to the question of what held us together: "When we
are touched by outside forces that reflect our worth we can
begin to struggle against the ruler's fascism and exploitation.
We even beg[i]n to fill up with ourselves."[17]

What Did the Women of TWWA Think about Children, the Home, and Their Roles?

We spent many of our young activist years engaged in having
babies, breastfeeding them, and beginning to raise them. We
were getting pregnant and having babies in our twenties *while*
we picketed and rallied, *while* we were in college or medical school, and *while* we worked. We believed that we could
have it all—family and work, activism and home life, intimate
coupling, and collective action. Some of us were married; some
were not. Many eschewed the idea of both government- and
church-sponsored marriages, questioning their legitimacy and
opting for personal commitments of our own making. We did
not believe children could be born "out of wedlock." We believed
strongly in the right to choose. We saw home as a place for
shared work, where women and men work together to make a
life. And we lived that reality. Our partners cooked and tended
to the children, did laundry, and other household chores. My
husband, Joaquín Rosa, was by far a better cook than I and
ironed even our jeans according to the form of military press
he had learned in the navy. While Melanie was simultaneously
in medical school and working in the Alliance, her husband
cooked, did the laundry, tended to the children, and kept the
house clean.

The norm was to share family and household responsibilities not only within our own family units but also between families. Sisters in California set up a whole arrangement where families helped each other with childcare needs.

What Mistakes Did You Make? Where Did You Go Wrong?

As with any entity comprising human beings, we made mistakes. From my perspective, some of the mistakes were not speaking up when we should have, and some were ongoing dynamics that were invisible to us. Some things we didn't see or just didn't talk about. One example was the abuse of a New York Alliance member by her partner. It took too long for this to come out and only then in the context of larger issues. Some sisters knew about it, but spousal abuse either in the abstract or in relation to our own lives was never talked about as a group in New York. We did not integrate our theories with our practice in this regard. We did not sit down together and think about how to address this problem, how to support our sister. In the New York Chapter, too often, our politics did not stay close enough to the personal. Ana Celia mentioned this in her recollections, saying that during her time in the Alliance, this was a conflict between her and Fran. She experienced herself as more sensitive to, and more interested in, integrating the personal into the work of the Alliance, while Fran was more focused on the big political picture. Fran's approach prevailed.

Another major shortcoming surrounds one of our strengths: the Alliance's position on lesbian and gay oppression. Our 1970 platform read, "The oppression and dehumanizing ostracism that homosexuals face must be rejected and their right to exist as dignified human beings must be defended." In New York, we honored this statement, which was clear and advanced for the time, by welcoming lesbian and bisexual women into membership. Still, gay identity was not discussed openly.

Lenore recalled, "I do remember it being uncomfortable. There were a couple of women who were lesbian or bisexual. Some I was unsure about and it was something not encouraged to be discussed. No one was openly disparaging, but we were aware." There were some same-sex encounters among members, but silence and invisibility reigned there, too, and heterosexual relationships and heteronormative thinking were the dominant paradigms.

Even more distressing, I was stunned to learn, were the Bay Area Alliance's statements and actions with regard to lesbian sisters, which stood in direct opposition to our clearly stated platform: "Women had the right to love others of their own sex without fear or shame." When lesbian women critiqued the organization for not being pro-lesbian enough, Bay Area sisters at first refused to take a stand and then stated that there were more important issues to discuss than sexual orientation. In that moment and in that way, sisters were hurt, and our political vision and work were also diminished.

Even at a reunion in 2012, some of us were not able to talk comfortably about the subject of sexual orientation. Melanie wisely pointed out that a discrepancy often exists between what people say they believe and what we are actually able to live. Fran made her usual "in for a penny, in for a pound" statement indicating that once we committed to fighting oppression, we committed to fighting all oppression, and there was an unacknowledged difference between the West Coast (where some lesbians felt pushed out of the organization) and the East Coast (where we had one or two out lesbians and at least one married lesbian who was in the closet). In my opinion, still not enough soul searching was done at that meeting. But the reality of sisters like myself, who now have lesbian and bisexual children whom we cherish and support, suggests that we have evolved in our thinking.

And then there was the gun! Reading *Triple Jeopardy* and looking at the Alliance symbol, one cannot miss the gun. Although the Alliance, as an organization, never took up arms, the gun, for us, was a statement about women's duty to defend themselves and their communities. It was considered a symbol of the revolution and of women's agency. The Alliance platform stated, "Whereas the struggle for liberation must be borne equally by all members of an oppressed people, we declare that women have the right and the responsibility to bear arms. Women should be fully trained and educated in the martial arts as well as in the political arena. Furthermore, we recognize that it is our duty to defend all oppressed people."

The fact that most "militant" organizations of the sixties spoke only of self-defense rather than aggression was well-known at the time, although it has been increasingly misrepresented in historical retrospective. In my opinion, radical organizations, including the Alliance, romanticized armed struggle. The youth of Alliance members buttressed our altruism and commitment; at the same time, it diminished our ability to fully appreciate the ramifications of "armed struggle." Writings of young intellectuals, like those of the Martinican psychiatrist Frantz Fanon, whom we all read, spoke of violence as psychologically and politically beneficial, and this influenced our thinking. In *The Wretched of the Earth*, Fanon wrote, "Violence alone, perpetrated by the people, violence organized and guided by the leadership, provides the key for the masses to decipher social reality."[18]

The "violence" of the radicals of that era was predominantly a response to the violence we witnessed daily—assassinations of revered political leaders, massacres of little children in Vietnam, murders of young men helping other Americans to vote, daily police brutality. It was an angry and violent period. And as with many liberation fighters from the time of the American Revolution, we saw taking up arms as a necessity.

I think now that Dr. Martin Luther King Jr.'s message of nonviolence held the moral high ground. It must also be acknowledged that the presence of activists and agitators like ourselves gave more negotiating power to people in the center and made it more likely that they would be listened to.

In the realm of theory, I believe our thinking lagged as well and, in hindsight, I see this as a shortcoming. We missed somehow that although our analysis was based on binaries, political and philosophical thinking had moved to the more intersecting and dialogic frame of "triple jeopardy." While dialectics centers on "either/or" thinking, the theory of dialogics envisions society as multivoiced (what Mikhail Bakhtin calls "polyphony")[19] and does not assume, as does Hegelian dialectics, that only two (usually polar opposite) perspectives exist. We remained dualistic while some of our thinking and the evolution of philosophy had moved to dialogics. We no longer think in polar opposites and, other than in the theory of contradictions, we did not then, as our organization's existence and praxis clearly reveal. Today, even the gender binary is falling away. Bakhtin's dialogical thinking asserts that there is no need to arrive at a synthesis or consensus and therefore leaves open the possibility of multiple outcomes. This important distinction reflects a significant shift in thinking that is more constitutive of the postmodern world.

I would also name the lack of spirituality as a shortcoming. Today, many of the women of the Alliance are no longer materialists who believe only in the world of matter. It is clear from the vantage point of age that turning away from religion as young twentysomethings is not uncommon and often takes the form of a temporary atheism. Some Alliance women were nonbelievers then and remain so now; the decision to believe in God or not is personal, but attempting to prohibit belief in God has historically been shown to fail. I think it is one element underlying the failure of the dictatorial socialist revolutions around the world.[20]

When I searched out Alliance women for interviews, one reality that could not escape observation was the widespread spirituality, and in some cases the religious observance, of many of these women. I am still moved by the devoted ethos of the Sunday services I attended with Georgette and her family in New Orleans. Although the Alliance had completely embraced a materialist philosophy that held that there was "no spirit," I found most sisters in their later years connected to their spiritual faith. Perhaps this is simply a sign of aging, as it is widely observed that most people become more religious and spiritual as they age, but reflecting on the shortcomings and invisibilities in the Alliance, I believe that the anger of the period, while it generated a great deal of agency and action on our part, also reflected a spiritual despair. We could not understand how God had allowed so much inequity.

We were angry. And well we should have been. It was important to be outraged at the injustices we saw. We spoke of rage, we spoke of self-defense, of having had enough, of not having had enough. We tried, as Ho Chi Minh had instructed, to turn anger into energy, but we did not speak of love, of caring, and we critiqued those who, like Dr. King, did. I think this is one reason, aside from FBI infiltration, why we imploded. A movement of anger and militancy cannot sustain itself over too long a period. This is not to suggest that our militancy did not have its accomplishments. As Joni Mitchell's "Both Sides, Now," a song of the era, proclaimed that "something's lost and something's gained in living every day."[21] We helped moved society forward toward liberation, although we may not always have done it in the most constructive ways. By the twenty-first century, many Alliance sisters, altered and enriched by their experiences, embraced more of a social gospel of justice, love, and liberation than they had before.

What Did We Accomplish? Did Our Work in the 1970s Make a Difference for Women of Color and Their Communities?

Linda's answer to this question was clear and compelling: "The Alliance was important in creating space for the leadership of women of color that wasn't there before. Leadership on programmatic issues. Demanding that space. Creating an agenda that for the first time looked at how race, class, and sex impacted women and made for different life experiences."

It can also be said that we advocated for the overall destruction of the system that we saw as racist, classist, and sexist. This did not come to pass. Racism, class oppression, sexual violence, and sexual discrimination still exist, seemingly unaffected by the principle of impermanence.

Numerous political theorists and philosophers give us important perspectives. In Fanon's terms, we discovered our mission, and we fulfilled it. Paraphrasing the words of writer and psychiatrist Paul Fleischman, we "did our job working in the common cause."[22] The Jewish passage Pirkei Avot 2:21

reads, "You are not obligated to complete the work, but neither are you free to desist from it." We did the work that we were called to do at that time. We did it through study, and writing, and action, and struggle. We were not the first or only women of color to take up the struggle for equal rights, but it is important to document this piece in the long history of women of color in the United States. In that way, we achieved much, yet the work is still incomplete.

We also accomplished the important task of coming together, of building community across identities, of operating as a political category, a unique political category in that historical moment. Members were Filipina, Puerto Rican, biracial, multiracial, Indian, African American, Japanese, West Indian, Korean, Mexican American, Chinese, Palestinian, and Lebanese. This alliance across ethnic and racial identities was unique then and now. Cherríe Moraga was correct when, in the foreword to the second edition of *This Bridge Called My Back*, she wrote about third world feminism, saying, "The *idea* of Third World feminism has proved to be much easier between the covers of a book than between real live women. There *are* many issues that divide us; and, recognizing that fact can make that dream at times seem quite remote."[23]

Yet for a period of time between 1970 and 1980, prior to Moraga's writing, the Alliance lived the philosophy of third world feminism. Many of these women still carry a dedication to those connections in their hearts and sow seeds of this unity across women and people of color in their everyday work. My own AmFam (Amherst Family) community of African American, Dominican, white, Cape Verdean, West Indian, Filipina, Puerto Rican, Indian, Korean, biracial, and multiracial men, women, and children exemplify that in my life.

What Alliance members achieved in the 1970s was both small and monumental—a few more drops in the oceanic wave of women of color who have and are changing the world. We took a stand for women. We took a stand for women's rights. We were internationalists. We were multicultural. We loved men of color, and we fought side by side with them to change the United States into a freer, more equitable nation.

Our most important achievements were our own self-development and contribution to what became an expanded conception of how women could and should participate in the movements of the 1970s and beyond. We educated women and men. We raised the questions and offered some solutions.

We were coming of age in a world permeated with inequity, war, and violence. We were trying to understand who we were and our place in the world. We lived in a crucible of questions about ourselves and the world around us. In response, we created an organization that provided us with the opportunity to study and connect with sister-friends who were asking the same questions. We engaged with one another, studied together, and became activists. In that way, we developed identities characterized by agency.

We educated ourselves about our bodies, our communities, about women internationally, about "the system," and about inequity and justice. We read, we discussed, we critiqued, we worked with our hands, and we connected with other groups. We traveled around the country and to other countries.

What we accomplished at first was self-actualization. We became change agents, third world women activists. Although it seems a little pretentious in retrospect, we considered ourselves revolutionaries, and this self-definition gave meaning to our lives. We knew what we stood for; we knew what we were fighting for; we knew where we were headed. We educated ourselves, kept active, developed hope, had a vision—and therefore did not succumb to drugs, to failure, or to despair.

We developed community. We had sisters. We had partners. We had purpose. We had people to hang with and something important to do, something upon which our lives and the lives of our communities and the future of our nation depended. We educated our children and our communities, teaching them the value of women, the need for involvement in the world around them, and the possibility of change. We showed our men what women could do, disabusing them of the idea that they had to support us or lead us and making it clear that they could not abuse us. We surprised them. We inspired them. And together, we built a partnership. And what we realized in the moment would stay with us all of our lives.

Unlike the women bell hooks described in 1981, we did not remain silent. Although *But Some of Us Are Brave* would not be published until 1982, two years after the Bay Alliance transitioned to the AAWO, and though "voice" in women's studies would not begin to be talked about until the publication of Carol Gilligan's groundbreaking 1982 book, *In a Different Voice*, we developed our voices and our courage in the 1970s. We were not silent among white women liberationists. We were not silent with third world men. We did not resign ourselves. We did not accept our lot. We joined together, and we got to work.

We saw (and still see) womanhood as an important aspect of our identity. We named sexism. We spoke out against la doble jornada. We educated our men and invited them to share in the drudgery of housework and the joy of raising children. Many of them, especially Black men, had done this kind of work historically. The testimony of Alliance women serves to document the participation of Asian, Black, and Latino men in the care and nurturing of women and children of color. Despite the current psychological and sociological "data" reporting that men of color, particularly Black and Latino men, are the worst culprits of inequality in the home by not sharing household duties with their wives, the brothers of the Alliance lived differently. We fought the battle against sexism while naming racism and classism and imperialism as evils that we also had to fight. We were a new generation of women, women who taught each other to resist, to speak up, and to fight for our rights.

We developed agency and power, the capacity to act on the world, and leadership qualities that enabled us to influence and engage our peers and decision makers of our era in attending to the needs and contributions of women of color, our families, and our communities. The words "I" and "me" were minimized. Initially, no bylines were published in the newspapers, no awards for individual accomplishment, and no personal accolades. We built community.

Loretta Ross, in her interview with Fran, remarked, "Your group of women were doing considerable theoretical development in the face of the charge that Black women don't do theory."[24] As mentioned earlier, the *Guardian* covered us; the Black Panther Party articles covered us; the Young Lords worked with us; we worked with numerous organizations in coalitions. According to *Paving the Way*, "TWWA was also a foundational source of new thinking about the powerful intersections among gender, race, and class."[25] All of this suggests that we influenced the conversation about the role of women in the liberation struggles of people of color on the left and about the role of women in the movement overall.

The Alliance demonstrated to our families and communities that we were part of an organization that uplifted us as women, and we showed them that there was a role for them in the struggle. Although they sometimes critiqued us, Panther women and the Young Lords women (whom we sometimes derisively called "the Young Ladies" when they criticized us) developed more of a voice and a greater sense of their own power as women after reading *Triple Jeopardy* and seeing us work. Barbara Christian, who was on campus and felt guilty about Black feminists' roles in terms of what men were saying, said the words of the Alliance gave them courage. I believe our influence was quite widespread.

The Alliance met four out of five of the stated goals and objectives in our platform: We created "a sisterhood of women devoted to the task of developing solidarity among the peoples of the third world based on a socialist ideology." We promoted "unity among third world people in the United States." We collected, interpreted, and distributed "information about the Third World, both at home and abroad and particularly information affecting its women." We re-created and built "solid relationships with our men, destroying myths that have been created by our oppressor to divide us from each other, and to work together to appreciate human love and respect." We did these in small ways, but we did them. We did not "establish an education fund to be used to promote educational projects, to publish articles, and to employ such other media as is necessary to carry out such educational projects," but we did publish, and we did educate.

Looking at our ideological platform, I conclude that we had mixed success. In our own families, we were clear that we did not own one another. Women worked and carried their economic share, and men joined women in tending to children and the household and did their share in the domestic domain. We certainly supported the idea of extended family, which was not hard since it was a cultural tradition for so many of us. Parents and siblings came to live with us as needed, as did cousins and other family members.

We maintained our right to decide if and when to have children. None of our children were ever seen as illegitimate; our decisions to have them were unconnected to our marital status. We were among the first women of color for whom the legality of marriage meant very little. We supported *Roe v. Wade* and worked also to expand the dialogue beyond abortion to a full support of all reproductive freedoms.

We have not done so well with employment. Women of color are still underpaid and too often involved in exploitative work. Miriam's book *Sweatshop Warriors* educates about this issue historically, looking at Mexican, Chinese, and Korean factory workers, and Linda presses for change in her work with the National Domestic Workers Alliance. We are nowhere near having achieved adequate income for all. Racism and sexism still exist, although some of us (not all) would argue that we have seen progress. We have more professors who are women and of color and more women of color in all professional positions, but all we need to do is look at the high numbers of immigrant women who are at the lowest end of the wage scale and the nannies and housekeepers who have little or no healthcare or retirement funding to see how far we still have to go.

Sex roles are more fluid and nonnormative today. Gay rights have become more prominent, and gay marriage is the law of the land after the US Supreme Court decision on June 26, 2015. And although we did not make these changes (or any of the changes discussed here) alone, we contributed to the dialogue and the activism—especially when in New York we withstood the taunts and assaults that we were lesbians because we chose to organize ourselves as women. We understood this as a direct expression of not only homophobia and heterosexism but also as a clear manifestation of sexism.

Concha answers the question of our impact this way, "In the long term I really think it's shaped the voice of third world women, probably the way most of us have participated in our respective worlds. Many of us have gone on to be influential, and it sort of started out on this pebble and continued to grow out in different directions."

I agree with Concha, and perhaps the most complete answer about what we accomplished can be gleaned from reading the individual portraits distributed throughout this book. The Alliance went on to inspire many organizations that came after it. To that degree, the contributions are incalculable and ongoing.

Are You Still a Socialist?

When I asked this question of former Alliance members, some said, "Yes absolutely," while others said they no longer consider themselves to be socialists. You can see the range of responses in the portraits.

My own answer is mixed. I would say yes and no. No to the type of socialism that created the horrendous hardship and oppression of the Soviet Union. No to socialism that strips citizens' rights to freedom of religion, as happened for a long while in Cuba.[26] Freedom, as a Vietnamese woman I recently met reminded me, is not something to assume one really understands unless one has lived under a regime where it is denied.

Perhaps out of loyalty to my grandmother, a Eugene Debs socialist, and to my own work in the seventies, for the most part, I still lean toward socialism. It has always connected economic equality to freedom, which I fully embrace. For me, it has been most recently articulated in the 2016 presidential candidacy of Bernie Sanders and the candidacy of Bronx democratic socialist Alexandria Ocasio-Cortez (AOC).

And although the word "socialist" strikes fear in the hearts of many, and although I must admit that too often socialism has been aligned with totalitarianism, one can be both socialist and believe in democracy, as Sanders illustrates. If we are talking about democratic socialism that includes a nationalized healthcare system (or Medicare for all), like the incredibly egalitarian systems found in Sweden and Finland, I support socialism. If democratic socialism involves tuition-free public education, as espoused by Ocasio-Cortez, I support socialism. If socialism is an ideology that champions social justice and progressive taxation and believes that each member of society should contribute to the maximum degree she is able so that those in need can be taken care of, then I am still a socialist. As long as we maintain the word "democracy" in the foreground and as long as we support people's freedom to worship (or not worship) as they choose, then democratic socialism is just fine with me. I would call myself a democratic socialist.

Perhaps a more relevant question is: Are the women of TWWA still activists? I would assert that they are. Readers may answer that question for themselves from the "A Luta Continua" sections in this book.

When You Think of the 2020 Election, Do You See Any Connections between the Ascension of Stacey Abrams, Kamala Harris, AOC, and the Squad and the Seeds TWWA Planted?

This was such a provocative question, not only after the presidential election but also after the runoffs in the Georgia senatorial elections, that I raised it with Alliance women and got an interesting and wide array of answers.

One response was definitive: "I know that TWWA was a historical force that contributed to this current climate." Another sister responded, "For myself, we are long past the stage when Black faces in high places is sufficient to solve the problems of Black women and other women of color. For heaven's sake, we had a Black president—what did he do for Black people? We need an agenda [like the one we developed in TWWA]: twenty-four-hour childcare, free education, decent jobs, and affordable housing."

Another wrote, "It is wonderful . . . that it seems to be coming full circle with new generations of activist third world women along with some of our contemporaries who keep on keeping on. The Trump era is not over, and we are still not safe. But the threat has ignited a new wave of activism that could turn the tide and bring great hope."

Another sister volunteered, "One of my daughters is the first Asian American to win an elected county-wide seat. I never pushed her to be an activist, but it seems to be in her spirit. Role models matter." Another said, "I feel proud when I see and hear women of color speaking out in almost the same language we used in *Triple Jeopardy*. These are extraordinary times, and COVID-19 has escalated our struggle for justice and equality to new heights. There is indeed a renewed sense of hope that the evils of capitalism and an international system based on exploitation and profit might come to an end. But let's get real. We all still need to more clearly understand and oppose a world system that allows profit to be more important than people, especially people of color. We still need to understand why it is that Black and Brown people can be killed and incarcerated on a whim or an impulse just because they have darker skin. Lastly, it is still refreshing to see young folks of color amongst the sea of whiteness that makes up governmental entities in this country. There is an opportunity now to continue to grow our presence and our consciousness. The struggle continues!"

All of their answers resonate with me. We need programs, and we need structural change. We need to work at the electoral level, and we need activism in our communities and in our workplaces. We need individual action, and we need a groundswell of community action. All left political activism can work together for the common good, as long as the goal is equity and justice for all.

Yes, the Squad and AOC and Stacey Abrams were influenced by the work we did, but we didn't plant the seeds. The seeds were planted long before we came along—all we did was continue to water the seeds of justice, as these young women are doing now. The answer is deceptively simple: "Somos hermanas en la lucha."

To my mind, Nancy Wong said it best. "TWWA: An Organizing Model for Today's Anti-Racist and Progressive Movements."

The Alliance's model of organizing *is* truly worthy of study and emulation.

What Remains to Be Done?

It all remains to be done. Done and redone. And expanded.

The first issue of *Triple Jeopardy* in 1971 devoted six separate articles to prisons in the US. Two of the articles focused on the massacre at Attica. Yet as Michelle Alexander illustrates in *The New Jim Crow*—2020 marked the tenth anniversary of this important work—we continue to see mass incarcerations, largely of Black and Brown women and men, with drug convictions accounting for the majority of the surge. Alexander reported that the US incarceration rate at the time of publication of her book was 750 per 100,000 people, versus 161 in the United States in 1972 and 93 in Germany, saying, "No one imagined that the prison population would more than quintuple in their lifetime."[27] The number of women in prison also increased from 13,000 in 1980 to 114,000 in 2019, and in 2019, the imprisonment rate for African American women (83 per 100,000) was over 1.7 times the rate of imprisonment for white women (48 per 100,000).[28]

Blacks make up 13 percent of the US population but 40 percent of the US incarcerated population. A third of Black men will have served time in prison, based on 2001 rates, and "the Hispanic population has doubled since 1990 and in the last 10 years has become the only race that has also seen growth in prison inmates, a break from the trend in shrinking black and white prisoners, according to two new reports on Latin immigrants."[29]

Turning our view toward education in the United States, we see that women have become more and more educated. Today, there are more women in college than men, but people of color are still undereducated, and our boys are now falling behind. The Alliance demanded that education give us the tools to understand ourselves. Here, again, there's mixed success. In 2019, women represented 56 percent of college matriculates, and by 2016 and 2017 took just over half the seats in medical and law schools, respectively. Largely through the efforts of the activists of the sixties and seventies, ethnic studies and women's studies programs were created. There are few leading institutions today that do not have Latinx studies, Black or Africana studies, women studies, or gender studies departments. (Some of our sisters, Miriam on the West Coast and Ana Celia and Barbara on the East Coast, were involved in the creation of these departments.)

Self-knowledge for educated women of color is easier to come by when students take a course in one of those departments. Yet at the same time, as Brenda points out, the emphasis on testing at the secondary school level has removed the opportunity for kids to learn about themselves, especially in poor communities. In states like Arizona and New Mexico, which tend toward conservative government and have more limited resources, all manner of ethnic studies programs are under attack, whereas in more affluent liberal states like Massachusetts, we can find classes on African American, Latinx, or LGBT literature in high school.

We have made little progress with universal childcare. There is no free, universal day care. We have more day care available for working parents, but it is costly, with poor quality, inadequate safety, and even abuse quite widespread. Day-care teachers are underpaid and often undereducated. The deep-sixing of the push for universal and subsidized childcare in 1971 has left us behind the rest of the industrialized world; the United States is completely retrograde in terms of issues like paid parental leave and childcare. In 2017, the United States ranked fifth from the bottom among thirty-eight Organisation for Economic Co-operation and Development countries on public spending on family benefits.[30]

Finally, the Affordable Care Act, which expanded medical care to twenty million previously uninsured citizens, was still very costly as of 2018, and between 2016 and 2020, the Trump administration dedicated itself to dismantling it. Education and housing cost too much, and none of these services are controlled by the people. Lack of access to prenatal care and other vital health services is causing our maternal death rate to rise. In 2018, the United States was found to be the most dangerous place in the developed world to have a child. We lag far behind most industrial nations with an infant mortality rate of 5.8 percent deaths per one thousand live births.[31] This is not Sweden, where the child of the custodian sees the same doctor as the child of the surgeon in the well-baby clinics that serve all Swedish citizens. Infant mortality rates in the United States are an outrage.

According to the annual State of the World's Mothers Report in 2015, the United States ranked thirty-third in terms of the well-being of mothers and children, and children under five years old in the United States are three times as likely to die as same-aged children in Iceland.[32] Mothers here get eight to twelve weeks of family leave if they are lucky, most often without pay. My daughter got two weeks paid maternity leave from the University of Massachusetts when she gave birth in September 2018.

Mothers in European countries get up to a year, *with pay*, and a guarantee that their jobs will be there when they return. For example, Sweden is considered to have some of the highest quality childcare in the world, "with a very long, paid parental leave split equally between the two parents, a monthly allowance for children, free children's healthcare as well as free transportation for the little ones."[33]

We are seen in many places as women in our own right, but that is continually and continuously challenged when one is poor or Black or Brown, or when English is a second language, or when one wears a hijab, or when the shape of one's eyes suggest to the ignorant that one may not have been born in this country.

Our communities are just as poor and ravaged as they were fifty years ago, just as segregated—even more so. As Barbara Morita pointed out, in the United States, if you lose your job, "You're worried you're going to end up on the streets . . . and you live with that tension and that fear."

The virulence of racism endures and keeps our eyes focused there. Police in the United States killed 298 Black people during

2020.[34] The need for movements like Black Lives Matter and the pushback against that movement from large swaths of American society illuminate the enduring power of racist thought.

I am pained by the lack of democratic and democratic socialist attention to the American workers—farmers, carpenters, steel, and aluminum workers, etc. I remember when I stood with the Ford workers in Rahway, New Jersey, in the seventies and the striking workers at Winchester in New Haven in 1980. I remember when I did dialogue work with Ford workers in the nineties. The Gini index shows that economic inequality in the United States is steadily increasing. Clearly, there is more work to do.

I still see pockets of unity for women of color and people of color in general; my own social circle includes many. The University of Massachusetts at Amherst, for example, hosts a Women of Color Leadership Network. But this is not widespread. On women's college campuses, women of color are still fairly separate. There may be, for example, a campus group for African American women and another for Caribbean and/or African women. There may be an Asian Student Group, and, additionally, a Korean Women's Group, and so on. Students may choose only one and often there is conflict between the groups.

People of color from diverse groups, for the most part, do not come together in coalition. There is more fear and contention now between African American and Latino groups in major cities like Springfield, Massachusetts, where they live together and, in my experience, compete for resources rather than coming together and accessing them.[35] In California, the difficulties between these two groups in the prisons have resulted in moves to segregate them from one another.[36]

There is more acceptance of differences today—of color, of sexual orientation, and of gender expression. On the downside of gender equality, women now go to war and mothers leave their children to do so. Sometimes both fathers and mothers are deployed at the same time. It is chilling to me now to remember that the gun was so central to our collective imagery in the Alliance. Women carrying guns were pictured in *Triple Jeopardy* and in our platform. The logo we developed for our organization was a hand holding a rifle. Today, neither armed conflict nor women (or men) fighting in wars is something I advocate for or welcome.

If we look at women, race, and class, we have done our best in relation to women, and better than before with regard to race, but nowhere near our goal of class and economic security for those at the bottom of the income and wealth scales. We wished to defeat imperialism, not ignore or abandon American workers. Many progressives seem to have lost sight of issues of economic exploitation. As Lenore wrote to me, as the events of the storming of the Capitol building demonstrated, now, just as in the 1970s, it is clear that the use of divide and conquer the working class is still alive and well. Race, gender, and sexual orientation; immigration status; color; and religion—the same tools that were wielded against us then are effective now. For all of the aforementioned reasons, this intersection—the triple jeopardy of race, class, sex—we saw then is still required to be seen to create true systemic change now.

What Does the Work of the TWWA Suggest for the Future?

My goal here is to pull back the curtain that obscures the past so that future generations can learn from it. As Kahlil Gibran wrote about children, "You may give them your love but not your thoughts, for they have their own thoughts. You may house their bodies but not their souls, for their souls dwell in the house of tomorrow, which you cannot visit, not even in your dreams."[37] My call here is to promote and support activism.

I have shared my observations and hopes in this book. One hope is that we will still work to liberate girls of color and our whole community. I name our girls, not because they come first, but because this was our focus and because women are still oppressed by systems of male hegemony and dominance. Women are more capable every day of becoming leaders in the struggle for equity and liberation.

The #MeToo movement birthed in 2006 by Tarana Burke, an African American woman, demonstrates that it is not only the perpetrators of violence against women (and in some cases men) who are problematic but also the silence of those who turn a blind eye. An extreme example is the two hundred girls Boko Haram kidnapped in Nigeria in 2014, but there are many smaller-scale oppressions worldwide that still keep girls from realizing their potential.

The violence against Black men that began in the slave trade and continued through enslavement, reconstruction, and the civil rights movement—really relentlessly throughout American history—continues. In recent years, we have seen an increase in the murder of unarmed Black men—George Floyd, Michael Brown, Trayvon Martin, Eric Garner, and too many others—killed with the tacit approval of institutions that are supposed to guarantee the safety of all people. As the Alliance did, we must work for our entire communities.

Inequity and injustice remain, new challenges have emerged, and new movements have risen up in defiance. The Black Lives Matter movement, the women's marches, the Never Again movement, the Me Too movement, and the Resist movement are some of those. Also of note is the massive worldwide multi-racial explosion of grief and activism that followed the murder of George Floyd.

There is hope, but there is work to be done.

Who Are Young Women Today Trying to "Live Like"?

If the mantra "Live Like Her" were resurrected today, to whom would your eyes turn? Who preoccupies your thoughts and shapes your actions? As mentioned in the very first pages of this book, one of my research assistants, Shera Resch, responded to that question this way: "Sadly, I can't think of anyone on the contemporary scene . . . I live in an era that makes icons of Beyoncé and Rihanna—where consumerism and obsession with celebrity shape the images of my generation." I asked her about the impact of researching women for this project, and

LIVE LIKE HER: ANGELA DAVIS

Another model in the pantheon of women of color whom we desired to imitate and "live like" was our own US revolutionary, Angela Davis. "Hands Off Angela Davis" was the banner that TWWA sisters carried down Fifth Avenue during the fiftieth-anniversary march. Angela Davis was Black, a woman, and a member of the Communist Party. Like us, she had suffered the impact of racism. Like us, she had struggled to understand the "beast" of US capitalism and imperialism and had found an answer in progressive socialist theory. Like us, she studied, took a stand, and joined organizations that fought for justice. She was a woman and a socialist, and she spoke out against the political and economic system that profited from our oppression. And she was a leader. We wanted to live like her, and to that end, we emulated her focus on the importance of the broad social forces that impacted Black people and other oppressed groups.

Growing up in the Deep South of Alabama, Angela's early school years were marked by segregation and the diminished resources of a system that was separate and unequal. She witnessed the physical and psychological violence of racism and the rage and self-hatred that racism generated in southern Blacks. Her parents' civil rights activism and her time in New York studying at Elisabeth Irwin High School guided her toward socialist theory, and her time in Paris studying at the Sorbonne and working with the German Socialist Student League solidified this. She returned to the United States to become active in the Black Power movement and continued her studies with Herbert Marcuse and her work with James Forman.

She joined the Communist Party and became active in the defense of the Black Panther Party and the Soledad Brothers, three Black men imprisoned in Soledad Prison. When she was accused of being complicit in the prison break attempt of George Jackson and the murder of a judge by Jackson's younger brother, Jonathan, she was hunted and spent two months underground until she was eventually exonerated of all charges. Her commitment, bravery, and righteous stance against racism and other forms of oppression were perfect embodiments of the women we wanted to live like.

then she lifted up Angela Davis, one of the activists whose life and work she studied. Shera said, "Angela helped define my possibilities. What I, and my generation of young Black women, do with that awesome legacy is yet to be seen." More recently, the Black Lives Matter movement and the widespread resistance to the Trump agenda suggest that activism may be on the rise again.

On March 8, 2010, Michelle Obama became the first First Lady to celebrate IWD in the White House, and as part of that celebration, she introduced young people to Dorothy Height, founder of the National Council of Negro Women and lifelong champion of the civil rights of African Americans and women. Civil rights leader James Farmer described Height as one of the "Big Six" of the civil rights movement, though her role was frequently ignored by the press due to sexism.[38] (Height passed away soon after, on April 20, 2010, at the age of ninety-eight.) At that same event, President Barack Obama noted that women were still subject to unequal pay, earning seventy-seven cents for every dollar a man earned; that one in four women had an experience of domestic violence; and that although women made up half of the US population, they only represented 17 percent of people in Congress and 3 percent of Fortune 500 company leaders. IWD celebrations have continued through the Obama and Trump administrations. And although these commemorations in the White House are encouraging, recognition at local levels lags far behind. Perhaps a reestablishment of the IWD celebration in communities of color would reinvigorate our collective consciousness, revealing to us the many women we emulate.

Closing Thoughts

In 2002, I met Grace Lee Boggs in Flint, Michigan, at a weekend conference of the Animating Democracy initiative, an arts and civic dialogue project sponsored by Americans for the Arts. A Chinese American woman, Grace was then eighty-seven years old. I did not know her, although her last name was familiar.

I asked her if she was related to James Boggs, a writer whose work I had read and admired while in the Alliance.

"He was my husband," Grace responded, her face beaming.[39] That was how I learned that Grace's "Jimmy," a man who dedicated his life to the struggle for racial and economic justice, had died. His book, *Racism and the Class Struggle*, published in 1970, made a profound impression on me.

Grace and I saw each another again that evening at the Flint Cultural Center museum. She wanted to speak with me, and there was some urgency in her voice and her demeanor. We stood in a small corner of the museum as she talked to me about her life in Detroit, where she had lived for more than fifty years, working at first with her husband and then with other activists to strengthen the people and the community. She spoke of the devastation of Detroit and of the loss of income because of the decline of the auto industry, but mostly, she wanted to talk about the people there.

"There is an escalating crisis in public education," she said. "Teachers are angry, principals are threatened, and kids are rebelling. We need to abandon the top-down factory model and engage children in solving real community problems." She talked about what she called the "shadow side of identity politics," which in her view has left us focusing on victim status rather than human status. She spoke about how people today are "more concerned with our possessions and our careers than the state of our neighborhoods," adding, "our great system of democracy no longer engages the hearts and minds of our people." She was concerned about what had happened to the youth particularly. "They will kill you for a pair of sneakers," she said. Neither her words nor her tone was judgmental. She simply spoke about what was happening to the communities of Detroit and the people in it, the ruined economy, and the loss of opportunity that had led inner-city youth to desperate and damaging behaviors.

She told me that something must be done about this situation, that it was essential to let people know, and that it was imperative that activists stop denying these realities. She said that we should be willing to shine the light of truth on this phenomenon and deal with it, not just talk about "isms" and let the destructive behavior of our communities go unacknowledged or unchallenged. She ended her conversation with me, a person about twenty-five years her junior, by saying, "So if you've got the courage, talk about this. Do something about this; if you've got the courage." This writing is my attempt to do just that—to continue to restate the call for activism and to remind us that our communities have internal problems that must be faced and addressed.

As Milagros remarked in our interview, we are at a point in our lives when we must begin to question a lot of what we accepted as truth. This is true. For me, I have come to question the role of guns and armed struggle. I would like all of us to look at our communities and ask if and when and who should be held accountable, and I do not see this as counter to being an activist.

In the close of her 2016 book, *Freedom Is a Constant Struggle*, Angela Davis wrote, "We have to go to great lengths. We cannot go on as usual. We cannot pivot the center. We cannot be moderate. We have to be willing to stand up and say no with our combined spirits, our collective intellects, and our many bodies."[40]

It is said that "the arc of the moral universe is long but it bends toward justice." To my mind, this is only true if WE THE PEOPLE bend that arc! In the 1970s and beyond, women of TWWA took a stand for justice. We strived to emulate our role models. Today, in this era of sexual assault; of wall-building; of the murder of Black men, women, and children; of violence perpetrated on innocents in schools, theaters, and the streets; of suicides by dairy farmers and the everyday hardships of American workers; and of the abandonment of hurricane-ravaged citizens in the US colony of Puerto Rico, many Americans are taking a stand. It is not hard to find an injustice that is being perpetrated or fellow activists to stand with. *Where will you be? Who will you live like?*

Acknowledgments

IN THE COMPANY of women, I have accomplished much of my most important professional work, and this book is no exception. First and foremost, I lift up the sisters of the Third World Women's Alliance (TWWA), especially Frances Beal, who taught me about women and social change and, just as important, about leadership, political development, and hard work. To my Alliance sisters Stella Holmes Hughes, Cheryl Johnson Perry League, Milagros Pérez Huth, and Renata and Melanie Tervalon: thanks for staying close all of these years and providing me the opportunity to remember so much while basking in the sunshine of old friendship.

A big "thank you" to former Hampshire College faculty Ellie Donkin for reading and commenting on a complete draft of an early manuscript. To E. Francis White, Miriam Slater, and my former Hampshire College students for asking good questions and producing such progressive work. To Ximena Zúñiga, mi querida amiga, who reviewed this work and added her wisdom about contemporary feminist theories.

To Pat Schneider and the women of the Amherst Writers and Artists Thursday-night writing group. Up until her death in 2020, even while she was in a nursing home, Pat made time to act as a steadfast midwife to my work. Several women from the group, including Linda Meccouri, read and commented on parts of the manuscript. Carol Paul offered me a free week at her writing studio in Maine, and Terry Jenoure and the Augusta Savage Gallery gave me a scholarship for a writing retreat in New Mexico.

To Kathleen Banks Nutter, librarian at Smith College, who has helped preserve and oversee the TWWA archives, and who was kind enough to let me know that they are the most frequently requested archives in the collection.

To Joan M. Drury and the Norcroft Writing Retreat for Women: two weeks in 1995 was the beginning. Two weeks in 2005 allowed me to take up the project again. Joan gave me time on the North Shore of Lake Superior in the company of inspiring, mostly white, women, again reassuring me that although we are not without differences, a spirit of sisterhood remains. Joan's commitment to inclusion is exemplary. To Joon Pyo Lee, who wrote a master's thesis on TWWA and has conveyed the best information to date about who we really were. To Sandra Nelson and JoAnne Jones, who read the penultimate draft. To Farah Ameen, copyeditor par excellence. I asked her to read my manuscript as a reader to tell me what she thought and suggest any changes she'd like. Farah, a Bangladeshi American woman, helped me to perfect the manuscript as only a woman of color could. Then she agreed to write the foreword for the book! I am ever grateful to her for her skill and entendimiento of the value of this work and of what I was trying to accomplish.

My young students at Hampshire College, where I taught from 1986 to 1996, inspired my research, and I owe a debt of gratitude to several Hampshire College and Mount Holyoke students who were invaluable assistants in my research. Shalini and Deborah at Hampshire helped me begin. At Mount Holyoke, Eileen Dunn took serious interest in the project and reviewed and summarized all of the *Triple Jeopardy* papers that I had collected. Shera Resch researched the women covered in "Live Like Her." Esmeralda López Mendoza did archival research with me at the Women of Color Resource Center (WCRC) in Oakland, California. Cathy Kim did a literature review of relational-cultural theory (RCT), and Lauren Silver analyzed Alliance documents and interviews from the perspective of RCT. Tasnia Tahsin organized the electronic files of *Triple Jeopardy*. Jamie Daniels went with me to the Bay Area to interview several women and transcribed those interviews. Yolanda Aponte did a wonderful job of organizing my materials, as did my work-study student Vivienne Carlson.

A huge debt of gratitude goes to the former WCRC in Oakland, where the meticulous records of the Bay Area Chapter of TWWA were housed before being moved to Smith College in Northampton, Massachusetts, in 2012. The generosity of Linda Burnham, founder and former director of the Center, and former director Anisha Desai were unmatched. The eight boxed archives that Sharon Davenport organized in 2004 were the main event. Without those, nothing would have been adequately remembered.

Mount Holyoke College facilitated the writing of this book in more ways than I can mention. The Department of Psychology and Education provided me with Visiting Associate Professor appointments from 2001 to 2011. Along with those appointments came college resources—the library and information technology system, supportive colleagues in my department (especially Gail Hornstein) and the Gender Studies Department, bright and eager students, and even a small grant from the Office of the Dean of Faculty to cover research expenses. Ongoing financial support from Romney Associates, Inc., our family consulting company, was invaluable. And special thanks to Sharisse Hosein, Angelica Castro, and Molly Keehn for their assistance with the penultimate push.

Feminist Press was always my publisher of choice for *We Were There.* I knew this was exactly the right place for this work. Major gratitude goes to Jamia Wilson, who greeted the manuscript with tremendous enthusiasm, quickly connecting the Alliance's history to the activism of her own parents during the sixties and seventies, and declaring her commitment to having these stories told. Thank you also to Lauren Rosemary Hook, who was Feminist Press's first gracious respondent to my persistent queries.

My deepest appreciation goes to my family. To my husband and life partner, Paul Wiley, whose love and support have sustained and heartened me through all the challenges and opportunities of the last forty years. He told me right at the start, "I'll always be there for you." And he has.

To our children: Maceo, for holding a space for love while challenging me to grow; Jonathan, for sharing the joy of family; Maya, for supporting me in the office and for giving me so many reasons to smile; and my daughter and fellow writer Imani, for being an activist woman of color and for reading much of this manuscript and encouraging me to tell the story. And appreciation to Maceo and Imani's father, Joaquín Rosa Denis, my compañero in those early years, who first introduced me to the movement of the late 1960s and who has maintained his activism through the years, manifested in his love and support of family and community and his leadership in the Alliance for Puerto Rican Education and Empowerment.

Platform of the Third World Women

Transcript: Women in the Struggle
(Third World Women's Alliance Platform)

The Third World Women's Alliance has recently come out of a two-month retreat. The administrative structure was not sufficient to deal with the growing interest on the part of the third world women across the country to their call for united action around their oppression as workers, as third world people, and as women. It was also necessary to take time out to deal with the uneven political development that existed within the organization as well as to formulate an organizational position with stated goals & objectives. The following article is composed of excerpts of a booklet that the Third World Women's Alliance has prepared to inform people about their organization, its history, and its goals.

THIRD WORLD WOMEN'S ALLIANCE
346 West 20th Street
New York, NY 10011

History of the Organization

The foundation of our present organization was laid in December, 1968. Within SNCC, a Black woman's caucus was formed to begin to address itself to the problems that the women of SNCC encountered within the organization. Women were

TWWA Platform. Published in *Triple Jeopardy* 1, no. 1
(September–October 1971), 8–9.
Smith College Special Collections, Northampton, MA.

generally confined to secretarial and/or supportive roles and no matter what a woman's capabilities were, never seemed to be able to rise above this situation. The women in SNCC who had been meeting over a period of several months decided that the organization should be expanded beyond the confines of SNCC and that we should be drawing in women from other organizations, welfare mothers, community workers and campus radicals. An attempt was made to reach out to these women and the name of the organization was changed to the Black Women's Alliance. As of now, the organization is independent of SNCC and at the same time, SNCC has decided to retain its women's caucus.

We decided to form a Black women's organization for many reasons. One was and still is the widespread myth and a concept in the Black community of the matriarchy. We stated that the concept of the matriarchy was a myth and that it has never existed in the United States. A matriarchy denotes a society where the economic power of a group rests in the hands of the women and we all know where the economic power of this nation rests. Our position would be to expose this myth.

There was also the widespread concept that by some miracle, the oppression of slavery for the Black woman was not as degrading, not as horrifying, not as barbaric as it had been for the Black man. However, we state that in any society where men are not yet free, women are less free because we are further enslaved by our sex.

Now we noticed another interesting thing. And that is, that with the rise of Black nationalism and the rejection of the white middle class norms and values, that this rejection of whiteness—white culture, white norms and values took a different turn when it came to the Black woman. That is, Black men began defining the role of Black women in the movement. They stated that our role was a supportive one, others stated that we must become breeders and provide an army; still others stated that we had kotex or pussy power. We opposed these concepts stating that a true revolutionary movement must enhance the status of women.

Further discussion and study began to point out to us the intimate connection between the oppression of women and the form of government which was in control. We began to see the economic basis of our oppression and we became convinced that capitalism and imperialism were our main enemies. It is economically profitable to exploit and oppress third world women. We represent a surplus labor supply, a cheap labor supply, a free labor supply (in our homes.)

The development of an anti-imperialist ideology led us to recognize the need for the Third World solidarity. Although Asian, Black, Chicana, Native American and Puerto Rican sisters have certain differences, we begin to see that we are all affected by the same general oppressions. Industries employing mainly third world women are among the most exploitive in the country. Domestic workers, hospital workers, factory workers and farm laborers are prime objects of this exploitation as are the garment workers.

Stereotypes which are forced upon our peoples and which try to mold them with the acceptable white values, large use of drugs and alcoholism in our respective communities used as escapes from the daily oppression suffered by our people and other problems mentioned above gave us the realization that our similarities transcended our differences. We realized that we would be much more effective and unified by becoming a third world women's organization. So our group was expanded to include all third world sisters since our oppression is basically caused by the same factors and our enemy is the same. The name of the organization was changed to reflect this new awareness and composition of the group—THIRD WORLD WOMEN'S ALLIANCE.

Is a Third World Women's Group Divisive to the Liberation Struggle?

The third world woman must always be fighting against and exposing her triple exploitation in the society. A third world women's group can potentially be one of the most revolutionary forces confronting the U.S. ruling class. The third world woman consciously aware of the depth of her oppression and willing to fight against it will never give up until all forms of racist, sexist, and economic exploitation is eliminated.

An independent third world women's organization, rather than divide the national liberation struggle would actually enhance the struggle. The rulers of this society would like to keep us thinking that the problem is only one of racism or that men are inherently the enemy, thus diverting our attention from the economic basis of our oppression. Thus our brothers who tell us not to get involved in women's liberation fail to realize that this idea, if carried out, would tend to contain rather than expand the revolutionary fervor of third world women and would harm the liberation struggle as a whole.

An independent third world women's organization gives us the opportunity to reach women who might not ordinarily be reached by male-female organizations and thus heighten the political consciousness of third world women. An independent third world women's group creates an atmosphere whereby women who are overly shy about speaking in a mixed group about "women's problems" would not have the same hesitation in an all women's group. We can train third world women for leadership roles and help them gain confidence in their own abilities and help to eliminate the concept of what is "feminine" and "masculine."

It must be understood that we are not just for civil rights for women or civil rights for third world people, but for the elimination of all forms of sexist & racist oppression—liberation for women and the third world. We understand that national liberation can come about under an atmosphere of economic equality and economic equality cannot be achieved under the system. We understand that the elimination of our oppression as women can only be achieved from a revolutionary government who understands with the help of women the need for women to be liberated.

Goals & Objectives

Our purpose is to make a meaningful and lasting contribution to the Third World community by working for the elimination of the oppression and exploitation from which we suffer. We further intend to take an active part in creating a socialist society where we can live as decent human beings free from the pressures of racism, economic exploitation and sexual oppression.

1. To create a sisterhood of women devoted to the task of developing solidarity among the peoples of the Third World, based on a socialist ideology of struggling for the complete elimination of any and all forms of oppression and exploitation based upon race, economic status, or sex and to use whatever means are necessary to accomplish this task.
2. To promote unity among Third World people within the United States in matters affecting the educational, economic, social and political life of our peoples.

3. To collect, interpret, and distribute information about the Third World, both at home and abroad, and particularly information affecting its women.
4. To establish an education fund to be used to promote educational projects, to publish articles, and to employ such other media as is necessary to carry out such educational projects.
5. To recreate and build solid relationships with our men, destroying myths that have been created by our oppressor to divide us from each other, and to work together to appreciate human love and respect.

Ideological Platform

We recognize the right of all people to be free. As women, we recognize that our struggle is against an imperialistic sexist system that oppresses all minority peoples as well as exploits the majority. The United States is ruled by a small ruling class clique who use the concepts of racism and chauvinism to divide, control and oppress the masses of people for economic gain and profit.

We want equal status and a society that does not exploit and murder other people and smaller nations. We will fight for a socialist system that guarantees full, creative, non-exploitative lives for all human beings, fully aware that we will never be free until all oppressed people are free.

Family

WHEREAS in a capitalist culture, the institution of the family has been used as an economic and psychological tool, not serving the needs of people, we declare that we will not relate to the private ownership of any person by another. We encourage and support the continued growth of communal households and the idea of the extended family. We encourage alternative forms to the patriarchal family and call for the sharing of all work (including housework and childcare) by men and women.

Women must have the right to decide if and when they want to have children. There is no such thing as an illegitimate child. There should be free and SAFE family planning methods available to all women, including abortions if necessary.

There should be no forced sterilization or mandatory birth control programs which are presently used as genocide against third world women and against other poor people.

Employment

WHEREAS third world women in a class society have been continuously exploited through their work, both in the home and on the job, we call for:

1. Guaranteed full, equal and non-exploitative employment, controlled collectively by the workers who produce the wealth of the society.
2. Guaranteed adequate income for all. This would entail the sharing of non-creative tasks and the maximum utilization of a revolutionary technology to eliminate these tasks.
3. An end to the racism and sexism which forces third world women into the lowest paying service jobs and which ensures that we will be the lowest paid of all.
4. The establishment of free day care centers available to all including facilities for pre-school and older children.

Sex Roles

WHEREAS behavior patterns based on rigid sex roles are oppressive to both men and women, role integration should be attempted. The true revolutionary should be concerned with human beings and not limit themselves to people as sex objects.

Furthermore, whether homosexuality is societal or genetic in origin, it exists in the third world community. The oppression and dehumanizing ostracism that homosexuals face must be rejected and their right to exist as dignified human beings must be defended.

Education

WHEREAS women historically have been deprived of education, or only partially educated and miseducated in those areas deemed appropriate for them by those ruling powers who benefit from this ignorance, we call for:

1. The right to determine our own goals and ambitions.
2. An end of sex roles regarding training and skills.
3. Self-Knowledge—the history of third world women and their contributions to the liberation struggle, the relation to society and the knowledge of their bodies.

Services

WHEREAS the services provided for the masses of third world people have been inadequate, unavailable, or too expensive, administered in a racist, sexist manner, we demand that all services necessary to human survival—health care, housing, food, clothing, transportation and education—should be free and controlled and administered by the people who use them.

Women in Our Own Right

WHEREAS we do not believe that any person is the property of any other and whereas all people must share equally in the decisions which affect them, we hereby demand:

1. That third world women have the right to determine their own lives, not lives determined by their fathers, brothers, or husbands.
2. That all organizations & institutions (including all so-called radical, militant and/or so-called revolutionary groups) deal with third world women in their own right as human beings and individuals, rather than as property of men and only valued in relationship to their association or connection with some man.

3. That third world women be full participants on all levels of the struggle for national liberation, i.e., administrative, political and military.

Self-Defense

WHEREAS the struggle for liberation must be borne equally by all members of an oppressed people, we declare that third world women have the right and responsibility to bear arms.

Women should be fully trained and educated in the martial arts as well as in the political arena. Furthermore, we recognize that it is our duty to defend all oppressed peoples.

Notes

Author's Note

1. "Editorial: What Is the Third World?," *Triple Jeopardy* 1, no. 2 (November 1971): 16, https://www.jstor.org/site/reveal-digital/independent-voices/. Unless otherwise noted, all *Triple Jeopardy* citations refer to the Independent Voices online archive found on JSTOR.
2. Women in the Struggle, The Third World Women's Alliance History and Platform, Third World Women's Alliance Records, box 3, file 9, Sophia Smith Collection, Smith College, Northampton, MA. Unless otherwise noted, all quotes referring to the Third World Women's Alliance platform are from this document.
3. Max Elbaum, *Revolution in the Air: Sixties Radicals Turn to Lenin, Mao and Che* (New York: Verso, 2002), 2.
4. Mike Giglio, "A Pro-Trump Militant Group Has Recruited Thousands of Police, Soldiers, and Veterans," *The Atlantic*, September 30, 2020, https://www.theatlantic.com/magazine/archive/2020/11/right-wing-militias-civil-war/616473/.
5. Madison J. Gay, "Black Gun Ownership Surges Amid 2020 Racial Tensions," BET, August 4, 2020, https://www.bet.com/news/national/2020/08/04/gun-sales-african-americans.html.
6. "About Black Lives Matter," Black Lives Matter (website), https://blacklivesmatter.com/about/.
7. Eric Sherman, "America Is the Richest, and Most Unequal, Country," *Fortune*, September 30, 2015, http://fortune.com/2015/09/30america-wealth-inequality/.
8. Zora Neale Hurston, *Dust Tracks on a Road* (New York: Harper Perennial, 2006), 87.
9. Audre Lorde, *Sister Outsider: Essays and Speeches* (Berkeley, CA: Crossing Press, 2007), 44.
10. Jean-Paul Sartre, introduction to *The Colonizer and the Colonized*, by Albert Memmi, trans. Howard Greenfeld (London: Souvenir Press, 1974), xxiii.

Introduction: The Need for This Story

1. bell hooks, *Ain't I a Woman: Black Women and Feminism* (Boston: South End Press, 1981), 1–2.
2. The term "second wave" has come under important critique in recent years. It is true that, as Kristan Poirot stated, the wave terminology does "fail to describe aptly how women's movements continually emerge in U.S. history." Kristan Poirot, *A Question of Sex: Feminism, Rhetoric, and Differences That Matter* (Amherst: University of Massachusetts Press, 2014), 131n54. Think, for example, of the #MeToo movement and the women's marches that have emerged in the last two years to protest Donald Trump's election. I have retained the phrase here because it is a familiar and well-known phrase referring to that period of intensive activism and change during the sixties and seventies.
3. These were the terms we used to describe ourselves in the 1970s. Today, we would likely describe ourselves as African American, Caribbean American, Asian American, Arab American, and Latina or Latinx.
4. See, for example, William L. Andrews, ed., *Sisters of the Spirit: Three Black Women's Autobiographies of the Nineteenth Century* (Bloomington: Indiana University Press, 1986); Ida B. Wells, *Crusade for Justice: The Autobiography of Ida B. Wells* (Chicago: University of Chicago Press, 2013); Pauli Murray, *Pauli Murray: The Autobiography of a Black Activist, Feminist, Lawyer, Priest, and Poet* (Knoxville: University of Tennessee Press, 1989). Also, the National Black Feminist Organization formed in the spring of 1973.
5. Kristin Anderson-Bricker, "'Triple Jeopardy': Black Women and the Growth of Feminist Consciousness in SNCC, 1964–1975," in *Still Lifting, Still Climbing: African American Women's Contemporary Activism*, ed. Kimberly Springer (New York: New York University Press, 1999), 49–69.
6. Rosalyn Baxandall and Linda Gordon, eds., *Dear Sisters: Dispatches from the Women's Liberation Movement* (New York: Basic Books, 2000), 65.
7. Linda Burnham, "The Wellspring of Black Feminist Theory," *Southern University Law Review* 28, no. 3 (2001): 265–70.
8. Linda Burnham, interview by Loretta J. Ross, March 18, 2005, Oakland, CA, transcript, Voices of Feminism Oral History Project, Sophia Smith Collection, Smith College, Northampton, MA, https://www.smith.edu/libraries/libs/ssc/vof/transcripts/Burnham.pdf.
9. Max Elbaum, *Revolution in the Air: Sixties Radicals Turn to Lenin, Mao and Che* (New York: Verso, 2002), 82.
10. Stephen Michael Ward, "'Ours Too Was a Struggle for a Better World': Activist Intellectuals and the Radical Promise of the Black Power Movement, 1962–1972" (PhD diss., University of Texas at Austin, 2002), 223–67.

11. Benita Roth, *Separate Roads to Feminism: Black, Chicana, and White Feminist Movements in America's Second Wave* (New York: Cambridge University Press, 2004), 91.
12. Joon Pyo Lee, "The Third World Women's Alliance, 1970–1980: Women of Color Organizing in a Revolutionary Era" (master's thesis, Sarah Lawrence College, 2007).
13. Iris Morales, *Through the Eyes of Rebel Women: The Young Lords, 1969–1976* (New York: Red Sugarcane Press, Inc., 2016).
14. Becky Thompson, "Multiracial Feminism: Recasting the Chronology of Second Wave Feminism," *Feminist Studies* 28, no. 2 (Summer 2002): 337.
15. Thompson, "Multiracial Feminism," 337.
16. Thompson, "Multiracial Feminism," 337.
17. Linda Burnham, "Doing Double Duty: Linda Burnham Recounts the Analysis and Histories of Women of Color Feminists as They Head into the UN Conference," *ColorLines* 4, no. 3 (2001): 23.
18. bell hooks, *Feminist Theory: From Margin to Center* (Boston: South End, 1984), xi–xii.

Chapter 1: August 26, 1970

1. Betty Friedan, quoted in Linda Charlton, "Women March Down Fifth in Equality Drive," *New York Times*, August 27, 1970, 1.
2. "A Place in the Sun," *Triple Jeopardy* 1, no. 1 (September–October 1971), 6.
3. Kathleen Thompson and Hilary Mac Austin, eds., *The Face of Our Past: Images of Black Women from Colonial America to the Present* (Bloomington: Indiana University Press, 2000), 40.
4. Nadia Kareem Nittle, "The U.S. Government's Role in Sterilizing Women of Color," ThoughtCo., last modified February 4, 2021, https://www.thoughtco.com/u-s-governments-role-sterilizing-women-of-color-2834600.
5. "Sterilization of Black Women Is Common in US," *Triple Jeopardy* 3, no. 1 (September–October 1973), 1; "Sterilization: Dominican Women in NYC," *Triple Jeopardy* 3, no. 2 (November–December 1973), 8; "Sterilization: La Operacíon: The Doctor May Need It More Than You," *Triple Jeopardy* 3, no. 4 (January–February 1975), 1; "Puerto Rican Women Sterilized," *Triple Jeopardy* 4, no. 1 (January–February 1975), 3.
6. Alice Steinbach, *The Miss Dennis School of Writing and Other Lessons from a Woman's Life* (Baltimore, MD: The Bancroft Press, 1996), 123.
7. "Part II—1956," Feminist Majority Foundation, accessed April 9, 2021, https://feminist.org/resources/feminist-chronicles/the-feminist-chronicles-2/part-ii-1956/.
8. Mabel Newcomer, *A Century of Higher Education for American Women* (New York: Harper & Brothers, 1959).

9. Charlayne Hunter, "Many Blacks Wary of 'Women's Liberation' Movement in U.S.," *New York Times*, November 17, 1970, 47.

10. "Women's Equality Day," National Woman's History Museum, August 26, 2013, http://www.nwhm.org/blog/happy-womens-equality-day/.

11. Jo Freeman, *The Politics of Women's Liberation: A Case Study of an Emerging Social Movement and its Relation to the Policy Process* (Lincoln, NE: iUniverse.com, Inc., 2000), 156.

Chapter 2: From Double Jeopardy to Triple Jeopardy: The Genesis of the TWWA

1. "Home," SNCC 1960–1966: Six Years of the Student Nonviolent Coordinating Committee, accessed April 9, 2021, https://www. ibiblio.org/sncc/index.html.

2. Frances M. Beal, interviews by Patricia Romney, 1995, 2005, 2008, and 2011, Oakland, CA. Unless otherwise noted, all quotes from Frances M. Beal are from these interviews.

3. "SNCC Position Paper (re women), November, 1964," Civil Rights Movement Archive, http://www.crmvet.org/docs/6411w_us_women. pdf.

4. Gwen Patton, interview by Patricia Romney, September 9, 2005, telephone interview. Unless otherwise noted, all quotes from Gwen Patton are from this interview.

5. Jacqueline Jones, *Labor of Love, Labor of Sorrow: Black Women, Work, and the Family, from Slavery to the Present* (New York: Basic Books, 2009), 260.

6. Elaine Brown, *A Taste of Power: A Black Woman's Story* (New York: Anchor Books, 1994), 357.

7. Michelle Bernard, "Despite the Tremendous Risk, African American Women Marched for Suffrage, Too," *Washington Post*, March 3, 2013, http://www.washingtonpost.com/blogs/she-the-people/ wp/2013/03/03/despite-the-tremendous-risk-african-american- women-marched-for-suffrage-too/.

8. Mae Jackson, interview by Patricia Romney, December 26, 2020, telephone interview. Unless otherwise noted, all quotes from Mae Jackson are from this interview.

9. Gwen Patton, "Letter to Sisters," January 6, 1969, National Council of Negro Women—Beal Papers, Third World Women's Alliance Records, box 3, folder 24, Sophia Smith Collection, Smith College, Northampton, MA.

10. Patton, "Letter to Sisters," 1969.

11. Frances Beal to Julia Hervé, April 23, 1969, National Council of Negro Women—Beal Papers, Third World Women's Alliance Records, box 3, folder 24, Sophia Smith Collection, Smith College, Northampton, MA.

12. *Black Woman's Manifesto*, Third World Women's Alliance Records, box 4, file 19, Sophia Smith Collection, Smith College, Northampton, MA.

13. First appeared in *Black Woman's Manifesto* and then in Robin Morgan's 1970 anthology, *Sisterhood Is Powerful*, and in Toni Cade Bambara's 1970 anthology, *The Black Woman*. Published again in 1995 in *Words of Fire*, edited by Beverly Guy-Sheftall.

14. "SNCC's International Bureau," SNCC Digital Gateway, accessed April 9, 2021, https://snccdigital.org/inside-sncc/international-connections/international-bureau/.

15. "College Coeds Are Dismissed," *Kingsport News*, May 13, 1968, 8.

16. Yemaya Rice Jones, interview by Patricia Romney, May 10, 2016, telephone interview. Unless otherwise noted, all quotes from Yemaya Rice Jones are from this interview.

17. Stella Holmes Hughes, interview by Patricia Romney, March 7, 2009, New York, NY. Unless otherwise noted, all quotes from Stella Holmes Hughes are from this interview.

18. "Women in the Struggle," *Triple Jeopardy* 1, no. 1 (September–October, 1971), 8–9.

19. For a history of the term, see Gérard Chaliand's "Third World: definitions and descriptions," Third World Traveler (website), accessed April 9, 2021, http://www.thirdworldtraveler.com/General/ThirdWorld_def.html.

20. "Editorial: What Is the Third World?," *Triple Jeopardy* 1, no. 2 (November 1971), 16.

21. Nancy Ordover, "Puerto Rico," Eugenics Archives, February 24, 2014, http://eugenicsarchive.ca/discover/connections/530ba18176f0db569b00001b.

22. Theresa Vargas, "Guinea Pigs or Pioneers? How Puerto Rican Women Were Used to Test the Birth Control Pill," *Washington Post*, May 9, 2017, https://www.washingtonpost.com/news/retropolis/wp/2017/05/09/guinea-pigs-or-pioneers-how-puerto-rican-women-were-used-to-test-the-birth-control-pill/.

23. "Que Viva Puerto Rico Libre," *Triple Jeopardy*, 1 no. 2 (November 1971), 5.

24. Elaine H. Kim and Janice Otani, *With Silk Wings: Asian American Women at Work* (San Francisco: Asian Women United, 1983), 97.

25. "Anti-War Demonstrations," *Triple Jeopardy* 1, no. 1 (September–October 1971), 5.

26. Brian Lanker, *I Dream a World: Portraits of Black Women Who Changed America* (New York: Stewart, Tabori & Chang, 1989), 8.

27. Brenda Boho Beato, interview by Patricia Romney, May 1, 2010, Brooklyn, NY. Unless otherwise noted, all quotes from Brenda Boho Beato are from this interview.

28. Milagros Pérez Huth, interview by Patricia Romney, December 1, 2005, Shushan, NY. Unless otherwise noted, all quotes from Milagros Pérez Huth are from this interview.

29. Georgette Ioup, interview by Patricia Romney, 2006, New Orleans, LA. Unless otherwise noted, all quotes from Georgette Ioup are from this interview.

Chapter 3: The New York Chapter (1970–1977): Platform, Theory, and Praxis

1. *Triple Jeopardy*, Third World Women's Alliance Records, box 3, file 9, Sophia Smith Collection, Smith College, Northampton, MA. Unless otherwise noted, all quotes referring to the Third World Women's Alliance platform are from this document.
2. See complete TWWA platform on p. 253.
3. Marilyn Aguirre and Anneris Goris, "Sterilization: Dominican Women in N.Y.C.," *Triple Jeopardy* 3, no. 2 (November–December 1973), 8–9.
4. Jesús Papoleto Meléndez, "junkies are very skillful people," *Triple Jeopardy* 1, no. 3 (January 1972), 8.
5. Boston Women's Health Collective, *Our Bodies, Ourselves: A Book by and for Women* (New York: Simon & Schuster, 1984), xi.
6. "Anatomy and Physiology," *Triple Jeopardy* 1, no. 1 (September–October, 1971), 7.
7. Cheryl Johnson Perry, interview by Patricia Romney, July 19, 2011, Oakland, CA. Unless otherwise noted, all quotes from Cheryl Johnson Perry are from this interview.
8. Frances M. Beal, "Double Jeopardy: To Be Black and Female," in *The Black Woman: An Anthology*, ed. Toni Cade Bambara (New York: Simon & Schuster, 2010), 109–22.
9. Christine Choy, interview by Patricia Romney, March 6, 2009, New York, NY. Unless otherwise noted, all quotes from Christine Choy are from this interview.
10. Harlem Fight Back was founded in 1964 by A. Phillip Randolph to organize for the inclusion of Black and Latino workers in construction unions and construction projects. Lawrence Mishel, "Diversity in the New York City Union and Nonunion Construction Sectors," Economic Policy Institute, March 2, 2017, https://www.epi.org/publication/diversity-in-the-nyc-construction-union-and-nonunion-sectors/.
11. Ana Celia Zentella, interview by Patricia Romney, Summer 2008, University of California, San Diego. Unless otherwise noted, all quotes from Ana Celia Zentella are from this interview.
12. Stokely Carmichael, "Black Power," November 1966, UC Berkeley, transcript, Civil Rights Movement Archive, http://crmvet.org/info/stokely.htm.
13. Ernesto Che Guevara, "Man and Socialism in Cuba," trans. Margarita Zimmermann, March 1965, Marxists.org, https://www.marxists.org/archive/guevara/1965/03/man-socialism-alt.htm.
14. "Letter from Angela," *Triple Jeopardy* 1, no. 3 (January 1972), 3;

"Angela Davis: Repression and Resistance," *Triple Jeopardy* 2, no. 2 (January–February 1973), 4; "Angela Davis Raps with TWWA," *Triple Jeopardy* 2, no. 3 (March–April 1973), 4–6.

15. "El Teatro Guerilla," *Triple Jeopardy* 2, no. 4 (May–June 1973), 13.
16. "Editorial," *Triple Jeopardy* 1, no. 3 (January 1972), 16.
17. "Editorial," *Triple Jeopardy*, 16.
18. "El Movimiento and la Chicana," *Triple Jeopardy* 1, no. 5 (April–May 1972), 2.
19. *Manos a la Obra: The Story of Operation Bootstrap*, directed by Pedro Angel Rivera and Susan Zeig (New York: Center for Puerto Rican Studies, CUNY, 1983), 35 mm.
20. "Anti-War Demonstrations," *Triple Jeopardy* 1, no. 1 (September–October 1971), 5.
21. "Anti-War Demonstrations," *Triple Jeopardy*, 11.
22. "On the Job," *Triple Jeopardy* 1, no. 1 (September–October 1971), 14.
23. "On the Job: Third World Women & the Workforce," *Triple Jeopardy* 3, no. 1 (September–October 1973), 6.
24. "On the Job: Third World Women & the Workforce," *Triple Jeopardy*, 14.
25. "On the Job," *Triple Jeopardy* 2, no. 4 (May–June 1973), 4.
26. "Skills," *Triple Jeopardy* 1, no. 3 (January 1972), 14.
27. "Skills," *Triple Jeopardy* 1, no. 4 (February–March 1972), 6.
28. "Anatomy and Physiology," *Triple Jeopardy*, 7.
29. "Painless Childbirth: A Mother's Experience," *Triple Jeopardy* 1, no. 5 (April–May 1972), 8–9.
30. "International News," *Triple Jeopardy* 1, no. 2 (November 1971), 6.
31. "Que Viva La Revolución," *Triple Jeopardy* 1, no. 3 (January 1972), 5.
32. Jesús Papoleto Meléndez, "in a moment," *Triple Jeopardy* 1, no. 3 (January 1972), 9.
33. "Obituary of Josina Machel of FRELIMO," *Triple Jeopardy* 1, no. 7, Third World Women's Alliance Records, box 3, file 9, Sophia Smith Collection, Smith College, Northampton, MA.
34. "Que Viva La Revolución," *Triple Jeopardy*, 5.
35. Eileen Dunn, "What *Triple Jeopardy* Meant to Me" (unpublished paper, Spring 2007), Microsoft Word file.
36. "El Pueblo Vencerá," *Triple Jeopardy* 4, no. 2 (January–February 1975), 8–9.
37. D. L. Chandler, "Joan Little Cleared of Killing White Sexual Assaulter in Jail on This Day in 1975," NewsOne.com, August 15, 2013, http://newsone.com/2679256/joan-little-case/.
38. "Murder at San Quentin," *Triple Jeopardy* 1, no. 2 (September–October 1971), 3.
39. "Murder at San Quentin," *Triple Jeopardy*, 3.
40. "Live Like Her," *Triple Jeopardy* 1, no. 2 (November 1971), 14.
41. "Live Like Her," *Triple Jeopardy*, 14.
42. Manuel Roig-Franzia, "A Terrorist in the House," *Washington Post Magazine*, February 22, 2004, W12.

43. Roig-Franzia, "A Terrorist," W12.
44. Antonio Medina-Rivera, "Lolita Lebrón y Minerva Mirabel: mitificación y desmitificación del héroe político," in *Selected Proceedings of the Pennsylvania Foreign Language Conference*, ed. Gregorio C. Martin (Pittsburgh: Duquesne University, 2003), 119–29.
45. "Lolita Lebrón," *Triple Jeopardy* 3, no. 1 (September–October 1973), 5.
46. "Live Like Her," *Triple Jeopardy*, 14.

Chapter 4: Westward Expansion (1972–1980): Seattle Third World Women and the Bay Area Chapter

1. Melanie Tervalon, interview by Patricia Romney, November 3, 2010, Oakland, CA. Unless otherwise noted, all quotes from Melanie Tervalon are from this interview.
2. Bernice Davis, "Guinea-Bissau Declares Freedom," *Triple Jeopardy*, 3, no. 2 (November–December 1973), 7.
3. Michelle Mouton, interview by Patricia Romney, July 20, 2011, San Francisco, CA. Unless otherwise noted, all quotes from Michelle Mouton are from this interview.
4. Zelma Toro, interview by Patricia Romney, July 20, 2011, Oakland, CA. Unless otherwise noted, all quotes from Zelma Toro are from this interview.
5. Rebecca Carrillo, interview by Patricia Romney, September 10, 2011, Albuquerque, NM. Unless otherwise noted, all quotes from Rebecca Carrillo are from this interview.
6. Linda Burnham, interview by Patricia Romney, October 26, 2005, Oakland, CA. Unless otherwise noted, all quotes from Linda Burnham are from this interview.
7. Lucas Daumont, interview by Patricia Romney, January 15, 2008, Berkeley, CA. Unless otherwise noted, all quotes from Lucas Daumont are from this interview.
8. Miriam Ching Yoon Louie, interview by Patricia Romney, March 21, 2009, San Francisco, CA. Unless otherwise noted, all quotes from Miriam Ching Yoon Louie are from this interview.
9. Mao Tse-Tung, "Oppose Book Worship," Selected Works of Mao Tse-Tung, 1930, https://www.marxists.org/reference/archive/mao/selected-works/volume-6/mswv6_11.htm; Mao Tse-Tung, "Combat Liberalism," Selected Works of Mao Tse-Tung, September 7, 1937, https://www.marxists.org/reference/archive/mao/selected-works/volume-2/mswv2_03.htm; Mao Tse-Tung, "On Practice," Selected Works of Mao Tse-Tung, July 1937, https://www.marxists.org/reference/archive/mao/selected-works/volume-1/mswv1_16.htm.
10. Asian Women's History, Women in the Struggle, The Third World Women's Alliance History and Platform, Third World Women's Alliance Records, box 2, file 5, Sophia Smith Collection, Smith College, Northampton, MA.

11. National Report to Seattle and New York, January 1973, p. 1–2, box 3, file 21, Sophia Smith Collection, Smith College, Northampton, MA.
12. *Triple Jeopardy* 2, no. 1 (November–December 1972).
13. National Report to Seattle and New York, January 1973, box 3, file 21, Sophia Smith Collection, Smith College, Northampton, MA.
14. Agenda, January 29, 1975, Third World Women's Alliance Records, box 3, file 3, Sophia Smith Collection, Smith College, Northampton, MA.
15. Presentation at 1st General Meeting of TWWA, June 14, 1975, 2, Third World Women's Alliance Records, box 3, file 3, Sophia Smith Collection, Smith College, Northampton, MA.
16. Presentation at 1st General Meeting, 2.
17. *The Woman Question*, October 1977, 2/2/2/2, Third World Women's Alliance Records, box 2, file 17, Sophia Smith Collection, Smith College, Northampton, MA.
18. *The Woman Question*, 2/2/2/2.
19. *The Woman Question*, 2/2/2/2.
20. *The Woman Question*, 1. Note: this is another version of the paper previously published February 17. Third World Women's Alliance Records, box 2, file 17, Sophia Smith Collection, Smith College, Northampton, MA.
21. *The Woman Question*, 1.
22. *The Woman Question*, 2.
23. *The Woman Question*, 3.
24. *The Woman Question*, 3.
25. *The Woman Question*, 3.
26. Principles of Third World Women's Alliance, n.d., p. 4, box 3, folder 19, Sophia Smith Collection, Smith College, Northampton, MA.
27. Miriam Ching Yoon Louie, interview by Patricia Romney, July 19, 2011, Oakland, CA.
28. Towards Defining the Political Direction of the Third World Women's Alliance, Third World Women's Alliance Records, box 1, file 9, Sophia Smith Collection, Smith College, Northampton, MA.
29. Notice, 59 Fed. Reg. 8756 (Feb. 23, 1994).
30. Third World Women's Alliance songs, Third World Women's Alliance Records, box 4, file 13, Sophia Smith Collection, Smith College, Northampton, MA.
31. Coalition to Fight Infant Mortality, "Newsletter," 1, no. 1, April 1980, 1, Third World Women's Alliance Records, box 1, file 12, Sophia Smith Collection, Smith College, Northampton, MA.
32. Coalition to Fight Infant Mortality, "Newsletter," 3.
33. Coalition to Fight Infant Mortality, "The Woman Question," October 1977, 1, Third World Women's Alliance Records, box 2, file 17, Sophia Smith Collection, Smith College, Northampton, MA, "Newsletter," 3.
34. Coalition to Fight Infant Mortality, "The Woman Question," 1, 2/2/2/2.
35. Coalition to Fight Infant Mortality, "The Woman Question," 2/2/2/2.

36. Coalition to Fight Infant Mortality, "The Woman Question," 2/2/2/2.
37. "Summation of History of Third World Women's Alliance," 1980, 1, Third World Women's Alliance Records, box 3, file 9, Sophia Smith Collection, Smith College, Northampton, MA. Until otherwise noted, all subsequent quotes are from this same source.
38. Ric Ricard, interview by Patricia Romney, January 15, 2008, Oakland, CA, group interview with Lucas Daumont and Marty Price. Unless otherwise noted, all quotes from Ric Ricard are from this interview.

Chapter 5: International Women's Day

1. Ann-Ellice Parker, interview by Patricia Romney, 2011, telephone interview. Unless otherwise noted, all quotes from Ann-Ellice Parker are from this interview.
2. Concha Delgado Gaitán, interview by Patricia Romney, July 19, 2011, Oakland, CA. Unless otherwise noted, all quotes from Concha Delgado Gaitán are from this interview.
3. Nancy Hing Wong, interview by Patricia Romney, March 19, 2009, Oakland, CA. Unless otherwise noted, all quotes from Nancy Hing Wong are from this interview.
4. "History of International Women's Day," International Women's Day, accessed April 4, 2021, https://www.internationalwomensday.com/ Activity/15586/The-history-of-IWD/.
5. International Women's Day, Meeting Announcements, 1974–1975, Third World Women's Alliance Records, box 2, file 24, Sophia Smith Collection, Smith College, Northampton, MA.
6. International Women's Day, Bay Area Chapter Records, Third World Women's Alliance Records, box 6, file 21, Sophia Smith Collection, Smith College, Northampton, MA.
7. Bay Area Farah Strike Committee, Third World Women's Alliance Records, box 5, file 6, Sophia Smith Collection, Smith College, Northampton, MA.
8. International Women's Day, Bay Area Chapter Records, Third World Women's Alliance Records, box 2, file 23, Sophia Smith Collection, Smith College, Northampton, MA.
9. International Women's Day Pot Luck, March 1, 1975, Third World Women's Alliance Records, box 3, file 1, Sophia Smith Collection, Smith College, Northampton, MA.
10. International Women's Day, Bay Area Chapter Records, Third World Women's Alliance Records, box 2, file 1, Sophia Smith Collection, Smith College, Northampton, MA.
11. Marty Price, interview by Patricia Romney, January 15, 2008, Oakland, CA. Unless otherwise noted, all quotes from Marty Price are from this interview.

Chapter 6: Third World Women's Alliance Collaborators

1. "Puerto Rican Woman Visits China," *Triple Jeopardy* 2, no. 3 (March–April 1973), 1.
2. Joaquín Rosa, interview by Patricia Romney, December 5, 2020, telephone interview. Unless otherwise noted, all quotes from Joaquín Rosa are from this interview.
3. Elizabeth Garner Masarik and Averill Earls, "The Black Panther Party and the Free Breakfast Program: Feeding a Movement," July 19, 2020, in *Dig: A History Podcast*, produced by Elizabeth Garner Masarik and Averill Earls, podcast, 45:47, https://digpodcast.org/2020/07/19/black-panther-party/.
4. Iris Morales, *Through the Eyes of Rebel Women: The Young Lords, 1969–1976* (New York: Red Sugarcane Press, Inc., 2016), 45.
5. Morales, *Through the Eyes of Rebel Women*, 53.
6. "Third World Front against Imperialism," *Triple Jeopardy* 1, no. 3 (January 1972), 7.

Chapter 7: Reflecting Back/Looking Forward

1. John Legend and Common, vocalists, "Glory," by John Legend, Common, and Rhymefest, recorded 2014, Columbia Records, December 11, 2014.
2. FBI file of TWWA, 1971–1974, Third World Women's Alliance Records, box 4, files 11–12, Series I, Administration, Sophia Smith Collection, Smith College, Northampton, MA.
3. Linda Burnham, interview by Loretta J. Ross, March 18, 2005, Oakland, CA, transcript, Voices of Feminism Oral History Project, Sophia Smith Collection, Smith College, Northampton, MA.
4. Alice Walker, *In Search of our Mothers' Gardens: Womanist Prose* (San Diego: Harcourt Brace Jovanovich, 1983), xi.
5. Kimberly Springer, *Living for the Revolution: Black Feminist Organizations, 1968–1980* (Durham, NC: Duke University Press, 2005), 4.
6. Becky Thompson, "Multiracial Feminism: Recasting the Chronology of Second Wave Feminism," *Feminist Studies* 28, no. 2 (Summer 2002), 337–60.
7. Barbara Smith and Beverly Smith, "Across the Kitchen Table: A Sister-to-Sister Dialogue," in *This Bridge Called My Back: Writings by Radical Women of Color*, ed. Cherríe Moraga and Gloría Anzaldúa (London: Persephone Press, 1981), 61.
8. bell hooks, *Ain't I a Woman: Black Women and Feminism* (Boston: South End Press, 1981), 194.
9. Chimamanda Ngozi Adichie, *We Should All Be Feminists* (New York: Anchor Books, 2014), 48.

10. According to research by Kathleen Banks Nutter, Sophia Smith Collection Archivist, *Triple Jeopardy* contained seven articles about the Palestinian struggle, in discussion with the author, February 3, 2017.

11. Jean Baker Miller, *Toward a New Psychology of Women* (Boston: Beacon Press, 1976).

12. Jean Baker Miller and Irene Pierce Stiver, *The Healing Connection: How Women Form Relationships in Therapy and in Life* (Boston: Beacon Press, 1997), 26.

13. J. V. Jordan, A. G. Kaplan, J. B. Miller, I. P. Stiver, and J. L. Surrey, *Women's Growth In Connection: Writings from the Stone Center* (New York: Guilford Press, 1991).

14. Miller and Stiver, *The Healing Connection*, 27.

15. Jean Baker Miller, "How Change Happens: Controlling Images, Mutuality, and Power," *Women and Therapy* 31, no. 2/3/4 (2008), 109–27.

16. Patricia Hill Collins, *Black Feminist Thought: Knowledge, Consciousness and the Politics of Empowerment* (London: Routledge, 2008), 69.

17. "Revolt of Poor Black Women," *Triple Jeopardy* 2, no. 3 (March–April 1973), 16.

18. Frantz Fanon, *The Wretched of the Earth* (New York: Grove Press, 2007), 96.

19. Patricia Romney, "The Art of Dialogue," in *Civic Dialogue, Arts & Culture: Findings from Animating Democracy*, ed. P. Korza, B. Schaffer Bacon, and A. Assaf (Washington, DC: Americans for the Arts Press, 2005), 57–79.

20. Patricia Romney, "Cuba from Both Sides," *Journal of Feminist Family Therapy* 5, no. 2 (1994), 75–81.

21. Joni Mitchell, vocalist, "Both Sides, Now," by Joni Mitchell, track 5, side 2 on *Clouds*, Reprise, 1969.

22. Paul R. Fleischman, *The Healing Spirit: Case Studies in Religion and Psychotherapy* (London: SPCK, 1990), 261.

23. Cherríe Moraga and Gloría Anzaldúa, eds., *This Bridge Called My Back*, 2nd ed. (Boston: Kitchen Table/Women of Color Press), 41.

24. Frances M. Beal, interview by Loretta J. Ross, Voices of Feminism Oral History Project, March 18, 2005, 41, 3rd of 3 DVDs, 24:12, Sophia Smith Collection, Smith College, Northampton, MA.

25. *Paving the Way: A Teaching Guide to the Third World Women's Alliance* (Oakland, CA: Women of Color Resource Center, 2006), DVD.

26. Romney, "Cuba from Both Sides," 75–81.

27. Michelle Alexander, *The New Jim Crow: Mass Incarceration in the Age of Colorblindness* (New York: The New Press, 2010), 9.

28. "Fact Sheet: Incarcerated Women and Girls," The Sentencing Project, updated November 2020, https://www.sentencingproject.org/wp-content/uploads/2016/02/Incarcerated-Women-and-Girls.pdf.

29. Paul Bedard, "Only Hispanic Prison Population Rising, Blacks, Whites Down," *Washington Examiner*, May 2, 2019, https://www.

washingtonexaminer.com/washington-secrets/only-hispanic-prison-population-rising-blacks-whites-down.

30. Nancy L. Cohen, "Why America Never Had Universal Child Care," *New Republic*, April 24, 2013, https://newrepublic.com/article/113009/child-care-america-was-very-close-universal-day-care.

31. Allison Young, "Hospitals Know How to Protect Mothers. They Just Aren't Doing It," *USA Today*, updated March 23, 2021, https://www.ustoday.com/in-depth/news/investigations/deadly-deliveries/2018/07/26/maternal-mortality-rates-preeclmpsia-postpartum-hemmorrhage-safety/546889002/.

32. Save the Children, *State of the World's Mothers 2015*, May 2015, https://www.savethechildren.org/content/dam/usa/reports/advocacy/sowm/sowm-2015.pdf.

33. "Childcare in Sweden," Expat.com, October 29, 2018, http://expat.com/en/guide/europe/sweden/19295-childcare-in-sweden.html.

34. Khaleda Rahman, "From George Floyd to Breonna Taylor, Remembering the Black People Killed by Police in 2020," *Newsweek*, December 29, 2020, https://www.newsweek.com/george-floyd-breonna-taylor-black-people-police-killed-1556285.

35. Wendy Conklin, "Latinos and Blacks: What Unites and Divides Us?," *The Diversity Factor* 16, no. 1 (Winter 2008), 20–28.

36. Christie Thompson, "Are California Prisons Punishing Inmates Based on Race?," ProPublica, April 12, 2013, https://www.propublica.org/article/are-california-prisons-punishing-inmates-based-on-race.

37. Kahlil Gibran, *The Prophet* (Oxford, UK: Oneworld Publications, 1955), 26.

38. James Farmer, *Lay Bare the Heart: An Autobiography of the Civil Rights Movement* (Fort Worth: Texas Christian University Press, 2014), 215.

39. Grace Lee Boggs, conversation with Patricia Romney, October 9, 2003, at Animating Democracy's National Exchange on Art and Civic Dialogue in Flint, MI.

40. Angela Y. Davis, *Freedom Is a Constant Struggle: Ferguson, Palestine, and the Foundations of a Movement* (Chicago: Haymarket Books, 2016), 145.